Excel

Get the Results You Want!

Year 7 NAPLAN*-style Literacy Tests

Maya Puiu

* This is not an officially endorsed publication of the NAPLAN program and is produced by Pascal Press independently of Australian governments.

Reprinted 2011
New NAPLAN Test question formats added 2012
Reprinted 2014, 2015
Conventions of Language questions updated 2016
Reprinted 2017, 2018, 2019

Revised in 2020 for the NAPLAN Online tests

Reprinted 2021, 2022, 2023, 2024

ISBN 978 1 74125 365 8

Pascal Press Pty Ltd
PO Box 250
Glebe NSW 2037
(02) 9198 1748
www.pascalpress.com.au

Publisher: Vivienne Joannou
Project editor: Mark Dixon
Edited by Rosemary Peers
Proofread by Barbara Bessant
Answers checked by Dale Little and Peter Little
Cover and page design by DiZign Pty Ltd
Typeset by Precision Typesetting (Barbara Nilsson) and Grizzly Graphics (Leanne Richters)
Printed by Vivar Printing/Green Giant Press

Contents

WHAT IS NAPLAN?

- NAPLAN stands for National Assessment Program—Literacy and Numeracy.
- It is conducted every year in March and the tests are taken by students in Years 3, 5, 7 and 9.
- The tests cover Literacy—Reading, Writing, Conventions of Language (spelling, grammar and punctuation)—and Numeracy.

WHAT IS NAPLAN ONLINE?

Introduction

- In the past all NAPLAN tests were paper tests.
- From 2022 all students have taken the NAPLAN tests online.
- This means students complete the NAPLAN tests on a computer or tablet.

Tailored test design

- With NAPLAN paper tests, all students in each year level took exactly the same tests.
- In the NAPLAN Online tests this isn't the case; instead, every student takes a tailor-made test based on their ability.
- Please visit the official ACARA site for a detailed explanation of the tailored test process used in NAPLAN Online and also for general information about the tests: https://nap.edu.au/online-assessment.
- These tailor-made tests mean broadly, therefore, that a student who is at a standard level of achievement takes a test mostly comprised of questions of a standard level; a student who is at an intermediate level of achievement takes a test mostly comprised of questions of an intermediate level; and a student who is at an advanced level of achievement takes a test mostly comprised of questions of an advanced level.

Different question types

- Because of the digital format, NAPLAN Online contains more question types than in the paper tests. In the paper tests there are only multiple-choice and short-answer question types. In NAPLAN Online, however, there are also other question types. For example, students might be asked to drag text across a screen or listen to an audio recording of a sentence and then spell a word they hear.
- Please refer to the next page to see some examples of these additional question types that are found in NAPLAN Online and how they compare to questions in this book. As you will see, the content tested is exactly the same but the questions are presented differently.

NAPLAN ONLINE QUESTION TYPES

Additional NAPLAN Online question types	Equivalent questions in this book
Sequencing Drag these events to show the correct order. 1 [ ] 2 [ ] 3 [ ] 4 [ ] We usually visit the beach We go home to keep cool However, if it is too hot When summer comes	Sequence the following phrases in their correct order. **A** We usually visit the beach **B** We go home to keep cool **C** However, if it is too hot **D** When summer comes **Order** / **Phrase** 1 / 2 / 3 / 4 /
Click Which **two** phrases both complete this sentence correctly? When you walk the dog ______ you both benefit tremendously. **A** in the morning **B** park, beach or footpath **C** to get out of the house **D** while the sun **E** upside down	Which **two** phrases both complete this sentence correctly? When you walk the dog ______ you both benefit tremendously. **A** in the morning **B** park, beach or footpath **C** to get out of the house **D** while the sun **E** upside down
Drag and drop Which word correctly completes the sentence? The book you are looking for is ______ table. through the over a on a on the with the	Which option completes the sentence correctly? The book you are looking for is ______ table. **A** through the **B** over a **C** on a **D** on the **E** with the
Text entry People need to exercise ______ to stay in good physical condition. Click on the play button to listen to the missing word. 0.08 / 0.09 Type the correct spelling of the word in the box. [ ]	Ask your teacher or parent to read the spelling words for you. The words are listed on page 174. Write the spelling word on the line below. **Word** / **Example** properly / People need to exercise properly to stay in good physical condition. ______

STEP 1: USE THIS BOOK

How *Excel* can help you prepare for NAPLAN Online

Tailored test design

- We can't replicate the digital experience in book form and offer you tailored tests, but with this series we do provide Standard, Intermediate and Advanced NAPLAN Online–style Literacy tests.
- This means that a student using these tests will be able to prepare with confidence for tests at different ability levels.
- This makes it excellent preparation for the tailored NAPLAN Online Literacy tests.

Remember the advantages of revising in book form

There are many benefits to a child using books to prepare for the online test:

- One of the most important benefits is that writing on paper will help your child retain information. It can be a very effective way to memorise. High-quality educational research has shown that writing by hand is more effective than using a keyboard for remembering what you write and assisting in learning.
- Students will be able to prepare thoroughly for topic revision using books and then practise computer skills easily. They will only succeed with sound knowledge of topics; this requires study and focus. Students will not succeed in tests simply because they know how to answer questions digitally.
- Some students find it easier to concentrate when reading a page in a book than when reading on a screen.
- It can be more convenient to use a book, especially when a child doesn't have ready access to a digital device.
- You can be confident that ***Excel*** books will help students acquire the topic knowledge they need, as we have over 30 years experience in helping students prepare for tests. All our writers are experienced educators.

STEP 2: PRACTISE ON *Excel Test Zone*

How *Excel Test Zone* can help you practise online

We recommend you go to www.exceltestzone.com.au and register for practice in NAPLAN Online–style tests once you have completed this book. The reasons include:

- for optimal performance in the NAPLAN Online tests we recommend students gain practice at completing online tests as well as completing revision in book form
- students should practise answering questions on a digital device to become confident with this process
- students will be able to practise tailored tests like those in NAPLAN Online, as well as other types of tests
- students will also be able to gain valuable practice in onscreen skills such as dragging and dropping answers.

Remember that ***Excel Test Zone*** has been helping students prepare for NAPLAN since 2009; in fact we had NAPLAN online questions even before NAPLAN tests went online!

We also have updated our website along with our book range to ensure your preparation for NAPLAN Online is 100% up to date.

THE YEAR 7 NAPLAN ONLINE LITERACY TESTS

About the tests

In Literacy there are three NAPLAN tests:

- **Reading** (comprehension)—there are 48 to 50 questions in this test
- **Conventions of Language** (spelling, grammar and punctuation)—there are 50 questions in this test
- **Writing** (written expression)—there is one piece of writing in this test.

About the report

- When your child completes the NAPLAN tests, you and your child's school will receive a report indicating their standard of proficiency in literacy and numeracy. There are four levels of achievement:
  - **Exceeding** (advanced proficiency)
  - **Strong** (average to high-average proficiency)
  - **Developing** (not yet proficient)
  - **Needs additional support** (help is needed).

The report will also show the national average.

ABOUT THIS BOOK

The Mini Reading and Conventions of Language Tests

In the first part of the book you will find ten tests for each subject. These tests are divided into three levels of difficulty:

- Standard level
- Intermediate level
- Advanced level.

- You will be able to see what level your child is at by finding the point where they start having consistent difficulty with questions. For example, if your child answers most questions correctly up to the intermediate level and then gets most questions wrong from then onwards, it is likely your child's ability is at an intermediate level.
- You will be able to see your child's strengths and weaknesses in different topics by completing the **Strengths and weaknesses chart** (see page viii).
- You will also be able to give your child intensive practice in short tests which have time limits based on the actual Reading and Conventions of Language test times.
- There are quick answers for every question so you can easily mark your child's work.
- For the **Reading tests**, line references and explanations are provided. The line references will help you find exactly where the answer to the question is found in the text. Questions in the reading answer section have been divided into three types: fact-finding, inferring and judgement. Explanations are provided within these answer scaffolds to help you teach your child how to answer the different types of reading questions. If you turn to the inside back cover you will see all these types of explanations explained fully.
- For the **Conventions of Language tests**, tips and explanations are provided. Your child can then learn to apply these general tips to similar questions and the explanations will help you explain the answers to your child.

The Mini Writing Tests

- There are three **Writing tests**.
- There are tips for writing specific to the type of text of each question. These tips will provide guidelines for your child's writing.
- Each Writing Test has writing samples at intermediate and advanced levels. From this you will be able to see which level your child is writing at. For example, if your child's writing closely resembles the intermediate writing sample then their writing is at the intermediate level.
- Marking checklists are also provided so you can go through your child's writing and check that they have covered all of the necessary points.

The Sample Online-style Literacy Tests

- In the second part of the book we provide you with two sample tests which are modelled on actual NAPLAN Online Literacy tests.
- For the Conventions of Language and Reading tests there are answers, tips and explanations.
- For the Writing tests there are marking checklists and writing samples, one each at intermediate and advanced levels. From this you will be able to see what level your child is writing at by comparing their writing to the writing samples.

STRENGTHS AND WEAKNESSES CHART

- As your child completes each test, mark it using the answer section at the back and then fill in this chart to record their progress.
- You will be able to see at a glance your child's strengths and weaknesses in different topics and different strands of Literacy.
- If you find your child needs more practice on specific topics, use the checklist of ***Excel*** books on the back cover to find the book to help them.

Area of Learning	Level	Mini test	Mark
Spelling	Standard	1	/25
Spelling	Standard	2	/25
Spelling	Intermediate	3	/25
Spelling	Intermediate	4	/25
Spelling	Intermediate	5	/25
Spelling	Intermediate	6	/25
Spelling	Advanced	7	/25
Spelling	Advanced	8	/25
Spelling	Advanced	9	/25
Spelling	Advanced	10	/25
Grammar	Standard	1	/25
Grammar	Intermediate	2	/25
Grammar	Intermediate	3	/25
Grammar	Advanced	4	/25
Grammar	Advanced	5	/25
Punctuation	Standard	1	/25
Punctuation	Intermediate	2	/25
Punctuation	Intermediate	3	/25
Punctuation	Advanced	4	/25
Punctuation	Advanced	5	/25
Reading	Standard	1	/8
Reading	Standard	2	/8
Reading	Intermediate	3	/8
Reading	Intermediate	4	/8
Reading	Intermediate	5	/8
Reading	Intermediate	6	/8
Reading	Advanced	7	/8
Reading	Advanced	8	/8
Reading	Advanced	9	/8
Reading	Advanced	10	/8

SPELLING

Standard level questions

Mini Test 1

Please ask your parent or teacher to read to you the spelling words on page 169.
Write the correct spelling of each word in the box.

1. The earth has many large ______ of water.
2. The ______ luncheon was a huge success.
3. The gardener worked hard to rake up all the ______.
4. Take care when working with sharp ______.
5. I have twisted both ______ in my running career.
6. As an artist, I tend to use a lot of ______.
7. My ______ are growing so much, soon I'll need new shoes.
8. My daughter's favourite story is the one with the three ______.
9. The waiter found carrying multiple ______ difficult.
10. The ______ had chewed a large hole in the hessian sacking.
11. The Great Barrier ______ is gorgeous!
12. What are your favourite ______?
13. I am still waiting on a few ______ to my party invitation.
14. The number of ______ interested in sport is increasing.
15. People do many ______ to stay in good physical condition.

Answers and explanations on pages 120–121

Mini Test 1 (continued)

The spelling mistakes in these sentences have been highlighted. Write the correct spelling of each highlighted word in the box.

16 The term "sport" refers to all competitve physical activitys.

17 I find playing soccer and other ball-related sportes very enjoyable.

18 The doorbell rang and I ran quickly downstares.

19 I was pleased to see evrybody had arrived.

20 I hoped my mak-up looked all right.

21 I laughed to see a huge gift—a liffe like Homer Simpson doll!

Read the text *Salvaging*. Each line has a word that is incorrect. Write the correct spelling of the word in the box.

Salvaging

22 Salvaging is an xsellent way of saving energy and making a difference during your lifetime.

23 Alongsyde energy, there is still a great deal of waste, which could be recycled.

24 Mooreover, waste is harmful to the environment.

25 It is becoming more comenplace for people to buy more products and to create more waste.

Answers and explanations on pages 120–121

SPELLING

Standard level questions

Mini Test 2

Please ask your parent or teacher to read to you the spelling words on page 169. Write the correct spelling of each word in the box.

1. Getting a good result in the exam was my ______ concern.
2. I tried not to ______ during the politician's speech.
3. Thanks to Mum, the cake we ______ was a huge success.
4. You need to have your ______ to receive a refund.
5. ______ and vegetables are required in a healthy diet.
6. I had to visit an official office in order to ______ my certificate.
7. "You really ______ make an effort," I reminded myself.
8. Unless the traffic is bad, it doesn't ______ take long to get home.
9. The ______ coloured walls were unremarkable.
10. I have always wanted to study at a ______ school.
11. I couldn't wait to see ______ new computer.
12. "What are you doing over ______?" called the supervisor.
13. I sat down at the edge of the cliff to enjoy the ______.
14. The shop owner ______ and chased after the thief.
15. I needed to quickly set the ______ for dinner.

Answers and explanations on pages 121–122

Mini Test 2 (continued)

The spelling mistakes in these sentences have been highlighted. Write the correct spelling of each highlighted word in the box.

16 I was felling nervous when I realised I would be quite late.

17 The cieling fan moved slowly, barely moving the hot air.

18 I always seem to spill food and beverages on my whyte pants.

19 I was hoping to steele away before the end of the movie.

20 The gymnast moved with grace and perpose.

Each line has a word that is incorrect. Write the correct spelling of the word in the box.

21 The handle was lose so I was careful when closing the door.

22 The room was an unusually vivid shade of grean.

23 The book was so scary I almost let out a screem.

24 I was careful to hold onto my bag so I didn't loose it.

25 The room was strangely quite and unusually warm.

Answers and explanations on pages 121–122

SPELLING

Intermediate level questions

Mini Test 3

Please ask your parent or teacher to read to you the spelling words on page 170.
Write the correct spelling of each word in the box.

1. The train was ______ for twenty minutes.
2. Scones with ______ are my favourite type of cake.
3. The widow had been in ______ for two years.
4. "Go ______!" exclaimed the preacher.
5. The teacher's ______ was there to assist anyone who needed help.
6. The ______ was still smoky after the fires had cleared.
7. The light on the table threw a strong ______ of colour around the room.
8. The children were ______ from the cinema for unruly behaviour.
9. I couldn't ______ waiting a moment longer for my present!
10. The chair was a lovely golden ______ colour.
11. The tree's ______ was weakened in the storm.
12. It's important to know where the car's ______ is.
13. I think some people have a lack of common ______.
14. I love it when my ______ uncles come to visit us.
15. We had a group of people visit ______ house for lunch yesterday.

Answers and explanations on pages 122–123

Mini Test 3 (continued)

The spelling mistakes in these sentences have been highlighted. Write the correct spelling of each highlighted word in the box.

16 The family brought there dog to the park.

17 I got along well with Tommy while he stayed and he had a good thyme too.

18 Robert Bartlett (1875–1946), an Arctic explorer, was famous for his skill in piloting ships threw ice.

19 He commanded a navel ship for the explorer Robert E Peary from 1905 to 1909.

20 Bartlett led an expedition in 1913 on which the ship *Karluk* was crushed by ice in the South Poll.

21 He was not idol, and walked across the ice to Siberia and returned with rescuers for his companions.

Read the text *Diary*. Each line has a word that is incorrect.
Write the correct spelling of the word in the box.

Diary

22 The play tonight totally blue me away!

23 The seen with the dancing was amazing.

24 The storyline was very humerus too.

25 I don't want to sound vein but I think I look like the lead character.

Answers and explanations on pages 122–123

SPELLING

Intermediate level questions

Mini Test 4

Please ask your parent or teacher to read to you the spelling words on page 170.
Write the correct spelling of each word in the box.

1. The evenings are so ______ during summer.
2. I thought last night's play was simply ______.
3. He felt terrible about ______ the class but could no longer find time for it.
4. ______ a high result was her primary concern.
5. I sometimes have difficulty ______ the Internet.
6. Without ______ too much, I feel I did my best.
7. The actor ______ in the glory of winning an Oscar.
8. The soccer goalie ______ the ball and caught it.
9. My study workload has ______ now I'm in high school.
10. The town was completely ______ by the disaster.
11. She ______ into the narrow opening, hoping she could squeeze through.
12. A ______ singer is visiting our town.
13. We are thinking of ______ north this winter.
14. A Bunsen burner is a ______ piece of laboratory equipment.
15. It is commonly used for ______ chemical substances, sterilisation and combustion.

Answers and explanations on pages 123–124

The spelling mistakes in these sentences have been highlighted. Write the correct spelling of each highlighted word in the box.

16 It works by berning flammable gas, usually methane.

17 It is named after the very faymos Robert Wilhelm Bunsen, who was a German chemist.

18 Once there was a widower who married a proud and spytteful woman as his second wife.

19 She had two daughters who were equally vayn.

20 By his first wife, he had had a beautyful young daughter who was a girl of unparalleled goodness and sweet temper.

21 The stepmother, prefferring her daughters, forced the first daughter to complete all the housework.

Read the text *Boots the monkey*. Each line has a word that is incorrect. Write the correct spelling of the word in the box.

Boots the monkey

22 Boots the Monkey, whom Dora met one day in the forest, is her best freind.

23 He is friendly and enthusiastic, and usually wears nutheing but his beloved red boots, hence his name.

24 He is gray with a yellow stomach.

25 His parents look similarer, with variations in eyes, height, clothing and fur.

Answers and explanations on pages 123–124

SPELLING

Intermediate level questions

Mini Test 5

Please ask your parent or teacher to read to you the spelling words on page 171.
Write the correct spelling of each word in the box.

1 Everybody deserves ______ in their lives.

2 Such ______ in a person is difficult to excuse.

3 Last year held some ______ experiences for me.

4 You need to be ______ in today's job market.

5 By opening the door, the room was made ______.

6 The writing was so hard to read it was ______.

7 Take care around ______ materials.

8 Most accidents are ______.

9 The business was deemed a success when it became ______..

10 It is not ______ to be in two places at once.

11 I hope you are ______ for making your own bed.

12 Crossing the road against the lights is not ______.

13 The neighbour's ______ is disturbing my sleep.

14 Buddhism is one of the major ______ of the world.

15 There was a lot of ______ in the office when we learnt of his illness.

Mini Test 5 (continued)

The spelling mistakes in these sentences have been highlighted. Write the correct spelling of each highlighted word in the box.

16 My father had to call in a specialist to asses the extent of the damage to the wall.

17 I am fastest than you at running.

18 I am the sleepyest I have felt in a long time.

19 My cat is softest than yours.

20 She is the lazyerest of the two sisters and refuses to wash up.

Each line has a word that is incorrect.
Write the correct spelling of the word in the box.

21 I felt sader than ever when she finally left.

22 It is expected that you will maintain a high level of personal tidyness.

23 The two are so dissimilar they are uncompareible.

24 He is filled with gooddness and compassion.

25 Megan is the shorter girl in our class.

Answers and explanations on pages 124–125

SPELLING

Intermediate level questions

Mini Test 6

Please ask your parent or teacher to read to you the spelling words on page 171.
Write the correct spelling of each word in the box.

1 The ______ were more than happy to sign copies of their books.

2 I was unable to attend the event due to a ______ complaint.

3 The children's ______ was exceptionally good.

4 The sound of my voice ______ off the rocks and back towards me.

5 ______ is essential in a balanced diet.

6 I am hoping to see the ______ eclipse later tonight.

7 Prince Charles is the rightful ______ to the throne.

8 She insisted on ______ a career on the stage.

9 The police gave up their ______ of the thief.

10 There is a special ______ to life drawing.

11 The walkers came dangerously close to falling into the ______.

12 A ______ is a deceitful and unreliable person.

13 It is my dream to one day sail around the world in a ______.

14 Chicken ______ is my favourite meal for dinner.

15 I cannot agree with the mindless ______ of animals.

Answers and explanations on pages 125–126

Mini Test 6 (continued)

The spelling mistakes in these sentences have been highlighted. Write the correct spelling of each highlighted word in the box.

16 Work has become werysome and is no longer enjoyable.

17 My street runs parallell to yours.

18 A good sleep and proper nutrishion are essential.

19 We are concerned about higene and encourage handwashing before meals.

20 His voice was horse from shouting for assistance.

Each line has a word that is incorrect. Write the correct spelling of the word in the box.

21 The small mouse narwed easily through the potato sack.

22 The rains came and the drout was finally broken.

23 I like to be thorugh and doublecheck my work.

24 At the hight of summer the heat is unbearable.

25 The witch shreeked and cackled.

Answers and explanations on pages 125–126

SPELLING

Advanced level questions

Mini Test 7

Please ask your parent or teacher to read to you the spelling words on page 172.
Write the correct spelling of each word in the box.

1 The ________ was towed after being parked illegally.

2 I hope to get better ________ with the new boy on my street.

3 There was ________ space in my room for a desk and bookcase.

4 The bobbing red ________ marked the swimmer's turning point.

5 Your ________ tells you when you have done something wrong.

6 Rubble and ________ littered the road after the crash.

7 I am learning about ________ in geometry.

8 It is important that we take care of our ________ .

9 The teacher had an ________ manner that was very helpful.

10 A fuel ________ is an instrument used to indicate the level of fuel contained in a tank.

11 My new TV was ________ not to break down for three years.

12 The ________ is a device used to chop off people's heads.

13 The ________ told me I would win the lotto this year!

14 Courageous and daring, people born in the Year of the Tiger rarely ________ into shyness.

15 Some people can be unpredictable and ________ .

Answers and explanations on pages 126–127

The spelling mistakes in these sentences have been highlighted. Write the correct spelling of each highlighted word in the box.

16 Our dog is sometimes territorial and posessive.

17 2010 is the Year of the Metal Tiger, with Metal bringing addishional strength and determination.

18 Embroidery is the art or handicraft of decarating fabric or other materials with needle and thread or yarn.

19 Embroidery may also incorparrate other materials such as metal strips or pearls.

20 Some basic techniques or stitches of the earlyest work include chain stitch, buttonhole or blanket stitch, running stitch, satin stitch and cross stitch.

21 These remain the fundermental techniques of hand embroidery today.

Read the text *Blogs*. Each line has a word that is incorrect.
Write the correct spelling of the word in the box.

Blogs

22 Many blogs provide comentery or news on a particular subject.

23 Others function as more personal online daires.

24 A tipicle blog combines text, images and links to other blogs.

25 Readers now aknowledge that the ability to leave comments is an important part of many blogs.

Answers and explanations on pages 126–127

SPELLING

Advanced level questions

Mini Test 8

Please ask your parent or teacher to read to you the spelling words on page 172. Write the correct spelling of each word in the box.

1. ______ allows substances to enter the body through the skin.
2. ______ have a wide range of shapes including spheres.
3. The word ______ often means any food that is rich in starch.
4. An ______ is generally an area within the natural environment.
5. A heating ______ is a device that changes electricity to heat.
6. All living things depend on ______.
7. ______ in animals are often transported in the blood.
8. ______ is a word used to describe objects that are very small.
9. The ice ______ is the centre of an ice crystal.
10. I hope I don't get the ______ that's going around.
11. It is interesting to consider the ______ of humankind.
12. The doctor checked my ______ levels.
13. In science, a ______ needs to be tested to establish a new theory.
14. Our body's primary source of ______ takes the form of glucose.
15. This type of sugar comes from digesting carbohydrates into a ______ that we can easily convert to energy.

Answers and explanations on pages 127–128

Mini Test 8 (continued)

The spelling mistakes in these sentences have been highlighted. Write the correct spelling of each highlighted word in the box.

16 Sometimes glucose levels in the bloodstreeme aren't properly regulated.

17 People can develop a serious condishion, such as diabetes.

18 Australia is home to between 600,000 and 700,000 uneeke species, many of which are found nowhere else in the world.

19 About 84 per cent of plants, 83 per cent of mamels, and 45 per cent of birds are only found in Australia.

20 Changes to the native habatat as a result of human activity have put many of these unique species at risk.

21 Over the last two hundred years many species of plants and animals have become extinkt.

Read the text *Food energy*. Each line has a word that is incorrect. Write the correct spelling of the word in the box.

Food energy

22 Like other forms of energy, food energy is expressed in calouries or joules.

23 The kilojoule is the unit officially recommended by the World Healf Organisation.

24 The calorie is still the most common younit in many countries.

25 It is only when food reacts with oxygen in the sells of living things that energy is released.

SPELLING

Advanced level questions

Mini Test 9

Please ask your parent or teacher to read to you the spelling words on page 173.
Write the correct spelling of each word in the box.

1. I would like to one day open my own ______ .
2. There were four ______ holding the roof up.
3. Her leg was ______ by the flying glass.
4. The jogger followed a familiar ______ .
5. The tourist dropped his sunglasses down a ______ .
6. I hope ______ to travel to Paris next summer.
7. My new vacuum cleaner is quite ______ .
8. I find the natural world ______ .
9. The ______ is my favourite flower.
10. The queen was used to ______ and fine things.
11. In my ______ time I like to read.
12. Whether I like school or not is ______ as I have to go.
13. The students were concerned about ______ issues.
14. The visitor was ______ by the beauty of the harbour.
15. I love to breathe the uncontaminated ______ of the mountains.

Answers and explanations on pages 128–129

Mini Test 9 (continued)

The spelling mistakes in these sentences have been highlighted. Write the correct spelling of each highlighted word in the box.

16 A puraist is one who desires that an item remain true to its essence.

17 Blunt sissors make cutting difficult.

18 My move downstairs is only temparary at this stage.

19 I thurouhly enjoyed last night's movie.

20 We need to call the upholltsarer about the rip in the armchair.

Each line has a word that is incorrect. Write the correct spelling of the word in the box.

21 The child appeared vulnarable standing alone without his mother.

22 We were very happy when the sewarage system was connected to our house.

23 The fire began to smolder as the rain hit it.

24 I feel better now my flu symptoms have subcided.

25 Tom enjoyed this year's local council scavanger hunt.

Answers and explanations on pages 128–129

SPELLING

Advanced level questions

Mini Test 10

Please ask your parent or teacher to read to you the spelling words on page 173.
Write the correct spelling of each word in the box.

1. I find Egyptian ______ fascinating.
2. After breaking a leg, Henry moved ______ around.
3. ______ means having an aggressive or fighting attitude.
4. She was ______ during the whole ordeal.
5. The student ______ from the extra reading.
6. People described him as happy and ______.
7. I was ______ upon receiving excellent test results.
8. The ______ light flickered irritatingly.
9. The glass on the road ______ a hole in my tyre.
10. People who remain awake may experience ______.
11. The light was ______ and glowed with a white heat.
12. I love the pattern of shapes and colours in a ______.
13. The ______ discharged his soldiers at midday.
14. The ______ nature of the case made it controversial.
15. I had to ______ the car around the fallen bin.

Answers and explanations on pages 129–130

Mini Test 10 (continued)

The spelling mistakes in these sentences have been highlighted. Write the correct spelling of each highlighted word in the box.

16 The family ossilated between a local holiday and an overseas trip.

17 The mountain's plateo offered a welcome respite after the long hike.

18 I hope to one day study to become a psichiatrast.

19 He learned how to ressusitate at the water-safety school.

20 Water therapy is theraputic for the pain in my lower back.

Each line has a word that is incorrect. Write the correct spelling of the word in the box.

21 The dog attack was vishious and unpleasant.

22 The trip was reminisant of other trips taken during my childhood.

23 A sovereighn state is self-governing and independent.

24 The hotel's fasilities were excellent.

25 We visited a mediieval castle last year in Europe.

Answers and explanations on pages 129–130

GRAMMAR

Standard level questions

Mini Test 1

1 Which word correctly completes this sentence?

It was a ______ cushion and quite soft.

A my **B** late **C** cotton **D** high

2 Which verb correctly completes this sentence?

I ______ to travel to the Nile River.

wants	would like	could	want	haven't
A	**B**	**C**	**D**	**E**

3 Write the grammatical terms to label the words in the box according to how each is used in this sentence.

She is an excellent English teacher.

noun adjective adverb pronoun article

Word	**Grammatical term in this sentence**
She	
an	
excellent	
teacher	

4 Tick the two adjectives in this sentence.

The day was both cool and windy so I packed my jumper.

5 Tick the **three** nouns in this sentence.

Where is your red hat? I think it's on the table or bed.

6 Which of the following correctly completes the sentence?

You had a phone call but I can't remember ______ rang you.

A what **B** who **C** when **D** why

7 Which option correctly completes this sentence?

I could see the snow falling ______ bedroom window.

A in the **B** at the **C** from the **D** with the

 Answers and explanations on pages 130–131

8 Which word correctly completes this sentence?

I wanted to deliver some of this delicious cake to ______ .

A She **B** her **C** he **D** they

9 Which option correctly completes this sentence?

He was an old man who had trouble ______ .

A to walking **B** to walk **C** with walk **D** walking

10 Which option completes this sentence correctly?

The book you are looking for is ______ table.

through the	over a	on a	on the	with the
A	**B**	**C**	**D**	**E**

11 Which word in this text does *him* refer to?

Harry took the cat from the shelter. His brother and sister will be delighted with him.

Harry (**A**), cat (**B**), brother (**C**), sister (**D**)

12 Write the grammatical terms to label the words in the box according to how each is used in this sentence.

The tired students had to make their own beds at camp.

noun adjective verb pronoun article

Word	Grammatical term in this sentence
The	
tired	
their	
beds	

13 Which word correctly completes this sentence?

"You don't mean you met ______ Australian Prime Minister, do you?"

the	a	she	her	it
A	**B**	**C**	**D**	**E**

Answers and explanations on pages 130–131

14 Which word correctly completes this sentence?

The swimming team completed ________ final competition last week.

A its **B** it's **C** its'

15 Circle the main clause of this sentence.

During the sudden and unexpected storm, the students ran for cover, despite the severe wind.

16 Tick the **three** adjectives in this sentence.

When you swim, you don't get tired like with land-based exercise. Swimming is a cool and enjoyable activity.

17 Circle the two adverbs in this question.

I frequently swim in the mornings but never in the afternoons.

18 Which is a complete sentence?

A Thinking of running.
B That film was interesting.
C Near the edge of the mountain.
D Until the bell goes.

19 Which option correctly completes this sentence?

Swimming involves the use of all major muscle groups and ________ you a workout, regardless of your ability.

A they give **B** gives **C** she gives **D** you give

20 Which option correctly completes this sentence?

There are many reasons why you should choose swimming as your favourite ________ activity.

A recreate **B** recreational **C** recreated **D** recreation

Answers and explanations on pages 130–131

21 Which word is an adverb in this sentence?

22 Which option correctly completes this sentence?

Exercise ________ your chances of a long and healthy life.

A will increased **B** could increases **C** might increase **D** would increased

23 Circle the **two** verbs in this sentence.

The boy might enjoy a chocolate ice-cream after dinner.

24 Which option correctly completes this sentence?

I always feel ________ after a long swim in the pool.

A real refreshed **B** really refreshing **C** really refreshed **D** really refreshes

25 Circle the underlined word that is an article in this sentence.

Swimming is a low-impact, weightless activity where you can just tune out and relax.

Answers and explanations on pages 130–131

GRAMMAR

Intermediate level questions

Mini Test 2

1 Which word correctly completes this sentence?

We will go overseas ______ August.

A in **B** at **C** on **D** since

2 Which word correctly completes this sentence?

______ the weekend we went bushwalking.

A On **B** At **C** In **D** Since

3 Write the grammatical terms to label the words in the box according to how each is used in this sentence.

I found London to be a vibrant and exciting city.

noun adjective adverb pronoun article

Word	Grammatical term in this sentence
I	
found	
London	
vibrant	

4 Which word is a preposition?

A large crowd stood by the road, watching the accident.

A (large) B (by) C (watching) D (accident)

5 Tick the **three** prepositions in this sentence.

He went into the kitchen from the passage and then across the hall.

6 Which option correctly completes this sentence?

Actions ______ to ensure no damage was permanent.

A is taken **B** was taken **C** were taken **D** were took

7 Which option correctly completes this sentence?

If I'd known you were coming over, ______ cooked you dinner.

A I'd of **B** you'd have **C** I'd have **D** I wouldn't

Answers and explanations on pages 131–132

8 Which sentence is correct?

A The first John Marsden book I read have from the *Tomorrow* series.

B The first John Marsden book I reads will be from the *Tomorrow* series.

C The first John Marsden book I read were from the *Tomorrow* series.

D The first John Marsden book I read was from the *Tomorrow* series.

9 Which sentence is correct?

A Today, I'd like to speak to you about our new sports program.

B Today, I'm like to speak to you about our new sports program.

C Today, I'll like to speak to you about new sports program.

D Today, I've like to speak to you about the new sports program.

10 Which sentence is correct?

A We departs on Friday, regardless of the rain.

B We departing on Friday, regardless of the rain.

C We will departed on Friday, regardless of the rain.

D We will depart on Friday, regardless of the rain.

11 Which word or words in this text does *their* refer to?

The sister and brother were late to their tennis lesson with the instructors.

sister	brother	sister and brother	instructors	tennis lessons
A	B	C	D	E

12 Write the grammatical terms to label the words in the box according to how each is used in this sentence.

There were two red packages left for the family on the bench.

noun adjective adverb preposition article

Word	Grammatical term in this sentence
were	
red	
for	
family	

Answers and explanations on pages 131–132

13 Which one of these sentences indicates that the homework is completed?

A I will complete my homework by then.
B I am completing my homework.
C I have completed my homework.
D I will have completed my homework.

14 Which words correctly complete this sentence?

Bungy jumping is an activity that ________ jumping ________ a tall structure while connected to a large elastic cord.

A involves, from
B involved, above
C involved, into
D involve, up

15 Circle the main clause of this sentence.

It is also possible to jump from a movable object, such as a hot-air-balloon or helicopter, which has the ability to hover above the ground.

16 Which **two** phrases both complete this sentence correctly?

When you walk the dog ________ you both benefit tremendously.

A in the morning
B park, beach or footpath
C to get out of the house
D while the sun
E upside down

17 Which option correctly completes this sentence?

Both ________ are interested in seeing a movie this afternoon.

A Sharon and me
B Me and Sharon
C Sharon and I
D I and Sharon

 Answers and explanations on pages 131–132

18 Which is a complete sentence?

A Happen to walk past.
B The plant needs water.
C While on holidays in Kenya.
D Whenever you feel.

19 Which option correctly completes this sentence?

I ________ to have seen the show but the tickets were sold out.

A would have liked **B** wants **C** will want **D** wanted

20 Circle the word that is an adverb in this sentence.

Castles and forts were often placed on hilltops.

21 Circle the word that is an adverb in this sentence.

A lift was placed there so people in wheelchairs could catch it.

22 Which option correctly completes this sentence?

He worked ________ and was awarded an academic prize.

B good **B** bad **C** well **D** goodly

23 Circle the **two** verbs in this sentence.

The cat prowled slowly towards the frightened bird flapping its wings.

24 Which option correctly completes this sentence?

Today is ________ than yesterday.

A cloudiest **B** cloudier **C** more cloudier **D** clouderiest

25 Which conjunction correctly joins these sentences?

The astronauts are weightless. They are in space.

unless	until	because	or	then
A	**B**	**C**	**D**	**E**

 Answers and explanations on pages 131–132

GRAMMAR Intermediate level questions

Mini Test 3

1 Which word correctly completes this sentence?

I hope you will get ______ your operation quickly.

A under **B** down **C** over **D** up

2 Which **two** phrases both complete this sentence correctly?

I thought that she had gone ______!

far away	so far	a bit far	a bit strong	far and away
A	**B**	**C**	**D**	**E**

3 Write the grammatical terms to label the words in the box according to how each is used in this sentence.

By tomorrow, I will have done my assignment.

noun adjective adverb pronoun article

Word	**Grammatical term in this sentence**
By	
will	
my	
assignment	

4 Circle the word that is an article.

"Game on!" shouted the opposing soccer captain.

5 Tick the three verbs in this sentence.

I have half a mind to ring that café to complain!

6 Which sentence is correct?

A I will have been doing the dishes when the phone rang.

B I have been doing the dishes when the phone rang.

C I will be doing the dishes when the phone rang.

D I had been doing the dishes, when the phone rang.

Answers and explanations on page 132

7 Which option correctly completes this sentence?

In September, I ______ studying French for two years.

will be	will have been	have been	I would of been
A	B	C	D

8 Which word correctly completes this sentence?

Shoes and socks go ______ .

A hand in mouth
B fingers and gloves
C hand in hand
D shoes and feet

9 Which word correctly completes this sentence?

When we were poor, we lived hand to ______ .

A head **B** mouth **C** heart **D** eye

10 Which word correctly completes this sentence?

What a relief to be ______ off the hook!

A dropped **B** hung **C** lifted **D** let

11 Which options complete this question correctly?

The dog survived ______ operation and ______ clear that things are going well.

it's its they're their

12 Write the grammatical terms to label the words in the box according to how each is used in this sentence.

We regularly went downstairs to visit the elderly couple for lunch.

noun adjective adverb preposition article

Word	Grammatical term in this sentence
regularly	
visit	
elderly	
lunch	

Answers and explanations on page 132

13 Which word completes this sentence correctly?

Leonardo DiCaprio has a passion for the environment that ________ as far back as the *Titanic* days of his early twenties.

A extends **B** extending **C** extend **D** extended

14 Which word correctly completes this sentence?

It started with an environmental documentary that I ________ when I was very young.

A see **B** saw **C** sawed **D** seen

15 Circle the main clause of this sentence.

Although it was difficult, I decided to become more active and outspoken about these issues, because ultimately I wanted to make a difference.

16 Tick the **four** pronouns in this sentence.

He took time to talk to me about the issue of my health as I didn't really understand very much about it.

17 Choose the correct preposition.

From then ________ I was much more active in environmental activities.

A in **B** at **C** on **D** under

18 Which is a complete sentence?

A Over the years.

B The actor had been practising his lines.

C A man with global.

D The son of a German mother.

19 Which option correctly completes this sentence?

The individual, ________ on the board of the Natural Resources Defence Council, is a well-known actor.

A that sits **B** who sits **C** who's sits **D** that seating

20 Which option correctly completes this sentence?

In 2005 he bought Blackadore Caye, an idyllic island off the coast of Belize, which he ________ develop into an environmentally friendly resort.

A plan to **B** plans on **C** plans to **D** planning on

Answers and explanations on page 132

Mini Test 3 (continued)

21 Circle the word that is a conjunction in this sentence.

With renewable energy resources, the resort will be both environmentally friendly and luxurious.

22 Which option correctly completes this sentence?

My house is considered a __________ as I have solar panels on my roof.

A green
B building green
C green built
D green build

23 Circle the **two** words that are verbs.

I have been driving my hybrid car for six years now.

24 Which word in the sentence does 'them' refer to?

Hybrid cars reduce emissions and I liked mine so much that I bought three more of them for my mum, dad and stepmum.

A emissions
B mum, dad and stepmum
C hybrid cars
D mum and dad

25 Circle the underlined word that is an adverb in this sentence.

The students wholeheartedly enjoy their time in the library.

Answers and explanations on page 132

GRAMMAR

Advanced level questions

Mini Test 4

1 Which word correctly completes this sentence?

The waiter laid the table ______.

A carefully **B** careful **C** caring **D** care

2 Which word or words correctly complete this sentence?

I ______ rang the doctor as I felt there was something terribly wrong.

A most urgent **B** urgently **C** more urgently **D** urgent

3 Write the grammatical terms to label the words in the box according to how each is used in this sentence.

The sun is shining more brightly now that summer has arrived.

noun adjective adverb pronoun article

Word	Grammatical term in this sentence
The	
sun	
brightly	
has	

4 Circle the underlined word that is an adjective.

I <u>felt</u> <u>sadder</u> than ever <u>when</u> he <u>finally</u> left.

5 Tick the **three** verbs in this sentence.

She is the lazier of the two sisters and refuses to wash the dishes.

6 Which option correctly completes this sentence?

I am the ______ person I know as I am always eating!

A hungry **B** hungriest **C** most hungriest **D** hungrier

7 Which word correctly completes this sentence?

I've always wanted to be a vet; ______, I would also be happy being a teacher.

A otherwise **B** however **C** except for **D** unless

Answers and explanations on page 133

8 Which phrase correctly completes this sentence?

______, she is the slower of the two sisters when they race.

A Despite being the eldest in the family
B In spite being the elder
C However older
D Nevertheless being older

9 Which option correctly completes this sentence?

The aeroplane landed ______ with no bumps.

A smoothly B smoother C smooths D smooth

10 Which sentence is correct?

A They might be able to come if it don't rain.
B If the movie starts late, we will miss our dinner reservation.
C However you felt about me then, like me you will.
D I am looking forward to going to beach, it wasn't far away.

11 Which underlined word can be left out of this sentence?

<u>They</u> put the <u>yellow</u> curtains up in the <u>shop</u> before hanging the red <u>curtains</u>.

A (They) B (yellow) C (shop) D (curtains)

12 Write the grammatical terms to label the words in the box according to how each is used in this sentence.

The sales assistant made an honest mistake and accidentally overcharged me.

noun adjective adverb preposition article conjunction

Word	Grammatical term in this sentence
assistant	
honest	
and	
accientally	

 Answers and explanations on page 133

Mini Test 4 (continued)

13 Which words correctly complete this sentence?

When the bus ________, the students were ________ to stand for elderly passengers.

A is coming, required
B came, requiring
C came, required
D comes, required

14 Which words correctly complete this sentence?

The students worked ________ in the library.

A real quietly **B** most quiet **C** very quiet **D** very quietly

15 Circle the main clause of this sentence.

In the wild, males seldom live longer than 10 years, as injuries sustained from continuous fighting reduces their life span.

16 Tick the **three** verbs in this sentence.

Prepare yourself for a thrilling experience that will excite and terrify you!

17 Circle the three nouns in this sentence.

Lions live for around 10 to 14 years while in captivity.

18 Which is a complete sentence?

A Your licence with you.
B Prepare yourself for.
C Driving must be taken seriously.
D Make sure that whenever you.

19 Which option correctly completes this sentence?

Visually, the male lion ________ distinctive and easily recognised by its mane.

A is highest **B** is high **C** is highly **D** highly

20 Which option correctly completes this sentence?

The face of the male lion is one of the ________ recognised animal symbols in human culture.

A most widely **B** most wide **C** widely **D** widerest

Answers and explanations on page 133

Mini Test 4 (continued)

21 Circle the **two** prepositions in this sentence.

Lions have been kept in menageries since Roman times and have been a key species sought for exhibition.

22 Which option correctly completes this sentence?

Zoos worldwide ________ cooperating in breeding programs for ________ endangered Asiatic subspecies.

A is, the **B** are, a **C** are, the **D** will, the

23 Circle the **two** verbs in this sentence.

While the rabbit hopped slowly through the grass, the fox watched carefully and intently.

24 Which words in the sentence does 'them' refer to?

Avoid dangerous driving as your car and licence may be taken away and you may not have them returned.

A dangerous driving

B car

C licence

D car and licence

E driving

25 Circle the **two** pronouns in this sentence.

Make sure that whenever you exit the vehicle you turn off your lights.

Answers and explanations on page 133

Advanced level questions

Mini Test 5

1 Which word correctly completes this sentence?

Alan rested ______ the wall while he waited to be served at the cafe.

A along **B** over **C** against **D** upon

2 Which sentence is correct?

A The value of the goods has to be high enough to meet the criteria that is set by the local authority.

B The value of the goods have to be high enough to meet the criteria that is set by the local authority.

C The value of the goods has to be high enough to meet the criteria that are set by the local authority.

D The value of the goods have to be high enough to meet the criteria that are set by the local authority.

3 Write the grammatical terms to label the words in the box according to how each is used in this sentence.

Tori wanted to buy a sandwich but she had no money.

noun adjective verb conjunction article

Word	Grammatical term in this sentence
Tori	
but	
had	
money	

4 Circle the two words that are articles.

I went to get a hat from the cupboard as it was very hot.

5 Tick the **three** verbs in this sentence.

The noisy motorcyclist revved his engine then shot through the street, which annoyed the neighbours.

6 Which option correctly completes this sentence?

What's the name of ______ flowers?

A them **B** those **C** they **D** that

Answers and explanations on page 134

Mini Test 5 (continued)

7 Which option correctly completes this sentence?

I ________ my homework last night but I fell asleep.

A completed
B will have been completing
C would have competed
D would of completed

8 Which words correctly complete this sentence?

When deciding ________ the best course ________ action, we must consider the needs ________ others.

A in, of, to **B** on, of, of **C** to, in, of **D** on, in, at

9 Which option correctly completes this sentence?

The stars ________ down on me.

A brightly shined **B** brightly shone **C** brightness shone **D** brightly shining

10 Circle the two underlined words that are pronouns in this sentence.

We watched the soccer game with great anticipation of a win but sadly we didn't win it.

11 Which option correctly completes this question?

I ________ get a haircut before school begins next term.

A needs to **B** will need to **C** needed to **D** needing to

12 Sequence the following phrases in their correct order.

A We usually visit the beach
B We go home to keep cool
C However, if it is too hot
D When summer comes

Order	Phrase
1	
2	
3	
4	

Answers and explanations on page 134

13 How could this sentence be written correctly using indirect speech?

Helen told her dad: "I won't go unless you come too".

A Helen told her dad she wouldn't go unless he came too.

B Helen told her dad that she didn't want to go.

C Helen's dad told her that she didn't want to go unless he went too.

D Dad told Helen that he wouldn't go unless she came too.

14 Which word correctly completes this sentence?

The ancient village was interesting to visit ________ there were many tourists.

A after **B** because **C** but **D** or

15 Circle the main clause of this sentence.

The heat was stifling, despite the installation of a new air-con system, which didn't work as well as we'd hoped.

16 Tick the **two** conjunctions in this sentence.

I like hot drinks such as tea, yet I don't like hot chocolate because it is too sweet.

17 Which word correctly completes this sentence?

In the past, criminals were ________ for their crimes against society.

A hung **B** hanged **C** hunged **D** hanger

18 Which is a complete sentence?

A Nelson Mandela is a former.

B To be elected in a democratic election.

C He held office from 1994 to 1999.

D President of South Africa who.

19 Which option correctly completes this sentence?

During my lifetime I have dedicated ________ to the struggle of the African people.

A me **B** I **C** myself **D** him

20 Which option that correctly completes this sentence?

I have cherished the ideal of a democratic and free society ________ all persons live together in harmony and with equal opportunity.

A in which **B** by which **C** on which **D** at which

Answers and explanations on page 134

Mini Test 5 (continued)

21 Circle the conjunction in this sentence.

The weather was raining yet we still managed a brisk walk.

22 Which option correctly completes this sentence?

It is an ideal which I hope to live for and to achieve. ______ if needs be, it is an ideal for which I am prepared to die.

A Whatever **B** In addition **C** However **D** Also

23 Which two words in the following sentence are common nouns?

The brown cow ambled slowly down the slippery grassy slope.

24 Which word in the following sentence is a proper noun?

This Saturday is my birthday and I can't wait!

25 Who or what does 'them' refer to in this sentence?

The presents were placed carefully under two trees by Mrs Anderson and Mr Pugh who had given them special name tags.

A The presents

B Mrs Anderson and Mr Pugh

C two trees

D special name tags

Answers and explanations on page 134

PUNCTUATION Standard level questions

Mini Test 1

1 Where does the missing comma (,) go?

I was born on Monday 19 July 1996 in Paris a small town in Texas.
A B C D

2 Where does the missing colon (:) go?

The committee now includes the following people (A) the mayor (B) the chief of police (C) and a local (D) representative.

3 Which comma (,) should be replaced by a colon (:)?

Remember, (A) it's important to exercise, (B) eat healthy food, (C) avoid stress, (D) have a good work/life balance and enjoy life.

4 Which comma (,) should be replaced by a colon (:)?

There are five things you need to bring to school on Monday, (A) your pencil case, (B) a ruler, (C) a folder, (D) scissors and some crayons.

5 Where does the missing comma (,) go?

Wow (A) that was a great (B) movie! I'd like to see it (C) again (D) and again.

6 Where does the missing comma (,) go?

Recently (A) we moved houses (B) to a suburb (C) in a different (D) state.

7 Where does the missing comma (,) go?

Unless (A) I complete my assignment (B) I won't be able to go (C) out on (D) Saturday.

Answers and explanations on pages 134–135

Mini Test 1 (continued)

8 Which is the best way to combine the following sentences into one?

The boy's favourite cereal was weetbix. The boy's favourite cereal was cornflakes. The boy's favourite cereal was porridge.

A The boy's favourite cereal was weetbix. The boy's favourite cereal was cornflakes and the boy's favourite cereal was porridge.

B The boy's favourite cereals were weetbix, cornflakes and porridge.

C The boy's favourite cereals is weetbix, cornflakes and porridge.

D The boy's favourite cereal was weetbix. The boy's favourite cereal was cornflakes, and porridge.

9 Where does the missing colon (**:**) go?

There is ↑A only one thing ↑B to do now ↑C get out ↑D while you have the chance.

10 Which sentence has the correct punctuation?

A The teacher said, Make sure you complete all questions.

B The teacher said "Make sure you complete all questions".

C The teacher said, "Make sure you complete all questions

D The teacher said, "Make sure you complete all questions."

11 Which is the correct place in this sentence to put the following punctuation and words?

, who were fearless,

The sailors ↑A rescued many ↑B when ↑C the boat sank ↑D

12 Which punctuation is missing from this sentence?

At school we are studying Pride and Prejudice.

A ' (apostrophe) **B** , (comma) **C** ? (question mark) **D** *italics*

13 Which punctuation mark is missing from this sentence?

Her recipe for cupcakes included flour eggs and cocoa.

A . (full stop) **B** , (comma) **C** ? (question mark) **D** : (colon)

14 Which punctuation mark is missing from this sentence?

Don't leave yet, he said.

A . (full stop) **B** , (comma) **C** " " (speech marks) **D** : (colon)

Answers and explanations on pages 134–135

15 Which punctuation mark is missing from this sentence?

"That student," said Mrs Brown "needs to pay attention."

A . (full stop) **B** , (comma) **C** ? (question mark) **D** : (colon)

16 Which sentence has the correct punctuation?

A Plastics, glass bottles, paper and tins are accepted for recycling.
B Plastics glass bottles, paper and tins are accepted for recycling.
C Plastics glass bottles paper and tins are accepted for recycling.
D Plastics, glass bottles, paper, and tins are accepted for recycling.

17 Which sentence has the correct punctuation?

A Peter said I don't like that car.
B Peter said, "I don't like that car."
C Peter said "I don't like that car".
D "Peter said" I don't like that car.

18 Which sentence has the correct punctuation?

A The poem, The Man from Snowy River, is exciting.
B The poem 'The Man from Snowy River' is exciting.
C The poem *The Man from Snowy River* is exciting.
D The poem, 'The Man from Snowy River', is exciting.

19 Which sentence has the correct punctuation?

A The band played 'Advance Australia Fair' very well, said the Principal
B "The band played 'Advance Australia Fair' very well," said the Principal.
C The band played 'Advance Australia Fair' very well, "said the Principal"
D The band played Advance Australia Fair very well, said the Principal

20 Which sentence has the correct punctuation?

A He asked nicely Where did you put the hat?
B He asked nicely, "Where did you put the hat?"
C He asked nicely, Where did you put the hat?
D "He asked nicely, "Where did you put the hat?"

21 Paul said that Carol had taken his pen.

How is this sentence expressed correctly in direct speech?

A Carol took my pen said Paul
B "Carol took my pen," said Paul.
C Carol said "Paul took my pen"
D "Paul said Carol took my pen"

Answers and explanations on pages 134–135

22 Which punctuation is missing from this sentence?

The rabbit's long ears [ ] which can be more than 10 cm long, are probably an adjustment for identifying predators.

A , (comma) **B** : (colon) **C** ? (question mark) **D** ' (apostrophe)

23 Which punctuation is missing from this sentence?

They have large, powerful hind legs [ ]

A : (colon) **B** , (comma) **C** . (full stop) **D** ? (question mark)

24 Which punctuation is missing from this sentence?

Each foot has five toes [ ] with one greatly reduced in size.

A . (full stop) **B** ! (exclamation mark)
C , (comma) **D** : (colon)

25 Which punctuation is missing from this sentence?

Which is your favourite colour of rabbit [ ]

A ? (question mark) **B** , (comma) **C** . (full stop) **D** ' (apostrophe)

Answers and explanations on pages 134–135

PUNCTUATION

Intermediate level questions

Mini Test 2

20 MIN

1 Where do the two missing apostrophes (') go?

Who (A) s responsible (B) for the mess (C) they (D) re making?

2 Where does the missing ellipsis (...) go?

"I'm (A) wondering (B) " Susan (C) stated (D) bemusedly.

3 Which comma (,) should be replaced by an apostrophe (')?

"Let,(A)s get together,(B)" said Julie to her friends Bob,(C) Raad,(D) Lisa and Gisele.

4 Where does the missing ellipsis (...) go?

Tony thought (A) and thought (B) and then (C) thought (D) some more.

5 Where does the missing ellipsis (...) go?

"The man (A) who murdered me is (B) " gasped (C) the dying (D) man.

6 Which punctuation mark is missing from this sentence?

As John saw someone he thought he knew, he exclaimed,
"I know who that is! Their name is umm."

A , (comma) **B** : (colon) **C** . (full stop) **D** ... (ellipsis)

7 Which punctuation marks are missing from this sentence?

My two brothers Nic and Dom are fantastic tennis players.

A , (commas) **B** ... (ellipses) **C** — (dashes) **D** ! (exclamation marks)

8 Where does the missing apostrophe (') go?

The witches (A) cats (B) were missing (C) from the house (D) .

Answers and explanations on pages 135–136

9 Where does the missing apostrophe (') go?

A B C D

You(A)re invited(B) to our home(C) for dinner(D) tonight.

10 Where does the missing apostrophe (') go?

A B C D

She would(A) have called(B) for assistance(C) if there(D)d been a problem.

11 Where does the missing apostrophe (') go?

A B C D

It(A)s okay if it(B)s hat fall(C)s off(D).

12 Which punctuation mark is missing from this sentence?

Theyd better hurry up or they'll miss the show.

A , (comma) **B** ? (question mark) **C** ' (apostrophe) **D** : (colon)

13 Where does the missing apostrophe (') go?

A B C D

He entered(A) the men(B)s room(C) looking for his(D) friend.

14 Which punctuation mark is missing from this sentence?

Joseph was pleased to get four As last term.

A , (comma) **B** ? (question mark) **C** ' (apostrophe) **D** : (colon)

15 Where does the missing apostrophe (') go?

A B C D

One of her sister(A)s(B) feet(C) was longer(D) than the other.

16 Which sentence has the correct punctuation?

A The children's shoes were lined up neatly outside.

B The childrens' shoes were lined up neatly outside.

C The childrens shoes were lined up neatly outside.

D The childrens shoe's were lined up neatly outside.

Answers and explanations on pages 135–136

Mini Test 2 (continued)

17 Which two words if joined would form the contraction *they'll*?

A they will **B** he will **C** I will **D** she is

18 Which two words if joined would form the contraction *would've*?

A would be **B** won't have **C** would have **D** wouldn't have

19 Which contraction is punctuated correctly?

A had'nt **B** arent' **C** wouldn't **D** theyl'l

20 Which word correctly completes the sentence?

I think ______ never be a greater dancer than Baryshnikov.

A she'll **B** they'll **C** there'll **D** it's

21 Which word correctly completes the sentence?

You ______ tell Tom about the surprise party, did you?

A didn't **B** haveno't **C** would't **D** shouldn't

22 Which punctuation is missing from this sentence?

A boy was hunting for locusts. He had caught a goodly number, when he saw a Scorpion and, mistaking him for a locust ______ reached out his hand to take him.

A , (comma) **B** ... (ellipsis) **C** . (full stop) **D** ? (question mark)

23 Which punctuation is missing from this sentence?

The Scorpion, showing his sting, said ______ If you had but touched me, my friend, you would have lost me, and all your locusts too!"

A . (full stop) **B** " (speech mark) **C** , (comma) **D** ... (ellipsis)

24 Which punctuation is missing from this sentence?

A Lion was awakened from sleep by a Mouse running over his face ______

A ... (ellipsis) **B** , (comma) **C** . (full stop) **D** ? (question mark)

25 Which punctuation is missing from this sentence?

Rising up angrily ______ he caught him and was about to kill him, when the Mouse piteously entreated.

A . (full stop) **B** " (speech mark) **C** , (comma) **D** ... (ellipsis)

Answers and explanations on pages 135–136

PUNCTUATION

Intermediate level questions

Mini Test 3

1 Where does the missing question mark (?) go?

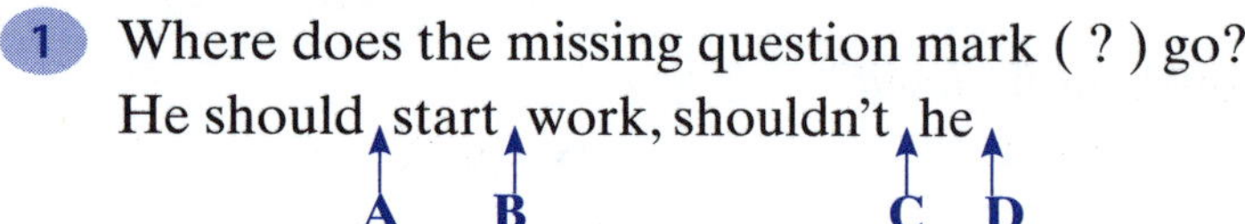

2 Where does the missing question mark (**?**) go?

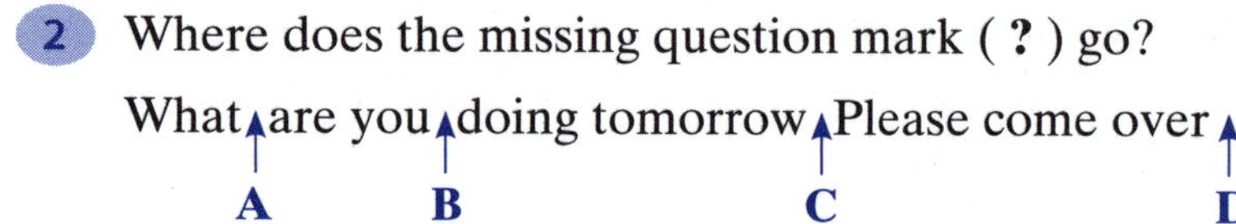

3 Which comma (**,**) should be replaced by a speech mark (**”**)?

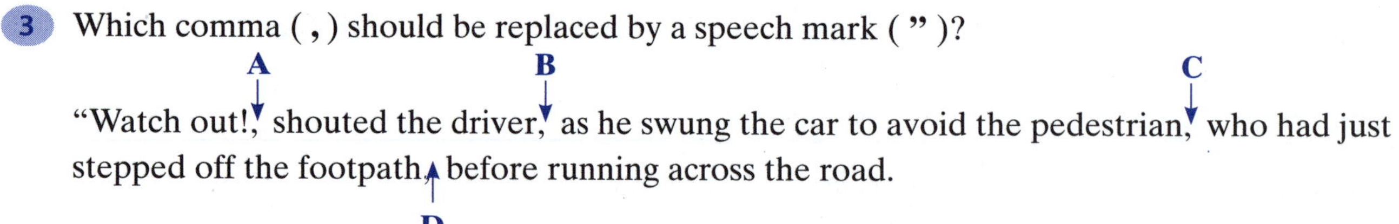

4 Which speech marks (**“ ”**) should be replaced by apostrophes (**’**)?

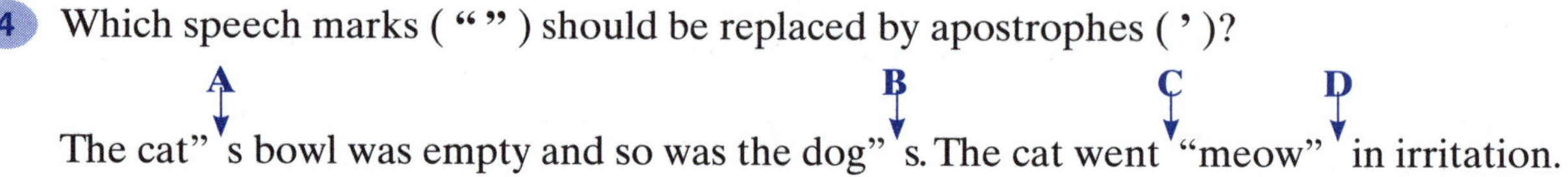

5 Where does the missing question mark go (**?**)?

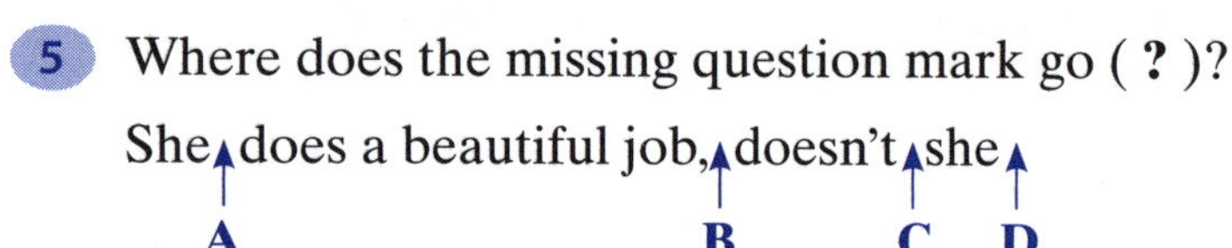

6 Where does the missing question mark go (**?**)?

“What **↑A** are you doing **↑B** tomorrow **↑C** ” Steve asked **↑D** Ken.

7 Where does the missing speech mark (**”**) go?

Mum shouted **↓A** after me, **↓B** “Don't forget **↓C** your lunch! **↓D**

8 Where do the missing speech marks (**“ ”**) go?

↓A I'm so tired! **↓B** exclaimed **↓C** Lucy. **↓D**

9 Which punctuation mark is missing from this sentence?

“Louise can come along, can't she” said Lucy.

A , (comma) **B** **?** (question mark) **C** **’** (apostrophe) **D** **“ ”** (speech marks)

10 Which punctuation mark is missing from this sentence?

“Do you want some ice cream” asked the woman.

A ’ (apostrophe) **B** ? (question mark) **C** , (comma) **D** . (full stop)

Answers and explanations on pages 136–137

Mini Test 3 (continued)

11 Which punctuation mark is missing from this sentence?

The mother shouted Wait! as her child crossed the road.

A ’ (apostrophe) **B** ? (question mark) **C** “ ” (speech marks) **D** . (full stop)

12 Which sentence has the correct punctuation?

A Sarah asked, “Which movie did you see?”
B Sarah asked which movie did you see?
C Sarah asked “Which movie did you see”
D Sarah asked, “Which movie? Did you see”

13 Which sentence has the correct punctuation?

A “Terry has been to Spain? Hasn’t he?” asked James.
B “Terry has been to Spain, hasn’t he?” asked James.
C “Terry? Has been to Spain hasn’t he.” asked James.
D “Terry has been to Spain hasn’t he.” asked James.

14 Which sentence has the correct punctuation?

A “Oh no! I think I may have dropped my keys?” said Ehab.
B “Oh no? I think I may have dropped my keys,” said Ehab.
C “Oh no! I think I may have dropped my keys,” said Ehab.
D “Oh no. I think I may have dropped my keys,” said Ehab.

15 Which sentence has the correct punctuation?

A The waiter asked me if I would like water or juice.
B The waiter “asked me” if I would like water or juice.
C The waiter asked me if I would like “water or juice”.
D The waiter asked me if I would like water or juice?

16 Which sentence has the correct punctuation?

A The walker said he “saw a huge snake on the track”.
B The walker “said he saw a huge snake on the track”.
C The walker said he saw a huge snake on the track.
D The “walker said” he saw a huge snake on the track.

17 Which sentence has the correct punctuation?

A Dinner was delicious, Mum, thanks! said Peter.
B “Dinner was delicious”, Mum, thanks! said Peter.
C Dinner was delicious, Mum,” thanks!” said Peter.
D “Dinner was delicious, Mum. Thanks!” said Peter.

18 Which sentence has the correct punctuation?

A Go away said Sally to her brother. “I don’t want you here.”
B “Go away” said Sally to her brother. I don’t want you here.
C Go away said Sally to her brother. I don’t want you here.
D “Go away,” said Sally to her brother. “I don’t want you here.”

Answers and explanations on pages 136–137

19 How is this sentence expressed correctly in indirect speech?

"I want to go on the ride!" screamed the boy toddler.

A I want to go, screamed the toddler, on the ride!
B The toddler screamed that he wanted to go on the ride.
C "I want to go on the ride!" screamed the toddler.
D He wanted to go on the ride, screamed the toddler.

20 How is this sentence expressed correctly in direct speech?

He said that he wanted them all to enter, immediately.

A Immediately he said, "Enter now".
B He said enter immediately now.
C "He said I want you to enter immediately"
D He said, "I want you all to enter immediately."

21 Which punctuation is missing from this sentence?

"Mum said that we can't go to the Show unless we tidy our room, ____ Tina told her sister Gina.

A , (comma) **B** . (full stop) **C** " (speech mark) **D** ' (apostrophe)

22 Which punctuation is missing from this sentence?

"Oh yuck", Gina said in reply, but stood up anyway ____ She really wanted to go to the Show.

A , (comma) **B** . (full stop) **C** " (speech mark) **D** ' (apostrophe)

23 Which punctuation is missing from this sentence?

"I'll get out the vacuum if you get the duster, ____ she said.

A . (full stop) **B** ' (apostrophe) **C** " (speech mark) **D** , (comma)

24 Which punctuation is missing from this sentence?

Mum came in, looked around ____ and declared their work a success.

A , (comma) **B** . (full stop) **C** " (speech mark) **D** ' (apostrophe)

25 Which punctuation is missing from this sentence?

"Woohoo ____ " shouted Gina. "We did it!"

A . (full stop) **B** , (comma) **C** ! (exclamation mark) **D** " (speech mark)

Answers and explanations on pages 136–137

PUNCTUATION

Advanced level questions

Mini Test 4

25 MIN

1 Where do the two missing apostrophes (’) go?

Steven [A] s team [B] s win was a shock to the coach [C] and train [D] er.

2 Where does the missing colon (:) go?

Here’s [A] what I need you [B] to get me [C] apples, oranges [D] and flour.

3 Where does the missing speech mark go (”)?

When the teacher [A] said [B] “Put your pens down! [C] we did. [D]

4 Sarah rushed over after seeing her friend Maria fall down.

Which way of punctuating the sentence makes the meaning clear?

A Seeing Maria fall, Sarah hurried forward.
B Seeing Maria fall Sarah, hurried forward.
C Seeing Maria, fall Sarah hurried forward.
D Seeing Maria fall Sarah hurried, forward.

5 Which sentence shows the correct punctuation of direct speech?

A “Where are you?” screamed the mother, “as she looked for her son.”
B The teacher said, “we will be returning to the classroom now.”
C When the bell rang, she looked up and exclaimed, “Is it the end of the lesson already?”
D “Where is the remote?” asked Dad “from his chair in the living room.”

6 Which sentence uses the apostrophe (’) correctly?

A The rocks’ rolled down the mountain.
B I could’ve gone if I’d made the time.
C The baby’s waited patiently in their strollers.
D Weve decided to postpone the event after all.

7 Which sentence correctly uses brackets?

A There are several ways of beginning to write an essay (all of them equally helpful) and it depends on writers which they prefer.
B There are several ways (of beginning to write an essay) all of them equally helpful and it depends on writers which they prefer.
C There are several ways of beginning to write an essay all of them equally helpful (and it depends on) writers which they prefer.
D There are several ways of beginning to write an essay all of them equally helpful and it depends on writers (which they prefer.)

Answers and explanations on pages 137–138

8 Which of the following words have quotation marks (‘ and ’) to tell the reader not to take them literally?

A He said to her, “I thought ‘Casablanca’ was a good film.”

B The teacher described his student as ‘a motivated and conscientious worker’.

C The poem is about the ‘unsinkable’ *Titanic*.

D Therese was not familiar with the word ‘officious’.

9 Which punctuation mark is missing from this sentence?

There are two main sports—soccer and league that are popular in this country.

A , (comma) B — (dash) C ... (ellipsis) D : (colon)

10 Which punctuation mark is missing from this sentence?

Our party is on Saturday night it will begin at 7 pm.

A , (comma) B — (dash) C ... (ellipsis) D ; (semicolon)

11 Which punctuation mark is missing from this sentence?

Theyll be okay if we leave them alone for five minutes.

A ’ (apostrophe) B — (dash) C ... (ellipsis) D ; (semicolon)

12 Which punctuation mark is missing from this sentence?

You have only two choices dinner or bed.

A ’ (apostrophe) B — (dash) C ... (ellipsis) D : (colon)

13 Which punctuation mark is missing from this sentence?

As a toddler she was messy as a teenager she’s even worse!

A ’ (apostrophe) B — (dash) C ... (ellipsis) D ; (semicolon)

14 Which sentence has the correct punctuation?

A I watched the winter Olympics every night it was on.

B I watched the Winter Olympics every night it was on.

C I watched the winter olympics every night it was on.

D I watched the winter Olympics Every Night it was on.

15 Which sentence has the correct punctuation?

A “I like Baker’s Taste bread better,” said Sandra to the sales assistant.

B “I like Baker’s Taste bread better said Sandra” to the sales assistant.

C “I like baker’s taste bread better” said Sandra to the Sales Assistant.

D I like Baker’s Taste bread better said Sandra to the sales assistant.

Answers and explanations on pages 137–138

16 Which sentence has the correct punctuation?

A The school principal was not pleased to see me arriving late.
B The school Principal was not pleased to see me arriving late.
C The School Principal was not pleased to see me arriving late.
D The School principal was not pleased to see me arriving late.

17 An apostrophe (') has been left out of this sentence. Where should the missing apostrophe go?

The children (A) (B) s shoes (C) were strewn (D) all over the floor.

18 Which sentence has the correct punctuation?

A I would've completed it but I ran out of time.
B I would h've completed it but I ran out of time.
C I w'have completed it but I ran out of time.
D I would'of completed it but I ran out of time.

19 Which sentence has the correct punctuation?

A There's no ice cream left! shouted Isabel.
B "Theres no ice cream left shouted Isabel".
C "There's no ice cream left!" shouted Isabel.
D There's no ice cream left shouted Isabel.

20 Which punctuation mark is missing from this sentence?

The gaunt man with the scarred lip was the first to speak ____

A ... (ellipsis) **B** , (comma) **C** " (speech mark) **D** . (full stop)

21 Which punctuation mark is missing from this sentence?

"Nowhere," he said ____ with a sigh of disappointment in his voice. "But after all, they had a full day's start."

A , (comma) **B** ! (exclamation mark) **C** ' (apostrophe) **D** ? (question mark)

22 Which punctuation mark is missing from this sentence?

"They don't know we are after them ____ " said the little man on the white horse.

A ... (ellipsis) **B** , (comma) **C** " (speech mark) **D** : (colon)

23 Which punctuation mark is missing from this sentence?

"SHE would know," said the leader bitterly ____ as if speaking to himself.

A ... (ellipsis) **B** , (comma) **C** " (speech mark) **D** : (colon)

24 Which punctuation mark is missing from this sentence?

"Even then they can't go fast. They've got no beast but the mule, and all today the girl's foot has been bleeding ____ "

A ... (ellipsis) **B** ! (exclamation mark) **C** ? (question mark) **D** – (dash)

25 Which punctuation mark is missing from this sentence?

"It helps ____ anyhow," whispered the little man to himself.

A ... (ellipsis) **B** , (comma) **C** " (speech mark) **D** : (colon)

Answers and explanations on pages 137–138

Mini Test 5

1 Which letters or words from this sentence should be in brackets ( )?

London is the capital of England and is located in the United Kingdom UK. It remains an important cultural centre in England today.

A London **B** England **C** United Kingdom **D** UK

2 Where does the missing apostrophe go?

The traffic was slow and the car (A) s (B) driver (C) s (D) were tired.

3 Which is the correct place in this sentence to put the following punctuation and words?

, which was the family's treasured pet,

The cat (A) had (B) been lost (C) for a fortnight. (D)

4 Which sentence uses punctuation correctly?

A "How was your day at work?" Paul asked worriedly.
B "How was your day at work? paul asked," worriedly.
C How was your day at work? Paul asked worriedly.
D How was your day at work? "Paul asked worriedly".

5 Where do the two missing speech marks go (" ")?

Sarah said, (A) I think (B) *Interpol* (C) was the best movie I have ever seen! (D) when I last saw her.

6 Where do the two missing apostrophes go?

The women (A) s (B) shoes were lined up outside Melinda (C) s (D) house.

7 Where do the two commas go?

The sun shone (A) unlike during last winter (B) for three (C) weeks (D) in a row.

8 Where does the missing apostrophe go?

When we pass (A) out the children (B) s (C) desserts they will be (D) so pleased.

9 Where does the missing colon go?

Elizabeth (A) has only (B) one thing (C) on her mind (D) profit.

Answers and explanations on pages 138–140

Mini Test 5 (continued)

10 Which punctuation mark should be used in the sentence below?

Don't go near the lions they might attack you.

A ? (question mark) **B** ! (exclamation mark) **C** ; (semicolon) **D** : (colon)

11 Which punctuation mark is missing from this sentence?

The mother shouted, "Don't go near the edge"

A ! (exclamation mark) **B** " " (speech marks) **C** ; (semicolon) **D** : (colon)

12 Which punctuation mark is missing from this sentence?

"Buy these things: tea, coffee … do we need sugar" said Dad.

A ? (question mark) **B** ' (apostrophe) **C** ; (semicolon) **D** : (colon)

13 Which punctuation mark is missing from this sentence?

Lisa said, "Umm umm can we go tomorrow instead?"

A ... (ellipsis) **B** . (full stop) **C** ; (semicolon) **D** : (colon)

14 Which punctuation mark is missing from this sentence?

The teacher said, "Remember to bring your pens You will probably need paper too."

A ? (question mark) **B** . (full stop) **C** ; (semicolon) **D** : (colon)

15 Which sentence has the correct punctuation?

A "The crowd went wild" said Tony, "when the band came on stage."
B "The crowd went wild," said Tony, "when the band came on stage."
C "The crowd went wild," said Tony. "When the band came on stage."
D "The crowd went wild"; said Tony, "when the band came on stage."

16 Which sentence has the correct punctuation?

A "Can you get the door, he shouted, I'm in the shower!"
B "Can you get the door" he shouted "I'm in the shower!"
C "Can you get the door?" he shouted. "I'm in the shower!"
D "Can you get the door?" He shouted. "I'm in the shower!"

17 Which sentence has the correct punctuation?

A When we were in the bush, we were warned to stick together.
B When we were in the bush we were warned to 'stick together'.
C When we were in the bush we were 'warned to stick together'.
D When we were in the bush, "we were warned to stick together".

18 Which sentence has the correct punctuation?

A To make the cake we need eggs, sugar and cream but we don't need flour or cocoa.
B To make the cake we need eggs sugar, and cream but we don't need flour or cocoa.
C To make the cake we need eggs sugar and cream but we don't need flour, or cocoa.
D To make the cake we need eggs, sugar, and cream but we dont need flour or cocoa.

Answers and explanations on pages 138–140

19 Which sentence has the correct punctuation?

A "Remember your umbrella said Mum" It looks like rain.

B "Remember your umbrella," said Mum. "It looks like rain."

C Remember your umbrella "said Mum"."It looks like rain".

D "Remember your umbrella said Mum. It looks like rain".

20 Which sentence has the correct punctuation?

A Paul said to Sarah, "I've really enjoyed reading *The Man from Snowy River* this year."

B Paul said to Sarah, I've really enjoyed reading "The Man from Snowy River" this year.

C Paul said to Sarah "I've really enjoyed reading The man from snowy river this year."

D Paul said to Sarah, "I've really enjoyed reading The man from Snowy river" this year.

21 Which sentence has the correct punctuation?

A Our school is performing along with five other schools at the Sydney Opera House.

B Our school is performing along with five other schools at the Sydney opera house.

C Our school is performing, along with five other schools, at the Sydney Opera House.

D Our School is performing, along with five other schools, at the Sydney Opera House.

22 Which punctuation mark is missing from this sentence?

The train station was built for three main purposes ▭ to bring people and goods from the city to the town; to provide a stable supply of food to the town; and to provide transportation for travelling employees.

A : (colon) B ; (semicolon) C , (comma) D . (full stop)

23 Which punctuation mark is missing from this sentence?

Some people type using their computer ▭ others write with a pen or pencil.

A : (colon) B ; (semicolon) C . (full stop) D " " (speech marks)

24 Which punctuation mark is missing from this sentence?

However they choose to write, people develop their own style ▭ as a result, there are many products available to assist them.

A : (colon) B ; (semicolon) C , (comma) D . (full stop)

25 Which punctuation mark is missing from this sentence?

There are basically two ways to get there ▭ take the train, which is inexpensive and fairly easily accessible, or take a taxi, which costs more but is faster.

A : (colon) B ; (semicolon) C , (comma) D . (full stop)

Answers and explanations on pages 138–140

READING

Standard level questions

Mini Test 1: Information report

An information report:

- presents information about a particular topic or subject. Some examples of information reports include textbooks and reference articles such as Wikipedia entries
- is made up of factual information and may describe features of the topic such as appearance, features or qualities
- is structured by a general opening statement that introduces the topic, a series of paragraphs on the topic and then a final summarising conclusion
- has language features that include technical language (jargon) related to the topic and use of the timeless present tense.

Read the information report *Caring for dogs responsibly* and answer the questions.

Caring for dogs responsibly

Dog ownership is a lifetime commitment and a responsible dog owner knows that caring for pets is a top priority. A well-cared-for dog is happy, healthy, friendly and well balanced.

Identification

Law requires that owners register their dogs with their local council. Additional identification in the form of a microchip helps dog and owner find each other if they become separated.

Health care

Yearly veterinarian trips for a medical exam and annual vaccinations keep dogs happy and healthy. A dog that shows symptoms of illness needs to see a vet for diagnosis and treatment.

Safety

Many cities require owners to leash their dogs at all times. Leash laws protect dogs from getting hit by cars or hurting anyone. A fenced-in backyard allows dogs to run freely without the risk of escape.

Nourishment

Dogs need fresh water daily, as well as one or two meals per day. The type of food depends on the dog's tastes, and the amount depends on the dog's weight, appetite and metabolism.

Training

Obedience training helps teach dogs the rules of the house and helps them to become well-behaved pets. Many dogs take to training quickly as they want to please their owner or earn a reward, such as a treat or favourite toy.

Source: <http://www.ehow.com/facts_6040228-responsibility-dog-care_.html>

Note: the numbers in the margin are line references to help you use the answer section more effectively.

1 Which of the paragraphs is about feeding a dog?

A Health care **B** Safety **C** Nourishment **D** Training

2 Paragraph 2, *Identification*, is concerned with

A identifying dog owners.
B informing readers about microchip technology.
C promoting local councils.
D getting dogs registered so that they can be identified if lost.

3 What are the main features of dog health care? You may choose more than one correct option.

A diagnosis and treatment
B a happy and healthy dog
C yearly veterinarian trips for a medical exam and annual vaccinations
D fresh water and two daily meals
E earning a reward

4 The heading *Nourishment* (line 15) refers to

A what a dog needs in order to be happy.
B what a dog needs in order to survive.
C what a dog needs in order to be safe.
D the dog's domestic conditions.

5 A *fenced-in backyard* (line 13) is important as it

A allows dogs to run around.
B stops dogs from running away.
C keeps dogs on leashes.
D stops dogs from getting hit by cars.

6 In *The type of food depends on the dog's tastes* (lines 16–17), which word suggests that dogs have individual tastes?

A type **B** depends **C** tastes **D** food

7 *Many dogs take to training quickly* (line 20). This means that

____

____

8 What is the purpose of the **first paragraph** of the text?

A to persuade people to like dogs
B to explain what dogs like and don't like
C to discuss different points of views about dog ownership
D to teach people about the best care for their dog

Answers and explanations on page 140

READING

Standard level questions

Mini Test 2: Explanation

An explanation:

- tells you how something occurs, why something happened or possibly how to solve a problem
- is more than just an order of events and should contain reasons
- usually contains an opening general statement, followed by paragraphs that explain the how or why of the topic and lastly a concluding idea
- has language features that include examples of technical language, or jargon, as well as words that show cause and effect.

Read the explanation *What are clouds and why does it rain?* and answer the questions.

What are clouds and why does it rain?

Almost all the air around us is moist. This means that it contains water in the form of vapour. You can't see it because water vapour is a gas, but it's still water.

Water can exist in three states: liquid (water), solid (ice) and gas (water vapour). Obviously, you can see and touch water and ice, but water vapour has no smell, you can't pick it up, and it's invisible. This doesn't mean that you can't feel it though.

Perhaps you can remember a hot and sticky day in summer, or a cold foggy day in winter, or even being in a hot shower full of steam? In each of those situations you will have felt water vapour all around you.

If you stopped and really looked at that fog or steam you would have spotted millions and millions of tiny water droplets floating in the air. What you saw was the same process that makes clouds—millions of tiny water droplets condensing out of the air to form liquid water.

We've all seen fog and steam, but why does water condense out of air and become visible? Well, warm air can hold more water vapour than cool air, so if warm air starts to cool, it can no longer hold as much water vapour. The extra water vapour has to go somewhere, so it condenses out as water.

Source: <http://www.geography-site.co.uk/pages/physical/climate/why%20does%20it%20rain.html>

Mini Test 2 (continued)

1 According to the text, what is *water vapour*? You may choose **more than one correct option**.

a gas	something you can see	moist air	a liquid	ice
A	**B**	**C**	**D**	**E**

2 Line 3 says *Water can exist in three states*. In this sentence, *states* means

A conditions. **B** places. **C** people. **D** types.

3 What are the main features of water vapour?

A It can't be felt or seen.
B It can be seen and smelled.
C It has no smell, can't be picked up and is invisible.
D It has no smell, can be picked up and is invisible.

4 *This doesn't mean that you can't feel it though* (lines 4–5) suggests that

A you can feel the water vapour in the air.
B you can't feel the water vapour in the air.
C you can see the water vapour in the air.
D you can touch the water vapour in the air.

5 What is the process that makes clouds?

A vapour **B** floating **C** liquid **D** condensation

6 Which technique is used in the first sentence of the third paragraph?

A exaggeration
B emotive words
C rhetorical question
D scientific theory

7 The sentence *We've all seen fog and steam, but why does water condense out of air and become visible?* (line 11) contains a question mark because

A the writer is asking the reader to confirm this fact.
B the reader should know the answer.
C the writer doesn't know the answer.
D the writer is asking a question that they will then answer.

8 Read both *What are clouds and why does it rain?* and *Caring for dogs responsibly* (page 57). For which purposes were these texts written? Choose **two** purposes for each text.

Purpose	***What are clouds and why does it rain?***	***Caring for dogs responsibly***
to inform		
to persuade		
to explain		

Answers and explanations on pages 140–141

READING

Intermediate level questions

Mini Test 3: Book blurb

A book blurb:

- is the short text that is usually written on the back of a book, or maybe printed on the inside cover
- provides basic information about the book. This is usually delivered in an exciting way, often by focusing on a dramatic event from the book, in order to gain readers' interest and entice them to purchase it
- is usually brief, spanning only a few paragraphs. A summary of the book is often included. The text may be supported by a visual or graphic that captures readers' imaginations.

Read the book blurb and answer the questions.

Asian-Australians have often been written about by outsiders, as outsiders.

In this collection, compiled by award-winning author Alice Pung, they tell their own stories with verve, courage and a large dose of humour.

They tell tales of leaving home, falling in love and finding one's feet.

A young Cindy Pan vows to win every single category of Nobel Prize.

Tony Ayres blows a kiss to a skinhead and lives to tell the tale.

Benjamin Law has a close encounter with some angry Australian fauna, and Kylie Kwong makes a moving pilgrimage to her great-grandfather's Chinese village.

Here are well-known authors and exciting new voices, spanning several generations and drawn from all over Australia.

In sharing their stories, they show us what it is really like to grow up Asian, and Australian.

From *Growing Up Asian in Australia*, ed. Alice Pung, Black Inc, 2008

Mini Test 3 (continued)

1. The text mentions 'outsiders' who write about Asian-Australians. Who are they?
   A Asians
   B non-Asian Australians
   C Alice Pung
   D Benjamin Law

2. *Verve* means
   A energy.
   B sadness.
   C humour.
   D patience.

3. In lines 6–7, ... *finding one's feet* means
   A looking at your feet.
   B looking for your feet.
   C discovering who you are.
   D deciding what you like.

4. Who has an unfortunate experience with an Australian animal?
   A Tony Ayres
   B Cindy Pan
   C Benjamin Law
   D Kylie Kwong

5. *Kylie Kwong makes a moving pilgrimage* (lines 13–14). *Moving* in this sentence means that she
   A relocated overseas.
   B moved to her great-grandfather's village.
   C had a moving sale.
   D had an emotional experience.

6. The writers are described as *exciting new voices*. This means that they
   A are excellent singers.
   B have new and interesting perspectives.
   C are excited about writing.
   D are just learning to speak English.

7. In what way does this book show the reader what ... *it is really like to grow up Asian*?
   A by telling tales of leaving home
   B by sharing experiences of Australian nature
   C by showing stories from all over Australia
   D by sharing the experiences of a range of Asian-Australians

8. Place the following examples of events that occur to the authors in the order in which they occur in the text. Use numbers 1 to 5 to order the sentences.

   ☐ A young Cindy Pan vows to win every single category of Nobel Prize.

   ☐ Kylie Kwong makes a moving pilgrimage to her great-grandfather's Chinese village.

   ☐ Tony Ayres blows a kiss to a skinhead and lives to tell the tale.

   ☐ They tell tales of leaving home, falling in love and finding one's feet.

   ☐ Benjamin Law has a close encounter with some angry Australian fauna.

Answers and explanations on page 141

READING

Intermediate level questions

Mini Test 4: News report

A news report:

- is a factual account of current affairs. Its purpose is to report on topics and issues of interest in a way that is informative and interesting
- follows a particular structure. It has a strong headline and answers questions such as what happened, who was involved, where and when the event occurred, as well as why
- may also include statements from participants, an authority on the topic (such as a scientist) or observers. A photo or graphic may accompany the report and supports the information given.

Read the news report *Aboriginal students make short work of success* and answer the questions.

Aboriginal students make short work of success

Anna Patty, Education Editor

A SYDNEY private school's investment in Aboriginal children is starting to pay off, with dramatically improved literacy and numeracy results.

St Andrew's Cathedral School in the central business district established a special school called Gawura for Aborigines just under two years ago in a spare classroom on its rooftop.

The school, established with donations, has reached its maximum number of enrolments of 25 pupils in kindergarten to year 6 for this year and next.

A snapshot of results for this year's first national literacy and numeracy tests shows the year 5 Gawura pupils achieved results in writing that bettered the state average and were less than one point below the school average.

Reading results were below the state average but well above the state average for indigenous students. Overall literacy was 491 points compared with the state average of 497.4.

The school's headmaster, Phillip Heath, said he was still concerned about numeracy test results that remained well below the state average for all students and those of indigenous background.

Overall, numeracy results were 411.6 compared to the state average of 489.1 for all students and 426.8 for indigenous students.

Mr Heath said that when students first arrived at Gawura, they were one to two years behind the average performance of other NSW students.

The NSW Government is aiming to lift the performance of all Aboriginal students to meet the state average.

Four of the Gawura students will enter high school at St Andrew's next year where they will continue to gain extra support.

While the Gawura children join other school children for cultural and sporting activities, Mr Heath said he had been criticised for teaching them separately from the others and creating a small 'apartheid' at the school. But he argues that this was necessary to give the Aboriginal students the level of individual attention they needed to improve their results.

By high school age, it was expected that the Gawura students would be confident enough to join the rest of the school in mixed classrooms.

'They are really proud of who they are and they haven't lost their cultural identity,' Mr Heath said. 'They haven't had a "whitefella" culture imposed on them.'

Source: *Sydney Morning Herald*, 29 November 2008.

1 What language technique is used in the article's title?
A exaggeration **B** simile **C** metaphor **D** alliteration

2 What is the name of the special school operating within St Andrew's?
A St Andrew's **B** Gawura **C** Special School **D** Heath

Answers and explanations on page 142

3 In line 1, what is the *investment* the school makes in its Aboriginal students?

A educational
B financial
C social
D educational, financial and emotional

4 In line 13, what is a *snapshot of results*?

A an overview of results
B a photo of results
C a detailed report on the results
D a description of results

5 According to the text, some Aboriginal students will attend St Andrew's Cathedral School. Place the following events in the order in which they occur in the article. Use numbers 1 to 4 to order the sentences.

☐ Four of the Gawura students will continue to gain extra support when they begin high school at St Andrew's.

☐ St Andrew's Cathedral School established a special school called Gawura for Aborigines in a spare classroom on its rooftop.

☐ The Gawura students would be confident enough to join the rest of the school in mixed classrooms when they reached high school age.

☐ A private school's investment in Aboriginal children is starting to become successful, with improved literacy and numeracy results.

6 Read both *Aboriginal students make short work of success* and the book blurb on page 61. Write three features of each text. Choose from: headline, quotation, anecdote, statistics and emotional language.

Aboriginal students make short work of success	***Book blurb***

7 Read both *Aboriginal students make short work of success* and the book blurb on page 61. For which purposes were these texts written? Choose two purposes for each text.

Purpose	***Aboriginal students make short work of success***	***Book blurb***
to inform		
to persuade		
to criticise		
to explain		
to report		

8 Read both *Aboriginal students make short work of success* and the book blurb on page 61. Choose the correct words to complete the sentence.

It is most likely that the book blurb would appear in a (magazine / newspaper / novel), while *Aboriginal students make short work of success* would appear in a (newspaper / poster / novel).

Answers and explanations on page 142

READING

Intermediate level questions

Mini Test 5: Interview

An interview:

- is a structured dialogue or discussion between two people—an interviewer (person who asks the questions) and an interviewee (person who answers the questions)
- gathers information from one person, usually a person of interest such as a celebrity or politician
- has an introduction which should contain some general background information about the interviewee and the subject. A series of questions and answers then follow and lastly the conclusion, which may appear only as a final concluding question and answer. The language should contain simple and direct questions that are 'open' and that allow for more detailed answers.

Read the interview with Saskia Burmeister and answer the questions.

BEHIND THE NEWS: Interview with Saskia Burmeister, 15 March 2005

Hating Alison Ashley

The classic Australian novel by Robin Klein has been made into a movie. *Hating Alison Ashley* deals with issues like friendship and acceptance. Things that young people understand. Kerry speaks to one of the stars, Saskia Burmeister.

Erica Yurkin may not be too thrilled with her life, but Saskia Burmeister, who plays Erica, couldn't be happier with how hers is turning out. Saskia is considered one of Australia's rising stars after scoring the lead role in *Hating Alison Ashley*.

You're twenty at the moment and the character you're playing is fourteen. Was it difficult to go back those few years?

No, not really. It was there on the page for me and certainly I did relate to her in the sense that I could look back and go that was me and I felt that as well and I remember my first kiss.

So what else did she have in common with her character?

She has this obsession with *Romeo and Juliet* and I read the script and went 'that's me'.

The hours may be long, but Saskia says it's all worth it. She's doing what she's always wanted to do.

I was about five years old and I saw this film with an actor Meryl Streep in it. It was just something that I went these aren't people living inside the TV; this is acting and what is acting?

And yeah it was that moment that it clicked and I had a name for something that I knew I was going to be doing for the rest of my life.

Mini Test 5 (continued)

1 The movie *Hating Alison Ashley* deals with issues like
- **A** friendship and young people.
- **B** acceptance.
- **C** friendship and acceptance.
- **D** understanding and friendship.

2 Who is Saskia Burmeister?
- **A** an actor from the film
- **B** the writer of the book
- **C** the director of the film
- **D** a character from the book

3 Choose the correct answer to complete the sentence.

The character Saskia plays is ______ years old.

A a few **B** fourteen **C** fifteen **D** twenty

4 What does she have in common with her character?
- **A** a first kiss
- **B** long hours
- **C** They are both thrilled with their lives.
- **D** a love of *Romeo and Juliet*

5 The word *clicked*, as it appears on line 16, means
- **A** to turn on a light switch.
- **B** when something suddenly makes sense.
- **C** when something is unclear.
- **D** to find a name.

6 What effect is used to highlight the questions within the text?

A italics **B** underlining **C** bold **D** spacing

7 Choose **two** answers to complete the sentence.

This interview is structured as ______ and in an ______ format.
- **A** question and answer
- **B** narrative
- **C** interview
- **D** report
- **E** description

8 The purpose of this text is to
- **A** persuade.
- **B** argue.
- **C** inform and persuade.
- **D** criticise.

Answers and explanations on pages 142–143

READING

Intermediate level questions

Mini Test 6: Narrative

A narrative:

- tells a story that is entertaining and informative. Some examples of narratives include science fiction novels, spoken stories or stories based on history
- is made up of an orientation that tells the reader the who, when and where of the story. Narratives are also made up of events, complications (problems) and resolutions (where the problems are solved)
- is made up of descriptive language, dialogue and time words to indicate when events are taking place.

Read the narrative *How the leopard got his spots* and answer the questions.

An extract from *How the leopard got his spots* by Rudyard Kipling

In the days when everybody started fair, Best Beloved, the Leopard lived in a place called the High Veldt. 'Member it wasn't the Low Veldt, or the Bush Veldt, or the Sour Veldt, but the 'sclusively bare, hot shiny High Veldt, where there was sand and sandy-coloured rock and 'sclusively tufts of sandy-yellowish grass.

The Giraffe and the Zebra and the Eland and the Koodoo and the Hartebeest lived there: and they were 'sclusively sandy-yellow-brownish all over; but the Leopard, he was the 'sclusivest sandiest-yellowest-brownest of them all—a greyish-yellowish catty-shaped kind of beast, and he matched the 'sclusively yellowish-greyish-brownish colour of the High Veldt to one hair.

This was very bad for the Giraffe and the Zebra and the rest of them: for he would lie down by a 'sclusively yellowish-greyish-brownish stone or clump of grass, and when the Giraffe or the Zebra or the Eland or the Koodoo or the Bush-Buck or the Bonte-Buck came by he would surprise them out of their jumpsome lives. He would indeed!

And, also, there was an Ethiopian with bows and arrows (a 'sclusively greyish-brownish-yellowish man he was then), who lived on the High Veldt with the Leopard: and the two used to hunt together—the Ethiopian with his bows and arrows, and the Leopard 'sclusively with his teeth and claws—till the Giraffe and the Eland and the Koodoo and the Quagga and all the rest of them didn't know which way to jump, Best Beloved. They didn't indeed!?

Mini Test 6 (continued)

1 Where did the leopard live?

A the Low Veldt **B** the High Veldt **C** the Bush Veldt **D** the Sour Veldt

2 The word *'sclusively* in the text is actually the word

A excuse. **B** exclusive. **C** exclusively. **D** disgusted.

3 Which Veldt has sand and sandy-coloured rocks?

A the Low Veldt **B** the High Veldt **C** the Bush Veldt **D** the Sour Veldt

4 According to the text, the leopard was what colour? You may choose **more than one.**

A sandiest-yellowest-brownest **B** sandy-yellow-brownish
C greyish-yellowish **D** greyish-brownish-yellowish

5 Why was this bad for the Giraffe and Zebra?

A The leopard looked like a clump of grass.
B They wanted to chase the leopard.
C They could easily see the leopard.
D They were unable to see the leopard as he was camouflaged.

6 Read both *Behind the news* (page 65) and *How the leopard got his spots.* Write three features of each text. Choose from: first-person perspective, conversational language, descriptive adjectives, made-up words, idiom, third-person perspective.

Behind the news	***How the leopard got his spots***

7 Read both *Behind the news* (page 65) and *How the leopard got his spots.* For which purposes were these texts written? Choose two purposes for each text.

Purpose	***Behind the news***	***How the leopard got his spots***
to tell a story		
to recount		
to inform		
to create interest		

8 Read both *Behind the news* (page 65) and *How the leopard got his spots.* Choose the correct words to complete the sentence.

It is most likely that *Behind the news* would appear in a (magazine / poster / novel), while *How the leopard got his spots* would appear in a (newspaper / website / novel).

Answers and explanations on page 143

READING

Advanced level questions

Mini Test 7: Diary entry

A diary entry:

- records personal experiences and allows the writer to reflect on those experiences
- usually contains a series of dated entries and is loosely structured, meaning there are no strict rules
- contains information about events, including when, where, who, what and why, and includes emotional language that allows the writer to focus on his or her feelings
- has language that reflects its loose structure and which can be conversational and colloquial with use of punctuation (dashes and ellipses) to show pauses and connections between ideas.

Read the diary entry and answer the questions.

February 24

It's a Sunday again. It seems that on Sunday afternoon the dorm separates, splits up, and all its parts go aimlessly in different directions, tracing out ragged and untidy paths. Then, around sunset, all the paths coalesce.

I like the word 'coalesce'. Though when I look at it for a long time it seems strange and ugly.

I've been here less than three weeks but it feels like three months. I've been reading back over this Journal, fragments of my life here, tears in the curtain. The routines of this school and the personalities of the people seem so familiar already, yet at first they seemed like a game of Dungeons and Dragons. So did the Hospital, back in the early days, I guess.

There are eight girls in the Dorm: Cathy, the thin, tall writer of poems; boyish, pretty Sophie, who's so bubbly and lively but who finds me so irritating; kind Anne of the spangled doona-cover; strong and silent Lisa, who stuck up for me that one time, but so private inside her cold Scandinavian marble mountain. All of these have found their way into this Journal already, though that was never my intention.

I write too much in this Journal. But it seems that I cannot help myself. I had trained myself to live without a voice and now I have almost to be forced into using one again. What if anyone reads this?

Extract reprinted with permission from *So Much to Tell You* by John Marsden, Lothian Children's Books, an imprint of Hachette Australia, 1998.

Mini Test 7 (continued)

1 *Coalesce* means

A come together.
B separate.
C depart.
D become well after an illness.

2 According to the text, the writer is describing the experience of being in a new place.

Place the following events in the order in which they occur in the extract. Use numbers 1 to 4 to order the sentences.

☐ It was never my intention to put all this into my journal.

☐ I've been here for about two weeks.

☐ All of the people and the routines seem so familiar already.

☐ I've been reading back over this Journal, fragments of my life here, tears in the curtain.

3 Which technique is used in the sentence *The routines … seemed like a game of Dungeons and Dragons* (line 14)?

metaphor	alliteration	simile	assonance	personification
A	B	C	D	E

4 Who finds the writer annoying?

A Lisa
B Cathy
C Sophie
D herself

5 *… but so private inside her cold Scandinavian marble mountain* (lines 18–19) implies that Lisa is

A friendly.
B disappointed.
C aloof.
D overseas.

6 *I had trained myself to live without a voice* (lines 21–22) means that the writer

A had stopped talking.
B had vocal training lessons.
C wanted to communicate with those around her.
D decided to stop communicating.

7 The diary entry ends with a question. The purpose of this is to

A consider what would happen if anyone read the diary.
B show the writer wants people to read her diary.
C reveal that the writer doesn't know the answer.
D allow the writer to ask a question that they will then answer.

8 The purpose of this text is to

A persuade people to like the writer.
B explain what boarding school is like.
C reveal emotions and feelings.
D give an opinion on school.

☞ Answers and explanations on pages 143–144

READING

Advanced level questions

Mini Test 8: Fable

A fable:
- is a short narrative that makes a moral point, traditionally by means of animal characters who speak and act like human beings
- conveys lessons or messages through symbolism. The tales usually achieve this by retelling the experiences of animals who make decisions and interact with each other, and whose behaviour is ultimately judged
- often has very simplistic language so that the moral is made clear.

Read the fable *The fox and the goat* and answer the questions.

The fox and the goat

A Fox one day fell into a deep well and could find no means of escape. A Goat, overcome with thirst, came to the same well, and seeing the Fox, inquired if the water was good.

Concealing his sad plight under a merry guise, the Fox indulged in a lavish praise of the water, saying it was excellent beyond measure, and encouraging him to descend.

The Goat, mindful only of his thirst, thoughtlessly jumped down, but just as he drank, the Fox informed him of the difficulty they were both in and suggested a scheme for their common escape. 'If,' said he, 'you will place your forefeet upon the wall and bend your head, I will run up your back and escape, and will help you out afterwards.'

The Goat readily assented and the Fox leaped upon his back. Steadying himself with the Goat's horns, he safely reached the mouth of the well and made off as fast as he could.

When the Goat upbraided him for breaking his promise, he turned around and cried out, 'You foolish old fellow! If you had as many brains in your head as you have hairs in your beard, you would never have gone down before you had inspected the way up, nor have exposed yourself to dangers from which you had no means of escape.'

Look before you leap.

From *Aesop's Fables*

Mini Test 8 (continued)

1 What happened to the fox?

A He was thirsty.

B He spoke to a goat.

C He fell into a deep well and was trapped.

D He asked if the water was good.

2 What is a *merry guise* (line 3)?

A a cheerful face B a sorrowful face C a costume D makeup

3 How did the fox escape the well?

A He helped the goat out first.

B The goat helped him out from above the well.

C He had a drink.

D He jumped on the goat's back.

4 What is the main message of this fable?

A You should help others.

B You should use your brains and assess situations before committing yourself.

C You should trust people you meet.

D You need brains to escape from tricky situations.

5 What does the fox mean when he says to the goat *If you had as many brains in your head as you have hairs in your beard* (lines 18–20)?

A The goat has lots of brains.

B The goat has a long beard.

C The goat is very smart.

D The goat is not very smart.

6 Read both the diary entry on page 69 and *The fox and the goat.* Write **three** features of each text. Choose from: simile, direct speech, coda, first-person perspective, third-person perspective, metaphor.

Diary entry	***The fox and the goat***

7 Read both the diary entry (page 69) and *The fox and the goat.* For which purposes were these texts written? Choose **two** purposes for each text.

Purpose	***Diary entry***	***The fox and the goat***
to reveal emotions and feelings		
to inform		
to entertain		
to instruct		
to report		

8 Read both the diary entry (page 69) and *The fox and the goat.* Choose the correct words to complete the sentence.

It is most likely that the diary entry would appear in a (magazine / newspaper / novel), while *The fox and the goat* would appear in a (newspaper / novel / collection of short stories).

Answers and explanations on page 144

READING

Advanced level questions

Mini Test 9: Narrative

Read the narrative *Marley's ghost* and answer the questions.

Go to page 67 to read about **Narratives**.

Marley's ghost

Marley was dead, to begin with. There is no doubt whatever about that. The register of his burial was signed by the clergyman, the clerk, the undertaker, and the chief mourner. Scrooge signed it. And Scrooge's name was good upon 'Change for anything he chose to put his hand to. Old Marley was as dead as a doornail.

Mind! I don't mean to say that I know of my own knowledge, what there is particularly dead about a doornail. I might have been inclined, myself, to regard a coffin-nail as the deadest piece of ironmongery in the trade. But the wisdom of our ancestors is in the simile; and my unhallowed hands shall not disturb it, or the country's done for. You will, therefore, permit me to repeat, emphatically, that Marley was as dead as a doornail.

Scrooge knew he was dead? Of course he did. How could it be otherwise? Scrooge and he were partners for I don't know how many years. Scrooge was his sole executor, his sole administrator, his sole assign, his sole residuary legatee, his sole friend, and sole mourner. And even Scrooge was not so dreadfully cut up by the sad event but that he was an excellent man of business on the very day of the funeral, and solemnised it with an undoubted bargain.

…

Scrooge never painted out Old Marley's name. There it stood, years afterwards, above the warehouse door: Scrooge and Marley. The firm was known as Scrooge and Marley. Sometimes people new to the business called Scrooge Scrooge, and sometimes Marley, but he answered to both names. It was all the same to him.

From *A Christmas Carol* by Charles Dickens

Mini Test 9 (continued)

1. How do we know that Marley is really dead?
   A Scrooge signed the register of burial.
   B The register of his burial had been signed by many important people.
   C Scrooge's name is good.
   D Marley is as dead as a doornail.

2. What is the *deadest piece of ironmongery* in the trade (lines 6–7)?
   A Marley **B** a doornail **C** Scrooge **D** a coffin-nail

3. What does the narrator mean when he says *Mind!* (line 5)?
   A therefore
   B on the other hand
   C in conclusion
   D equally

4. The phrase *dead as a doornail* (line 4) is an example of
   A exaggeration.
   B a metaphor.
   C a simile.
   D personification.

5. Another word for *emphatically* in line 8 is
   A always. **B** perhaps. **C** maybe. **D** definitely.

6. What is Scrooge's reaction to Marley's death, according to lines 12 to 14?
   A He wasn't very upset.
   B He cried.
   C He cut up things.
   D He was terribly upset.

7. What was Marley's relationship to Scrooge?
   A brother
   B business partner
   C employee
   D father

8. The purpose of the final paragraph of the extract is to
   A show that Marley was still important to Scrooge.
   B inform that the business name is both Scrooge and Marley.
   C provide an insight into Scrooge's personality.
   D remind us that Marley has died.

Answers and explanations on pages 144–145

READING

Advanced level questions

Mini Test 10: Poem

A poem:

- is a creative text that allows the poet to express his or her feelings or relate experiences. Some examples of poems include ballads, sonnets and song lyrics
- has a structure that can vary. They are all, however, made up of stanzas (paragraphs) and may be written using free verse (which doesn't follow any particular rules), or use rhyme and rhythm to communicate ideas.

Read the poem *In the playground* and answer the questions.

In the playground

In the playground
At the back of our house
There have been some changes.

They said the climbing frame was
NOT SAFE
So they sawed it down.

They said the paddling pool was
NOT SAFE
So they drained it dry.

They said the see-saw was
NOT SAFE
So they took it away.

They said the sandpit was
NOT SAFE
So they fenced it in.

They said the playground was
NOT SAFE
So they locked it up.

Sawed down
Drained dry
Taken away
Fenced in
Locked up

How do you feel?
Safe?

Michael Rosen

1 Where is the playground located?
A at the school
B in the garden
C in the local park
D behind the persona's house

2 Who are *they* in the poem?
A children B teachers C adults D parents

3 What feeling is created by the use of capital letters in *NOT SAFE*?
A The poet is shouting the words.
B The poet agrees with the words.
C They show that the playground is not safe.
D It reinforces the adult perspective on the dangers of the playground.

4 What happened to the see-saw?
A It was taken away.
B It was sawed down.
C It was locked up.
D It was drained dry.

5 In lines 19–23, information about what happened to the play equipment is
A questioned. B repeated. C shouted. D described.

6 Read both *Marley's ghost* (page 73) and *In the playground.* Write three features of each text. Choose from: old-fashioned language, exclamation, rhetorical question, third-person plural pronoun, instructional verbs.

Marley's ghost	***In the playground***

7 Read both *Marley's ghost* (page 73) and *In the playground.* For which purposes were these texts written? Choose two purposes for each text.

Purpose	***Marley's ghost***	***In the playground***
to question		
to entertain		
to recount		

8 Read both *Marley's ghost* (page 73) and *In the playground.* Choose the correct words to complete the sentence.

It is most likely that *Marley's ghost* would appear in a (magazine / newspaper / novel), while *In the playground* would appear in a (collection of poems / poster / novel).

Answers and explanations on page 145

TIPS FOR WRITING A PERSUASIVE TEXT

Check the Writing section (www.nap.edu.au/naplan/writing) of the official NAPLAN website for up-to-date and important information on the Writing Test. Sample Writing Tests and marking guidelines that outline the criteria markers use when assessing your writing are also provided. Please note that, to date in NAPLAN, the types of texts that students have been tested on have been narrative and persuasive writing.

The Australian Curriculum for English requires students to be taught three main types of texts:

- imaginative writing (including narratives and descriptions)
- informative writing (including procedures and reports)
- persuasive writing (expositions).

Informative writing has not yet been tested by NAPLAN. The best preparation for writing is for students to read a range of texts and to get lots of practice in writing different types of texts. We have included information on all types of texts in this book.

Persuasive texts

A **persuasive text** is sometimes known as an **exposition** or an **argument**. A persuasive text aims to argue a position and support it with evidence and reasons.

When writing persuasive texts it is best to keep the following points in mind. They will help you get the best possible mark.

Before you start writing

- Read the question carefully. You will probably be asked to write your reaction to a particular question or statement, such as *Excessive Internet usage is bad for teenagers.* Most of the topics that you will be asked to comment on are very general. This means you will probably be writing about something you know and can draw upon your experience.
- Give yourself a few minutes before you start writing to get your thoughts in order and jot down points.

Structure of persuasive texts

A persuasive text has a specific structure:

- The **introduction** is where you clearly state your ideas about the topic. You must ensure your position is clearly outlined. It is a good idea to list your main points in your introduction—three points is perfect.
- The **body** comprises a series of paragraphs where your opinions are developed. Evidence and/or reasons are given to upport your opinions about the topic. Each paragraph usually opens with a sentence that previews what the paragraph will focus on.
- The **conclusion** is a paragraph where the main points of your argument are summarised and where you restate your opinion on the topic. Your conclusion should not include any new information.

Language features of persuasive texts

You can use some or all of the following features:

- **Emotive language:** Use words or phrases that express emotion, e.g. *I find it shocking, terrible crime, terrific, heartless, desirable*.
- **Third-person narrative:** Avoid using *I* in your argument. The third person is more formal and appropriate to a persuasive text of this kind.
- **Connectives:** These words link your points together, e.g. *firstly, secondly, finally, on the other hand, however, furthermore, moreover* and *in conclusion.*
- **Modality:** Use modals to express different levels of certainty. High modal verbs, including *should, must, will not* and *ensure,* are strongly persuasive.
- **Repetition:** Repeat key words or phrases to have a dramatic effect on the reader by drawing emphasis to a point or idea.
- **Rhetorical questions:** These questions are designed to make the reader think, e.g. *Have you ever lost a loved one?*
- **Statements of appeal:** These affect the emotions of your readers and encourage action, e.g. *We owe it to our children to act now on climate change.*

Don't forget to:

- plan your argument before you start
- write in correctly formed sentences and take care with paragraphing
- choose your words carefully and pay attention to your spelling and punctuation
- write neatly but don't waste time
- make no more than three different points
- quickly check your argument once you have finished.

WRITING

Mini Test 1
Persuasive text

Before you start, read the Tips for Writing on page 77.

Today you are going to write a persuasive text.

Park or car park?

Should a local park be removed for the construction of a supermarket car park?

What do you think about this idea?

Write a Letter to the Editor of your local paper to convince a reader of your opinions.

Before you start writing, give some thought to:

- if you agree or disagree—you might see both sides of the argument
- an introduction—your opening paragraph should state clearly whether you agree or disagree with the topic
- your opinions—you should have reasons or evidence to support your opinions
- a conclusion—your letter should conclude with a summary of the main points of your argument.

Don't forget to:

- plan your writing
- write in full sentences
- use paragraphs to structure your letter
- pay attention to your spelling and punctuation
- choose words carefully that will help persuade your reader
- check that your work is clearly expressed.

Start writing here or type your answer on a tablet or computer.

☞ Turn to page 146 and use the Marking checklist to check the student's writing. Also go to pages 159–160 where the sample pieces of writing (Intermediate and Advanced levels) can be used to check at what level the student is writing. These writing samples have been analysed based on the marking criteria used by markers to assess the NAPLAN Writing Test.

TIPS FOR WRITING A NARRATIVE TEXT

Narrative texts

A **narrative** is a fiction text and is also known as a story. The purpose of a narrative is to entertain, amuse or inform.

Before you start writing

- Read the question and check the stimulus material carefully. *Stimulus material* refers to the topic, title, picture, words, phrases or extract of writing you are given to base your writing on.
- Decide if you are going to be writing in the first person (you become a character in your story) or in the third person (you are writing about other characters). When writing in the first person be careful not to overuse the pronoun *I* (e.g. *I did this*, *I did that*).
- Take a few moments to plan the structure of your story. Remember: Stories have a beginning, middle and end. It sounds simple but many stories fail because one of these three parts is not well written.

Structure of narrative texts

A narrative has a specific structure, containing:

- **Orientation**—the introduction of the setting and characters
- **Complication**—a problem faced by the character(s) that must be overcome
- **Climax**—a scene of increased tension where the character is faced with some kind of danger
- **Resolution**—the problem is overcome
- **Coda**—a lesson is learned and life returns to normal.

Language features of narrative texts

- **Engage the senses** of your reader through description of what can be seen, heard, felt, tasted or smelled. To do this you should include figures of speech such as similes, metaphors and personification.
- **Use strong action verbs** to capture mood and create tension. Instead of *The girl took the food* you could say *The girl lunged for the food*.
- **Use emotive words** to engage the emotions of your reader. It is important to consider what emotions you would like your reader to feel for a character in a specific situation. Once you have decided, use emotive words and phrases to evoke these emotions, e.g. *Lee sat alone feeling despair descend upon him* or *Rob's desire for the cookie caused his stomach to tangle*.
- **Use dialogue sparingly**. It should be used to develop a character or situation. Remember that dialogue tags should elaborate on the attitude of the speaker. Instead of writing *Jane said* you should be more specific, such as *Jane cried* or *Jane moaned, flicking her hair over her shoulder*.

Don't forget to:

- plan your narrative before you start
- write in correctly formed sentences and take care with paragraphing
- choose your words carefully and pay attention to your spelling and punctuation
- write neatly but don't waste time
- quickly check your narrative once you have finished.

WRITING

Mini Test 2
Narrative text

Before you start, read the Tips for Writing on page 79.

Today you are going to write a narrative.

You narrative will be about a **journey**. Look at the picture to give you some ideas. It could be a real or imagined journey. What sort of journey was it? Don't just think of physical journeys. Perhaps it was an emotional journey. When did the journey take place? Where was the journey to? Did anything interesting happen on the journey? Did you learn anything new or experience anything different?

Your narrative may be serious or humorous.

Your writing will be judged on expression and the structure of your narrative.

Before you start writing, give some thought to:

- where your narrative takes place (the setting)
- the characters and what they do in your narrative
- the events that take place in your narrative and the problems that have to be resolved
- how your narrative begins, what happens in your narrative, and how your narrative ends.

Don't forget to:

- plan your writing
- write in full sentences
- use paragraphs to structure your narrative
- pay attention to your spelling and punctuation
- check that your work is clearly expressed.

Start writing here or type your answer on a tablet or computer.

☞ Turn to pages 146–147 and use the Marking checklist to check the student's writing. Also go to pages 161–162 where the sample pieces of writing (Intermediate and Advanced levels) can be used to check at what level the student is writing. These writing samples have been analysed based on the marking criteria used by markers to assess the NAPLAN Writing Test.

TIPS FOR WRITING A RECOUNT TEXT

Recount texts

A **recount** tells about events that have happened to you or other people. It is usually a record of events in the order they happened. If it is a personal recount you will use the personal pronoun *I*. You could also write a recount of an event in the third person. A recount can conclude with a personal opinion of the event. Recounts are always written in the past tense.

Before you start writing

- Read the question and check the *stimulus material* carefully. Stimulus material means the topic, title, picture, words, phrases or extract of writing you are given to base your writing on.
- Give some thought to:
  - where your recount takes place
  - the characters and what they do in your recount
  - the events that take place in your recount
  - the problems that have to be resolved
  - how you and others reacted to the event. You may make brief personal comments on events as you write about them.
- Remember that a recount is usually told in the past tense because the events have already happened.
- When you have chosen your topic it might be helpful to jot a few ideas quickly on paper so you don't forget them. Decide if you will write a first-person recount (using *I* as the main character) or a third-person recount.

Structure of informative texts (recounts)

The introduction

- The first paragraph of a recount is important as it must provide the reader with a brief overview of the event being recounted. It must inform the reader about who, what, when and where.
- The introduction may feature proper nouns such as the names of places and people—this helps orient the reader.

The body

- Recounts recall events in the order in which they happened. The body of a recount is a series of chronological paragraphs detailing important aspects of the event being recounted.
- Conjunctions and connectives must be used to indicate when events occur. These include: *firstly, then, next, later, finally*.
- Correctly paragraph your writing. You need a new paragraph when there is a change in time or place or a new idea.
- Include personal comments, e.g. about your feelings, your opinions and your reactions, but only include comments that add to your recount.

The conclusion

- A conclusion is necessary as it informs the reader of how the event ended. It is also a good idea to include a final comment on the events or experiences. This may be as simple as reflecting on the impact that the event had on the individuals involved.

Language features of informative texts (recounts)

- **Engage the senses** of your reader through description of what can be seen, heard, felt, tasted or smelled. To do this you should include figures of speech such as similes, metaphors and personification.
- **Use strong action verbs** to capture mood and create tension. Instead of *The girl took the food* you could say *The girl lunged for the food.*
- **Use emotive words** to engage the emotions of your reader. It is important to consider what emotions you would like your reader to feel in a specific situation. Once you have decided, use emotive words and phrases to evoke these emotions, e.g. *Lee felt anxious having lost his wallet.*

Don't forget to:

- plan your recount before you start
- write in correctly formed sentences and take care with paragraphing
- choose your words carefully and pay attention to your spelling and punctuation
- write neatly but don't waste time
- quickly check your recount once you have finished.

WRITING

Mini Test 3
Recount text

Before you start, read the Tips for Writing on page 81.

A recount tells about events that have happened to you or other people. It is usually a record of events in the order they happened. If it is a personal recount you will use the word *I*. A recount can conclude with a personal opinion of the event.

Paragraphs are normally organised by time periods. Sometimes subheadings are used. Jot down events in the order they happened before you start.

Today you are going to write a personal recount about **your last holiday**. Explain where the holiday was and why you had to go. Where was the holiday? Did anyone go with you? How did you get there? Did anything happen along the way or while you were there? What was the weather like? What time of year was it? Was it a successful holiday?

Remember to stick to things that could be factual. This is not an opportunity to write a story.

Before you start writing, give some thought to:

- where your recount takes place (the setting)
- the characters and what they do in your recount
- the events that take place in your recount and the problems that have to be resolved
- how you and others reacted during your holiday. You may make brief personal comments on events as you write about them.

Don't forget to:

- plan your writing
- write in full sentences
- use paragraphs to structure your story
- pay attention to your spelling and punctuation
- choose words carefully
- check that your work is clearly expressed.

Start writing here or type your answer on a tablet or computer.

☞ **Turn to page 147 and use the Marking checklist to check the student's writing. Also go to pages 163–164 where the sample pieces of writing (Intermediate and Advanced levels) can be used to check at what level the student is writing. These writing samples have been analysed based on the marking criteria used by markers to assess the NAPLAN Writing Test.**

DIFFERENT TEST LEVELS

- There are six tests for students to complete in this section. These sample tests have been classified as either intermediate or advanced according to the level of the majority of questions. This will broadly reflect the NAPLAN Online tailored testing experience where students are guided into answering questions that match their ability.
- The following tests are included in this section:
  - two Reading Tests at intermediate and advanced levels
  - two Conventions of Language Tests at intermediate and advanced levels
  - two Writing Tests.

CHECKS

- The NAPLAN Online Conventions of Language and Reading tests will be divided into different sections.
- Students will have one last opportunity to check their answers in each section when they have reached the end of that section.
- Once they have moved onto a new section, they will not be able to go back and check their work again.

- We have included reminders for students to check their work at specific points in the Sample Tests so they become familiar with this process before they take the NAPLAN Online tests.

Excel Test Zone

- After students have consolidated their topic knowledge by completing this book, we recommend they practise NAPLAN Online–style questions on our website at www.exceltestzone.com.au.
- Students will be able to gain valuable practice in online skills.
- Students will also become confident in using a computer or tablet to complete NAPLAN Online–style tests so they will be fully prepared for the actual NAPLAN Online tests.

Sample Online-style Test 1

Intermediate level

1 Which sentence is correct?

A A large group of supporters stood by, watching the football.
B A large group of supporters stood by, watch the football.
C A large group of supporters stood behind, watched the football.
D A large group of supporters stood against, watching the football.

2 Which word correctly completes the sentence?

They both agreed that there ______ much to be gained by consultation.

A were **B** was **C** are **D** have

3 Which sentence indicates that something is not certain?

A I might call if you give me your number.
B I will call you when I have your number.
C I shall call you as I have been given your number.
D I did call you last Thursday, however you weren't there.

4 Which is the correct way to combine the following sentences into one?

Our house is near the park. Our house is behind the school. Our house is on Smith Street.

A Our house is near the park. Our house is behind the school and our house is on Smith Street.
B Our house is near the park, behind the school and on Smith Street.
C Our house is near the park and behind the school on Smith Street.
D Our house is near the park and behind the school. Our house is on Smith Street.

5 Write the grammatical terms to label the words in the box according to how each is used in this sentence.

The robber ran past before eventually getting caught.

Word	Grammatical term in this sentence
The	
robber	
ran	
eventually	

6 Which sentence contains an adverb?

A The class bookshelf contained novels, short stories and comics.
B The teacher turned to write on the whiteboard.
C She waited patiently for the bell to ring at the end of the lesson.
D Our local park is filled with excited children.

Answers and explanations on pages 148–150

7 Which sentence is correctly punctuated?

- **A** The turtle moved slowly along it's tank to its water bowl.
- **B** The turtle moved slowly along it's tank to it's water bowl.
- **C** The turtle moved slowly along its tank to it's water bowl.
- **D** The turtle moved slowly along its tank to its water bowl.

8 Which word or words are **not** needed in this sentence?

The store tried to tempt us with a free gift, but they were unsuccessful in getting us to buy their product.

A store **B** free **C** gift **D** unsuccessful

9 Which sentence shows the correct punctuation of direct speech?

- **A** "Who owns this book?" asked the librarian of her class.
- **B** "Who owns this book?" asked the librarian "of her class".
- **C** Who owns this book? "asked the librarian" of her class.
- **D** "Who owns this book? asked the librarian" of her class.

10 The dancers had a successful performance and the crowd really appreciated it. They showed their apreciation by throwing flowers on the stage.

In the second sentence, the pronoun *they* refers to

A dancers. **B** flowers. **C** crowd. **D** stage.

11 Which of the following correctly completes the sentence?

I learnt a lot about ________ at summer camp.

A me **B** am **C** I **D** myself

12 Tick the **two** prepositions in this sentence.

She climbed up the ladder to get into the attic.

13 Which word is a pronoun?

A liked **B** they **C** lots **D** cars

14 Which word or words could replace the highlighted word in this sentence?

The torn page was not noticed **during** the library's annual stocktake.

A within the period **B** on **C** at some point **D** in the course of

15 Which sentence uses the apostrophe (') correctly?

- **A** The dogs' walks were suspended by the wet afternoon.
- **B** The dogs' walks' were suspended by the wet afternoon.
- **C** The dog's walks were suspended by the wet afternoon.
- **D** The dogs' walks were sus'pended by the wet afternoon.

16 Where could the words 'to a certain extent' be placed in this sentence?

The young ^(A) man disagreed ^(B) with my proposal and requested ^(C) some further information ^(D)

Answers and explanations on pages 148–150

17 Which sentence includes an apostrophe (') of possession?

A The dog's leash was suspended from the coat rack. **B** Wasn't that a fantastic goal!
C Kameel's going on Wednesday—are you? **D** You didn't mean to say that, did you?

18 Which word in this text does *it* refer to?

Without really thinking about it, the older students helped the younger students to get on the bus.

A older students **B** thinking **C** younger students
D helped the younger students get on the bus **E** the bus

19 Which of the following correctly completes this sentence?

Gymnastics developed from exercises used by the ancient Greeks that ______ skills for mounting and dismounting a horse and circus routines.

A included **B** including **C** includes **D** will include

20 Circle the main clause of this sentence.

Due in part to the height of the apparatus, gymnastics is considered to be a hazardous sport, although it is considered safe in the right environment.

21 Which word is missing from the second clause?

A few of the students have lost their permission notes, ______ they will still be allowed to attend the event.

A while **B** whereas **C** however **D** in addition

22 Which sentence uses the apostrophe (') correctly?

A The doctors prescriptions' won't be filled by either pharmacist.
B The doctor's prescriptions won't be filled by either pharmacist.
C The doctors' prescriptions wont be filled by either pharmacists.
D The doctors prescriptions' wont be filled by either pharmacists'.

23 Which of the following correctly completes the sentence?

I haven't been on a bicycle ______ I was very young.

A since **B** although **C** because **D** meanwhile

24 Which of the following correctly completes the sentence?

The teenager was highly embarrassed ______ her father's behaviour.

A at **B** by **C** with **D** for

25 Which is the correct place in this sentence to put the following punctuation and words?

, who had been given free tickets,

Simon ↑(A) asked if Peter knew ↑(B) when the football ↑(C) was going to start ↑(D)

It would be a good idea to check your answers to questions 1 to 25 before moving on to the other questions.

Answers and explanations on pages 148–150

Year 7 Conventions of Language Sample Online-style Test 1

To the student

Ask your teacher or parent to read the spelling words for you. The words are listed on page 174. Write the spelling words on the lines below.

26 ______________________ 27 ______________________

28 ______________________ 29 ______________________

30 ______________________ 31 ______________________

32 ______________________ 33 ______________________

34 ______________________ 35 ______________________

36 ______________________ 37 ______________________

38 ______________________ 39 ______________________

40 ______________________

Read the text *Planting a tree*. The spelling mistakes have been highlighted.
Write the correct spelling for each highlighted word in the box

Planting a tree

41 The most common mistake when plantteing a tree is digging a hole that is too deep and too narrow.

42 Too deep and the roots don't have access to suficent oxygen

43 to ensure proper growf.

44 Two narrow and the root structure can't expand.

45 The tree will rekwire a deep watering after it is planted.

Each sentence has one word that is incorrect. Write the correct spelling of the word in the box.

46 Students at the school had many opoortunnities for leadership.

47 I wondered what the maxermum amount I could save in a year was.

48 The employees knew there were high standerds of appearance.

49 "What do you serpose is in the box?" asked Charles.

50 The mother worried about her child having an axedent on the bike.

Answers and explanations on pages 148–150

Year 7 Conventions of Language

Sample Online-style Test 2

Advanced level

1 Which word correctly completes the sentence?

Walking is different ______ other possible ways of getting home.

A than **B** from **C** in **D** of

2 Which is a complete sentence?

A Your birthday last week.
C If I'd have known.
B Jane spoke to Natalie excitedly.
D When the guests arrive.

3 Which comma (,) should be replaced by a colon (:) ?

The recipe requires five ingredients,(A) some flour,(B) cocoa,(C) eggs,(D) sugar and butter.

4 Which word correctly completes the sentence?

The liquid, once spilled, spread ______ and ruined the tablecloth.

A quick **B** quicker **C** quickly **D** quickest

5 Which word correctly completes the sentence?

Sarah was always a ______ pianist than me.

A gooder **B** better **C** more good **D** great

6 Which word correctly completes the sentence?

"Sally and ______ will take the lunch basket down," said Kate.

A myself **B** me **C** I **D** We

7 Which of the following should end with an exclamation mark?

A The show was fantastic and I loved it
B The show was pretty good
C The show was one of the best I have seen
D I enjoyed the show

8 Which word correctly completes the sentence?

______ free to play some cricket in the garden?

A Whose **B** Who's **C** Who'd **D** Who would've

Answers and explanations on pages 150–152

9 Which sentence uses speech marks (“ and ”) correctly?

A Tony wondered aloud, “Will this day ever end?”

B Tony “wondered aloud”. Will this day ever end?

C “Tony wondered aloud” Will this day ever end?

D Tony wondered “aloud. Will this day ever end?”

10 Highlight the word that is an adjective in this sentence.

Looking around, the policeman advanced cautiously towards the agitated woman.

11 Which is the correct way to combine the following sentences into one?

There’s a letter on the table for you. There’s a parcel on the table for you. They arrived today.

A Theres a letter and a parcel on the table for you. They arrived today.

B There’s a letter and a parcel on the table for you they arrived today.

C There’s a letter and a parcel on the table which arrived for you today.

D There’s a letter, and a parcel, on the table for you. They arrived today.

12 Which option correctly completes this sentence?

The origin of the name *film* ______ the words *photographic film*.

A comes **B** from **C** came from **D** is coming from

13 Which option correctly completes this sentence?

Film has ______ been the main form of recording and showing motion pictures.

A in history **B** historically **C** historical

14 Which sentence is correct?

A Neither the sport captain nor team is late for their soccer match last Saturday.

B Neither the sport captain nor team are late for their soccer match last Saturday.

C Neither the sport captain nor team was late for their soccer match last Saturday.

D Neither the sport captain nor team will be late for their soccer match last Saturday.

15 Where do the two missing speech marks (“ and ”) go?

The (A) boy at the back of the bus (B) shouted, (C) Stop the bus! I need to get off. (D)

16 Which option completes this sentence correctly?

A term that originally was given to humans ______ performed numerical calculations, the computer, was then used for the machines that did the same job.

A that **B** who **C** to **D** so

17 Circle the **three** nouns in this sentence.

A computer is not an acronym and is sometimes abbreviated as *’puter*.

Answers and explanations on pages 150–152

18 Which **two** options correctly complete this sentence?

A computer is an electronic device ______ allows you to input data and have it stored and processed ______ and efficiently.

A who, quick **B** that, quickly **C** which, quickly

19 Which option correctly completes this sentence?

Computers help make jobs much ______ than in times past.

A simple **B** simpler **C** more simpler **D** simplerer

20 Circle the word that is an adverb in this sentence.

I do not truthfully know what I would do without my little computer for study!

21 Fill in the grammatical terms to label the words in the box according to how each is used in this sentence.

The first computer was called the ENIAC, which was built during World War II.

verb	noun	adverb	adjective	preposition
A	**B**	**C**	**D**	**E**

Word	**Grammatical term in this sentence**
first	
computer	
called	
during	

22 Which word in the text does *they* refer to?

Computers first utilised vacuum tubes and were very large (sometimes room size). They were only found in businesses, universities and governments.

23 Circle the main clause of this sentence.

In addition to the use of transistors, computers also contained smaller and cheaper parts that allowed the common person to own their own computer.

24 Highlight the word or words from this sentence that should be enclosed in brackets ( ).

William Bill Henry Gates was born on 28 October 1955, and grew up in a comfortably off family with his two sisters in Seattle, Washington.

25 Where does the missing comma (,) go?

Peter↑leaving the shop, looked around↑to make sure he hadn't left anything↑behind

A B C

It would be a good idea to check your answers to questions 1 to 25 before moving on to the other questions.

Answers and explanations on pages 150–152

Year 7 Conventions of Language Sample Online-style Test 2

To the student

Ask your teacher or parent to read the spelling words for you. The words are listed on page 174. Write the spelling words on the lines below.

26 ______________________

27 ______________________

28 ______________________

29 ______________________

30 ______________________

31 ______________________

32 ______________________

33 ______________________

34 ______________________

35 ______________________

36 ______________________

37 ______________________

38 ______________________

39 ______________________

40 ______________________

Each sentence has a spelling mistake that is highlighted. Write the correct spelling of the word in the box.

41 "Can you **konfurm** your date of birth for me please?" [ ]

42 That dramatic **peformance** was the best I have ever seen! [ ]

43 My grandfather and I went **baoting** last weekend. [ ]

44 Peter believed his dog was unnecessarily **agressive** at the park that day. [ ]

45 The teacher recorded my **abcense** in a large diary. [ ]

Each sentence has one word that is incorrect. Write the correct spelling of the word in the box.

46 My uncle is an amature photographer who enjoys photographing wildlife. [ ]

47 My father ambarassed me in front of my friends. I'll never forgive him! [ ]

48 I have told you millions of times not to exagarate! [ ]

49 He found the cake irresistable and had two giant slices. [ ]

50 The maintenence department worked hard to fix the leaking water pipe. [ ]

Answers and explanations on pages 150–152

Year 7 Reading

Sample Online-style Test 1

Intermediate level

Read *Peafowl* and answer questions 1 to 8.

Peafowl

Behaviour

The peafowl are forest birds that nest on the ground. The Pavo peafowl are terrestrial feeders but roost in trees. There are two species of Pavo Peafowl: the Green Peafowl and the Indian Peafowl.

Both species of peafowl are believed to be polygamous. However, it has been suggested that 'females' entering a male Green Peafowl's territory are really his young and that Green Peafowl are really monogamous in the wild. The male peacock flares out its feathers when it is trying to get the female's attention. During mating season peafowl will often emit a very loud high-pitched cry.

Plumage

The male (peacock) Indian Peafowl has iridescent blue-green or green-coloured plumage. The so-called 'tail' of the peacock, also termed the 'train', is not the tail quill feathers but highly elongated upper tail coverts.

The train feathers have a series of eyes that are best seen when the tail is fanned. Both species have a crest atop the head.

The female (peahen) Indian Peafowl has a mixture of dull green, brown and grey in her plumage. She lacks the long upper tail coverts of the male but has a crest. The female can also display her plumage to ward off female competition or danger to her young.

The Green Peafowl is different in appearance to the Indian Peafowl. The male has green and gold plumage and has an erect crest. The wings are black with a sheen of blue.

Unlike the Indian Peafowl, the Green Peahen is very similar to the male, only having shorter upper tail coverts and less iridescence. It is very hard to tell a juvenile male from an adult female.

Many of the brilliant colours of the peacock plumage are due to an optical interference phenomenon, Bragg reflection, based on (nearly) periodic nanostructures found in the barbules (fibre-like components) of the feathers.

Source: <http://en.wikipedia.org/wiki/Peafowl>

Year 7 Reading Sample Online-style Test 1

1 *Terrestrial* means that

A the Pavo Peafowl roost in the trees.
B the Pavo Peafowl are forest birds.
C the Pavo Peafowl eat on the ground.
D the Pavo Peafowl nest on the ground.

2 The '*females*' in the Green Peafowl's territory are really his

A children. B mother. C mate. D sister.

3 The male peafowl is also known as a

A Green Peahen.
B Indian Peafowl.
C peacock.
D Pavo peafowl.

4 The Green Peafowl is different to the Indian Peafowl in that it

A has iridescent blue-green or green-coloured plumage.
B has highly elongated upper tail coverts.
C has shorter upper tail coverts and less iridescence.
D has green and gold plumage.

5 The tail of the peacock is really

A dull green, brown and grey.
B highly elongated upper tail coverts.
C black with a sheen of blue.
D blue-green or green coloured.

6 The Green Peafowl's wings are black with

A a blue lustre.
B a dull blue colour.
C an iridescent blue-green.
D green-coloured plumage.

7 Highlight the **two** sections of the text that include information about how the Pavo Peafowl looks.

A the headline
B the image
C the paragraph under the heading **Behaviour**
D the paragraphs under the heading **Plumage**

8 The dog's coat was shiny and *lustrous*.

Which word from the text is closest in meaning to *lustrous*?

A terrestrial B polygamous C iridescent D elongated

Answers and explanations on pages 152–153

Read the review of *Harry Potter and the Half-Blood Prince* and answer questions 9 to 16.

Movie review

Harry Potter and the Half-Blood Prince

Readers will know that *The Half-Blood Prince* is, by all accounts, the sparsest in the series. The film, quite rightly, follows suit. After the terrifying climax of *Order of the Phoenix*, wherein the wizarding world has finally had to accept that Voldemort (or 'He Who Must Not Be Named', for the squeamish among you) has returned, having had a tense battle with Dumbledore, Harry, and both the young and old incarnations of the Order of the Phoenix.

During this battle, Harry's godfather, Sirius Black (Gary Oldman), was killed by Bellatrix Lestrange (played with warped vigour by Helena Bonham Carter). This battle took place after it was revealed that Harry is 'the chosen one'. Meaning that either he has to kill Voldemort, or Voldemort has to kill him.

Honestly, there are so many spinning and whirling romantic entanglements in this film that you'd be forgiven for checking the book, just to make sure that any of this actually happened. But it did, and frankly, the stretches of *The Half-Blood Prince* which centre around everyday teenage angst and folly are executed brilliantly. Ron Weasley (Rupert Grint) and Hermione Granger (Emma Watson) not only do a wonderful job of convincing you that they really are Harry's oldest, dearest friends, but they manage to be pretty funny in the process.

So how does it compare to the book? Well, it's quite different in many ways, which is actually a good thing. Large portions of the book had to be omitted, which actually aided the progression of the tale. And the one ringing criticism of the Harry Potter films—that the kids can't act—can now be well and truly buried.

★★★★

Written by Paul Verhoeven, 15 July 2009, <www.thevine.com.au>

9 In line 1, *the sparsest* means that the book is
- **A** very long in comparison to the other books in the series.
- **B** brief in comparison to the other books in the series.
- **C** an average length.
- **D** concise.

10 Harry's godfather is
- **A** Gary Oldman.
- **B** Bellatrix Lestrange.
- **C** Sirius Black.
- **D** Helena Bonham Carter.

11 Harry is *'the chosen one'*. This means that he
- **A** is destined to die.
- **B** has been chosen by The Order of the Phoenix.
- **C** needs to go into battle.
- **D** needs to kill Voldemort or be killed by him.

12 Romantic entanglements are described as being *spinning and whirling*. This means that they are ________ .
- **A** constantly changing
- **B** turning around
- **C** predictable
- **D** boring

13 Which statement best supports the main argument of the text?
- **A** There are so many spinning and whirling romantic entanglements.
- **B** The *Half-blood Prince* is the sparsest in the series.
- **C** Ron and Hermione ... manage to be pretty funny in the process.
- **D** The one ringing criticism ... that the kids can't act—can now be well and truly buried.

14 In the final paragraph, the reviewer suggests that the acting ability of the younger characters is
- **A** excellent.
- **B** mundane.
- **C** terrible.
- **D** fairly good.

15 The overall reviewer's opinion is that
- **A** this film is terrible.
- **B** this film is just all right.
- **C** it's the best film he's ever seen.
- **D** everyone should see this film.

16 Read both *Peafowl* (page 92) and the movie review (page 94). For which purposes were these texts written? Choose **two** purposes for each text.

Purpose	***Peafowl***	***Movie review***
to inform		
to give an opinion		
to explain		

It would be a good idea to check your answers to questions 1 to 16 before moving on to the other questions.

Answers and explanations on page 153

Read *The Magic of Mulch* and answer questions 17 to 23.

The Magic of Mulch

Mulch is material that covers the soil to stop weed growth and promote healthy plants.

Mulch can be made from a wide variety of organic material.

Mulch helps retain nutrients and moisture in the soil when applied to the top of your garden.

Worms and microbes are examples of biological activity that mulch creates in order to make your garden healthier.

WEED-FREE MULCH

Take care when selecting material for your mulch. It is best not to include weeds, seedling plants and certain leaves in your mulch.

KILLER MULCH

Avoid making mulch with materials that have had weedkiller or pesticides used on them.

Mulch can be made from common organic items found around the garden and the kitchen. Some examples are:

LEAVES—Leaves provide a fibrous organic benefit to the soil.

GRASS CLIPPINGS—These are great for growing seedlings as they contain nitrogen and potash. This makes the clippings break down quickly.

STRAW—This can be purchased and used as mulch around larger plants.

SEAWEED—High in minerals, seaweed is sand-free and looks good on your garden!

NEWSPAPER—Wet or soiled newspaper that can no longer be recycled can be used as mulch.

It is important to try and increase the diversity of mulches you use on your garden.

17 The technique used in the poster's heading *The Magic of Mulch* is

A assonance. **B** repetition. **C** alliteration. **D** simile.

18 You read that *Mulch is* (lines 1–3)

A a substance used over soil that inhibits the growth of weeds.

B a material in soil that encourages the growth of healthy plants.

C a substance used over soil that encourages weed growth.

D something that decreases biological activity in the soil.

19 What will kill (destroy) your plants?

A grass clippings

B compost

C weedkiller or pesticides

D wood or bark chips

20 Using your own words, explain the meaning of *It's important to try and increase the diversity of mulches you use on your garden* (lines 36–37).

____

____

____

____

21 The poster encourages people to use mulch in their gardens by

A including detail about *killer mulch*.

B providing a list of items commonly found in mulch.

C including information about the benefits of mulch.

D providing information on what to leave out of mulch.

22 Grass clippings are good mulch as they *break down quickly* (line 30). This means that they

A travel down into the soil faster than other mulches.

B decompose faster than other mulches.

C contain nitrogen and potash.

D are special mulch for seedlings.

23 The purpose of this text is to

A inform. **B** entertain. **C** criticise. **D** persuade.

Answers and explanations on pages 153–154

Read *Dive Australia's depths* and answer questions 24 to 30.

Dive Australia's depths

Completely surrounded by water and rich in islands and reefs, Australia is a diver's dream. Our waters shelter a treasure trove of marine life, with more than 4000 species of fish and the world's highest diversity of sea grass. Swim with the giant, gentle whale shark on Ningaloo Reef or with sea-lions and dolphins on South Australia's Eyre Peninsula. Learn to dive on Queensland's Great Barrier Reef—the world's largest living organism. Or snorkel in sheltered and scenic Clovelly in Sydney. Discover kelp-encrusted submarines off the Mornington Peninsula or a maze of underwater caves along Tasmania's east coast. Our temperate waters are calling, so come dive in.

Great Barrier Reef, Queensland

Don't miss the World Heritage-listed Great Barrier Reef, a living masterpiece so big it can be seen from space. It stretches almost 2000 kilometres along the Queensland coast, from Cape York to Bundaberg. Discover the diving havens of Heron and Lizard Islands. Or stay in the Whitsundays and take a sea-plane to spectacular Heart Reef. Base yourself in Cairns or Port Douglas and visit the reef gardens of Green and Fitzroy Islands. Travel further to Agincourt Reef, on the edge of the continental shelf. Kick through coral canyons filled with turtles, sea stars and crabs at Lady Musgrave Island and Fitzroy Lagoon near Gladstone. Explore the SS *Yongala* shipwreck from Townsville and the *Llewellyn* shipwreck from Mackay.

Ningaloo, Western Australia

Join the tropical-coloured party at Ningaloo Marine Park, the world's largest fringing reef. It's home to 200 species of hard coral, 50 soft coral and over 500 species of fish. Snorkel or shallow dive with brightly adorned fish in the Bundegi Bombies reef sanctuary. Get up close to sci-fi sponges, gorgonians and sea whips at the entrance to the Exmouth Gulf. Mingle with turtles, manta rays, dolphins, dugongs, batfish, angelfish and clownfish, among others, at Lighthouse Bay. Discover spectacular reef diving and a glamorous underwater crowd at the Murion Islands. Between April and June you can even hang out with the whale shark, the world's largest fish.

24 What is *Completely surrounded by water and rich in islands and reefs* (line 1)?

A Great Barrier Reef **B** Ningaloo **C** Eyre Peninsula **D** Australia

25 In line 7, *temperate* means

A moderate and pleasant.

B angry.

C calm.

D cold.

26 How long is the Great Barrier Reef?

A 4000 kilometres **B** 200 kilometres **C** 2000 kilometres **D** 500 kilometres

27 *Kick through coral canyons* (line 19) means that you

A run. **B** swim. **C** snorkel. **D** dive.

28 Choose the correct option to complete the sentence. You may choose more than one.

In the text, the photographs are used to ________ .

A support the information given

B show people swimming and snorkelling

C show images of coral

D show you what you could be doing there

E advertise snorkelling equipment

29 Read both *The Magic of Mulch* (page 96) and *Dive Australia's depths*. Match the features to the text in which they are used. Choose **two** each.

The Magic of Mulch	*Dive Australia's depths*

A scientific terms **B** instructional verbs

C descriptive adjectives **D** images

30 Read both *The Magic of Mulch* and *Dive Australia's depths*. Choose the correct words to complete the sentence.

It is most likely that *The Magic of Mulch* would appear in a magazine / poster / novel, while *Dive Australia's depths* would appear in a newspaper / website / novel.

It would be a good idea to check your answers to questions 17 to 30 before moving on to the other questions.

Answers and explanations on page 154

Read *Beowulf* and answer questions 31 to 37.

Beowulf

PRELUDE OF THE FOUNDER OF THE DANISH HOUSE

LO, praise of the prowess of people-kings
of spear-armed Danes, in days long sped,
we have heard, and what honour the athelings
won!

Oft Scyld the Scefing from squadroned foes,
from many a tribe, the mead-bench tore,
awing the earls. Since erst he lay
friendless, a foundling, fate repaid him:
for he waxed under welkin, in wealth he throve,
till before him the folk, both far and near,
who house by the whale-path, heard his mandate,
gave him gifts: a good king he!

To him an heir was afterward born,
a son in his halls, whom heaven sent
to favour the folk, feeling their woe
that erst they had lacked an earl for leader
so long a while; the Lord endowed him,
the Wielder of Wonder, with world's renown.
Famed was this Beowulf: far flew the boast of him,
son of Scyld, in the Scandian lands.

31 The poem creates a feeling of

A drama.

B awe.

C inspiration.

D surprise.

32 A prelude is

A a pause.

B a chapter.

C a verse.

D an introduction.

33 The people spoken about in this poem are

A tribes.

B Danes.

C foes.

D lords.

34 Which word from the poem implies that Beowulf was special?

A prowess

B honour

C good

D famed

35 Beowulf's father's name is

A Lord.

B Wielder of Wonder.

C Scyld the Scefing.

D King.

36 The language technique used in line 1 is

A metaphor.

B simile.

C personification.

D alliteration.

37 The purpose of this text is to

A inform.

B entertain.

C criticise.

D persuade.

Answers and explanations on pages 154–155

Read the *Running infographic* and answer questions 38 to 41.

RUNNING INFOGRAPHIC

TIME

Studies show that running just 5 to 10 minutes each day at a moderate pace may help reduce your risk of death from heart attacks, strokes and other common diseases.

NUTRITION

Are you eating enough before a run? Running on an empty stomach can often lead to sluggish workouts and clawing hunger later in the day.

STRENGTH

Running is a weight-bearing exercise that develops more lower-body lean muscle mass. This also keeps your bones healthy, which is always a plus.

CALORIES

People frequently embrace running as a means to reach or maintain a healthy weight. Running burns more calories than weight training, swimming or cycling.

HEALTH

Running can significantly improve physical and mental health. As a form of aerobic exercise, running can reduce stress and improve heart health.

38 Which icon (pictogram) is used to represent ideas about 'strength'?

A running girl
B apple
C dumbbell
D stopwatch

39 During exercise, calories are ______________________.

A reduced
B burned
C developed
D improved

40 Which sentence best shows the purpose of the Infographic?

A Images are used to show the benefits of running.
B Dense information is provided to create a detailed understanding of the topic.
C Words and images are used to instruct readers on the best way to run.
D Simple graphics and words combine to create an overview of the benefits of running.

41 The tone of this text is

A persuasive.
B factual.
C entertaining.
D exciting.

Answers and explanations on page 155

Read *Tips to improve maths skills* and answer questions 42 to 47.

Tips to improve maths skills

Step 1

Make maths a regular part of your life by using it on a daily basis. This will help you to continue increasing your aptitude in the subject.

Step 2

Learn the mathematical terms in order to gain a better understanding of the concepts.

Step 3

Buy helpful maths guides or borrow books from the library that will assist you further in practising your maths skills.

Step 4

Make sure to doublecheck your work to make sure it is correct. If the answer is incorrect, take the extra time to figure out why and correct the work.

Step 5

Write out the numbers and mathematical concepts correctly, as this will help you see the work properly. It is easy to make a mistake if the work is written out sloppily or messy.

Step 6

Change your attitude to a positive one if you find that you do not like maths. It will help you increase your self-confidence. When you have confidence, it will help with completing the maths work. Even if you have the wrong answer to a problem, try to not get discouraged—but be encouraged to keep trying to solve the problem.

Source: <http://www.ehow.com/how_2314474_improve-math-skills.html>

42 Which step encourages a positive frame of mind?

A Step 1
B Step 3
C Step 5
D Step 6

43 The word at the beginning of each step is an example of a

A noun.
B verb.
C article.
D adjective

44 This text is an example of

A an instruction.
B a narrative.
C an exposition.
D a discussion.

45 *Aptitude* in line 4 means

A strength.
B weakness.
C ability.
D attitude towards.

46 What are the pictures surrounding the information called?

A mathematical symbols
B emoticons
C digits
D visual representations

47 What is the main message of Step 6?

A Self-confidence is the key to success.
B You need determination to solve problems.
C Your personal approach to maths influences success.
D Don't be discouraged by wrong answers.

48 Read both *Running infographic* (page 102) and *Tips to improve maths skills*. Choose the correct words to complete the sentence.

It is most likely that *Running infographic* would appear in a magazine / poster / novel, while *Tips to improve maths skills* would appear in a newspaper / website / novel.

Answers and explanations on page 155

Sample Online-style Test 2

Advanced level

Read *Origami* and answer questions 1 to 8.

Origami

Origami (from *ori* meaning 'folding', and *kami* meaning 'paper') is the traditional Japanese folk art of paper folding, which started in the 17th century AD and was popularised in the mid-1900s. It has since then evolved into a modern art form.

The goal of this art is to transform a flat sheet of material into a finished sculpture through folding and sculpting techniques, and as such the use of cuts and glue are not considered to be part of origami.

The number of basic origami folds is small, but they can be combined in a variety of ways to make intricate designs. The most well-known origami model is probably the Japanese paper crane. In general, these designs begin with a square sheet of paper which has sides that may be of different colours or prints. Contrary to popular belief, traditional Japanese origami, which has been practised since the Edo era (1603–1867), has often been less strict about the conventions, sometimes cutting the paper or using non-square shapes to start with.

Techniques

Many origami books begin with a description of basic origami techniques that are used to construct the models. These include simple diagrams of basic folds like valley and mountain folds, pleats, reverse folds, squash folds and sinks. There are also standard named bases, which are used in a wide variety of models, for instance the bird base is an intermediate stage in the construction of the flapping bird.

Origami paper

Origami paper is sold in pre-packaged squares of various sizes ranging from 2.5 cm to 25 cm or more. It is commonly coloured on one side and white on the other; however, dual-coloured and patterned versions exist and can be used effectively for colour-changed models. Origami paper weighs slightly less than copy paper, making it suitable for a wide range of models.

Normal copy paper can be used for simple folds, such as the crane and water bomb. Heavier weight papers can be wet-folded. This technique allows for a more rounded sculpting of the model that becomes rigid and sturdy when it is dry.

Source: <http://en.wikipedia.org/wiki/Origami>

Year 7 Reading Sample Online-style Test 2

1. The word *origami* stands for
   - **A** Japan.
   - **B** the word *ori* meaning 'folding'.
   - **C** the word *ori* meaning 'folding' and *kami* meaning 'paper'.
   - **D** the 17th century AD.

2. Which sentence best states that origami is popular in the present day?
   - **A** Origami is the traditional Japanese folk art of paper folding.
   - **B** It has since then evolved into a modern art form.
   - **C** The goal of this art is to transform a flat sheet of material into a finished sculpture.
   - **D** Traditional Japanese origami has often been less strict about conventions.

3. What is the most recognised origami model?
   - **A** one with an intricate design
   - **B** a finished sculpture
   - **C** one that uses a square piece of paper
   - **D** the Japanese paper crane

4. Some basic origami techniques include
   - **A** cutting and gluing.
   - **B** basic folds like valley and mountain folds, pleats, reverse folds and squash folds.
   - **C** using non-square shapes.
   - **D** using normal copy paper.

5. Choose the correct option to complete the sentence. You may choose more than one.

   According to the text, origami paper is commonly
   - **A** sold in pre-packaged squares of various sizes.
   - **B** features the use of both cuts and glue.
   - **C** weighs a little less than regular copy paper.
   - **D** is all dual coloured and patterned.
   - **E** wrapping paper or magazine pages.

6. Heavier paper than normal copy paper can be used for
   - **A** simple folds.
   - **B** the model of the crane.
   - **C** more rounded sculpting of the model.
   - **D** a wider range of models.

7. The purpose of this text is to
   - **A** persuade you to make origami.
   - **B** offer some basic instructions for how to make origami models.
   - **C** offer information about origami.
   - **D** offer the writer's opinion on origami.

8. The images have been included because they
   - **A** show you how to fold the paper.
   - **B** are very attractive.
   - **C** show the most difficult designs.
   - **D** show examples of materials and designs.

Answers and explanations on pages 155–156

Read *The cyclone* and answer questions 9 to 16.

Chapter 1: The cyclone

Dorothy lived in the midst of the great Kansas prairies, with Uncle Henry, who was a farmer, and Aunt Em, who was the farmer's wife. Their house was small, for the lumber to build it had to be carried by wagon many miles. There were four walls, a floor and a roof, which made one room; and this room contained a rusty looking cook stove, a cupboard for the dishes, a table, three or four chairs, and the beds. Uncle Henry and Aunt Em had a big bed in one corner, and Dorothy a little bed in another corner. There was no garret at all, and no cellar—except a small hole dug in the ground, called a cyclone cellar, where the family could go in case one of those great whirlwinds arose, mighty enough to crush any building in its path. It was reached by a trap door in the middle of the floor, from which a ladder led down into the small, dark hole.

When Dorothy stood in the doorway and looked around, she could see nothing but the great grey prairie on every side. Neither a tree nor a house broke the broad sweep of flat country that reached to the edge of the sky in all directions. The sun had baked the ploughed land into a grey mass, with little cracks running through it. Even the grass was not green, for the sun had burned the tops of the long blades until they were the same grey colour to be seen everywhere. Once the house had been painted, but the sun blistered the paint and the rains washed it away, and now the house was as dull and grey as everything else.

When Aunt Em came there to live she was a young, pretty wife. The sun and wind had changed her, too. They had taken the sparkle from her eyes and left them a sober grey; they had taken the red from her cheeks and lips, and they were grey also. She was thin and gaunt, and never smiled now. When Dorothy, who was an orphan, first came to her, Aunt Em had been so startled by the child's laughter that she would scream and press her hand upon her heart whenever Dorothy's merry voice reached her ears; and she still looked at the little girl with wonder that she could find anything to laugh at.

From *The Wonderful Wizard of Oz* by L Frank Baum

Year 7 Reading Sample Online-style Test 2

9 Uncle Henry's occupation is as a

A farmer's wife. B builder. C farmer. D Kansas prairie.

10 Their house could be described as

A small with four walls, a floor, a roof and a rusty-looking cook stove.
B small with three walls, a floor and only one big bed.
C small with four walls, no floor and a rusty-looking cook stove.
D small with four walls, a floor, no cook stove and beds.

11 Which phrase shows the strength of the cyclone?

A *great grey prairie* (line 13)
B *the sun blistered the paint and the winds washed it away* (line 24)
C *the house was as dull and grey as everything else* (line 25)
D *great whirlwinds arose, mighty enough to crush any building* (lines 7–8)

12 What had the sun done to the ploughed land?

A made the prairie grey and treeless
B rusted the cooking stove
C made the country a sweep of flat land
D baked the ploughed land into a grey mass

13 The sun had turned Aunt Em into

A a young and pretty wife.
B someone grey and serious.
C someone with a heart condition.
D someone who loved to listen to Dorothy's merry voice.

14 The purpose of this text is to

A offer a factual recount of life in Kansas.
B inform about life on a prairie.
C tell about Dorothy and her family.
D narrate a story that is not true.

15 Which pair of words best describes the environment of the story?

A austere and arid
B parched and decrepit
C grim and rigid
D serious and dry

16 Read both *Origami* (page 106) and *The cyclone*. Match the features to each text in which they are used.

Origami	*The cyclone*

past tense	jargon	descriptive adjectives	present tense	past tense
A	B	C	D	E

It would be a good idea to check your answers to questions 1 to 16 before moving on to the other questions.

Read *Seagrass* and answer questions 17 to 24.

Seagrass

Seagrass ...

- is a marine plant which grows like terrestrial grass
- is often found in shallow coastal waters
- is the main food source for Green Turtles and dugongs
- dugongs can eat up to 40 kg of seagrass every day
- animal feeding trails and troughs can be seen in the seagrass beds.

Detritus, formed by the breakdown of seagrass, supports a complex marine food chain which sustains a myriad of captivating and striking aquatic creatures.

These unusual marine flowering plants are called sea grasses because the leaves are long and narrow and are very often green, and because the plants often grow in large 'meadows' which look like grassland.

17 What is *terrestrial grass*?

- **A** grass that grows on the ocean floor
- **B** grass that grows on land, as opposed to the ocean floor
- **C** grass farmed by extra-terrestrials
- **D** a marine plant

18 How is *detritus* formed?

- **A** by a complex marine food chain
- **B** in shallow coastal waters
- **C** by the breakdown of seagrass
- **D** by feeding trails and troughs that are found in seagrass beds

19 What is *seagrass*?

- **A** mudflats
- **B** a terrestrial plant similar to marine grass
- **C** a marine plant similar to terrestrial grass and the main food source for Green Turtles
- **D** feeding trails and furrows

20 There are images of

- **A** plant life only.
- **B** plant and animal life.
- **C** plant, animal life and shells.
- **D** the ocean floor.

21 The images are used to

- **A** support the information presented in the text.
- **B** show pretty pictures of sea life.
- **C** allow you to see a dugong in its natural environment.
- **D** show you what sea animals eat.

22 *Myriad* in the sentence *sustains a myriad of captivating and striking aquatic creatures* (lines 12–13) could be replaced by the word

- **A** oceanic.
- **B** animal.
- **C** wonderful.
- **D** numerous.

23 The purpose of this text is to

- **A** inform readers about seagrass and its place in the ecosystem.
- **B** persuade readers to take care of the ocean.
- **C** suggest readers visit the ocean for a holiday.
- **D** encourage readers to take an interest in seagrass.

24 The area where the plants grow is called a 'meadow' because

- **A** flowers grow there.
- **B** the leaves are long and narrow.
- **C** the plants grow in a large field.
- **D** the plants need the sun to survive.

Answers and explanations on pages 156–157

Read *The song of wandering Aengus* and answer questions 25 to 32.

The song of wandering Aengus

I went out to the hazel wood,
Because a fire was in my head,
And cut and peeled a hazel wand,
And hooked a berry to a thread;
And when white moths were on the wing,
And moth-like stars were flickering out,
I dropped the berry in a stream
And caught a little silver trout.

When I had laid it on the floor
I went to blow the fire aflame,
But something rustled on the floor,
And someone called me by my name:
It had become a glimmering girl
With apple blossom in her hair
Who called me by my name and ran
And faded through the brightening air.

Though I am old with wandering
Through hollow lands and hilly lands,
I will find out where she has gone,
And kiss her lips and take her hands;
And walk among long dappled grass,
And pluck till time and times are done
The silver apples of the moon,
The golden apples of the sun.

WB Yeats

25 In line 2, what could a *fire was in my head* mean?

A Aengus was on fire.
B He had a burning head.
C Something was bothering him.
D He was content and at peace.

26 What is Aengus making in stanza 1?

A a stick B a fishing pole C a needle D a berry

27 Who calls Aengus's name in stanza 2?

A a young girl
B a little silver trout
C a berry
D an old and wandering man

28 Another word for *glimmering* in line 13 could be

A radiant. B shiny. C shady. D dark.

29 In the final stanza, Aengus has become

A a young girl.
B a little silver trout.
C an old man.
D the silver apples of the moon.

30 The technique used at the end of lines 18 and 20 is

A rhyme.
B rhythm.
C alliteration.
D simile.

31 *Wandering* in the text (line 17) means

A living. B travelling. C confused. D walking.

32 This text creates a feeling of

A desire for fishing.
B longing (nostalgia) about the past.
C yearning to walk among long dappled grass.
D searching for someone missing.

It would be a good idea to check your answers to questions 17 to 32 before moving on to the other questions.

Answers and explanations on page 157

Read *Eve's diary* and answer questions 33 to 40.

Eve's diary

by Mark Twain

SATURDAY.—I am almost a whole day old, now. I arrived yesterday. That is as it seems to me. And it must be so, for if there was a day-before-yesterday I was not there when it happened, or I should remember it. It could be, of course, that it did happen, and that I was not noticing. Very well; I will be very watchful now, and if any day-before-yesterdays happen I will make a note of it. It will be best to start right and not let the record get confused, for some instinct tells me that these details are going to be important to the historian some day. For I feel like an experiment, I feel exactly like an experiment; it would be impossible for a person to feel more like an experiment than I do, and so I am coming to feel convinced that that is what I *am*—an experiment; just an experiment, and nothing more.

Then if I am an experiment, am I the whole of it? No, I think not; I think the rest of it is part of it. I am the main part of it, but I think the rest of it has its share in the matter. Is my position assured, or do I have to watch it and take care of it? The latter, perhaps. Some instinct tells me that eternal vigilance is the price of supremacy. (That is a good phrase, I think, for one so young.)

Everything looks better today than it did yesterday. In the rush of finishing up yesterday, the mountains were left in a ragged condition, and some of the plains were so cluttered with rubbish and remnants that the aspects were quite distressing. Noble and beautiful works of art should not be subjected to haste; and this majestic new world is indeed a most noble and beautiful work. And certainly marvellously near to being perfect, notwithstanding the shortness of the time. There are too many stars in some places and not enough in others, but that can be remedied presently, no doubt. The moon got loose last night, and slid down and fell out of the scheme—a very great loss; it breaks my heart to think of it. There isn't another thing among the ornaments and decorations that is comparable to it for beauty and finish. It should have been fastened better. If we can only get it back again—

33 A usual feature of a diary is that it
- **A** is written from the first-person perspective (*I*).
- **B** contains mostly factual and objective information.
- **C** is a chronological list of events that happened in a day.
- **D** is a text that is written for a wide audience.

34 How old is Eve at the beginning of the diary entry?
- **A** a day old
- **B** less than a day old
- **C** very young
- **D** arrived yesterday

35 What is it that Eve feels like for a large section of the first paragraph?
- **A** watchful
- **B** convinced
- **C** an experiment
- **D** confused

36 The language technique used in line 10 is
- **A** alliteration.
- **B** metaphor.
- **C** exclamation mark.
- **D** rhetorical question.

37 In line 13, why is Eve impressed with her own phrase *eternal vigilance is the price of supremacy*?
- **A** It sounds impressive, given her age.
- **B** It sounds like a good phrase.
- **C** It makes her feel instinctive.
- **D** It makes her feel supreme.

38 The word *majestic* in line 20 could be replaced by
- **A** magnificent.
- **B** kingly.
- **C** noble.
- **D** exciting.

39 Read both *The song of wandering Aengus* (page 112) and *Eve's diary*. For which purposes were these texts written? Choose **two** purposes for each text.

Purpose	***The song of wandering Aengus***	***Eve's diary***
to reflect		
to recount		
to entertain		

40 Read both *The song of wandering Aengus* (page 112) and *Eve's diary*. Choose the correct words to complete the sentence.

It is most likely that *The song of wandering Aengus* would appear in a collection of poems / poster / novel, while *Eve's diary* would appear in a newspaper / website / collection of short stories.

Read *Butterflies* and answer questions 41 to 48.

Butterflies

A butterfly is any of several groups of mainly day-flying insects of the order *Lepidoptera*, the butterflies and moths.

Life spans

It is a popular belief that butterflies have very short life spans. However, butterflies in their adult stage can live from a week to nearly a year depending on the species. Many species have long larval life stages while others can remain dormant in their pupae or egg stages and thereby survive winters.

Eggs

Butterfly eggs consist of a hard-ridged outer layer of shell, called the *chorion*. This is lined with a thin coating of wax, which prevents the egg from drying out before the larva has had time to fully develop. Each egg contains a number of tiny funnel-shaped openings at one end, called *micropyles*; the purpose of these holes is to allow sperm to enter and fertilise the egg. Butterfly and moth eggs vary greatly in size between species, but they are all either spherical or ovate.

Butterfly eggs are fixed to a leaf with special glue, which hardens rapidly. As it hardens it contracts, deforming the shape of the egg. This glue is easily seen surrounding the base of every egg forming a meniscus. The nature of the glue is unknown and is a suitable subject for research. The same glue is produced by a pupa to secure the setae of the cremaster. This glue is so hard that the silk pad, to which the setae are glued, cannot be separated.

Eggs are usually laid on plants. Each species of butterfly has its own host plant range and while some species of butterfly are restricted to just one species of plant, others use a range of plant species, often including members of a common family.

Source: <http://en.wikipedia.org/wiki/Butterfly>

41 A butterfly is

A a creature that has a short life span.
B part of a number of groups of insects that fly mainly during the day.
C a species that has a long larval life stage.
D an insect that is fixed to a leaf with special glue.

42 How long do butterflies live?

A They have very short life spans.
B They all survive winters.
C Depending on the species, they could live for between seven days and a year.
D They live for about a week.

43 What is a micropyle?

A a series of holes in the butterfly egg that determine the size of the butterfly
B a series of holes in the butterfly egg that make the butterfly larger
C a series of holes in the butterfly eggs that allows the egg to be fertilised
D a hard-ridged outer layer of shell

44 In line 24 we are told that the special glue hardens. This results in the glue

A getting warm and then sticky.
B becoming firm and fixing the egg to a leaf.
C changing quickly.
D being unable to be separated from the egg.

45 Why is the special butterfly glue a suitable subject for research?

A The same glue is produced by a pupa to secure the setae of the cremaster.
B This glue is so hard that the silk pad, to which the setae are glued, cannot be separated.
C Particular details about the glue are still uncertain.
D This is an interesting topic for research.

46 In line 29, the word *host* in the sentence *Each species of butterfly has its own host plant range* means

A the animal or plant on which or in which another organism lives.
B a person who manages an inn or hotel.
C one who receives or entertains guests.
D the recipient of a transplanted tissue or organ.

47 The purpose of this text is to

A provide entertaining information on the life of a butterfly.
B provide factual information on butterfly life spans and reproduction.
C provide factual information on what butterflies eat and how they survive.
D to explain about the chorion and micropyle.

48 When a muscle *shrinks,* it pulls on the bone.

Which word from the text is closest in meaning to *shrinks*?

A stretches **B** rebounds **C** contracts **D** moves

Year 7 Writing

Sample Online-style Test 1

Before you start, read the Tips for Writing on page 77.

Today you are going to write a persuasive text.

School uniform or not?

Your school wants to introduce the rule that all students must wear a school uniform. What do you think about this idea?

Write a persuasive speech to your fellow students in order to convince them of your opinions.

Before you start writing, give some thought to:

- if you agree or disagree—you might see both sides of the argument
- an introduction—your opening paragraph should state clearly whether you agree or disagree with the topic
- your opinions—you should have reasons or evidence to support your opinions
- a conclusion—your speech should conclude with a summary of the main points of your argument.

Don't forget to:

- plan your writing
- write in full sentences
- use paragraphs to structure your speech
- pay attention to your spelling and punctuation
- choose words carefully that will help persuade your audience
- check that your work is clearly expressed.

Start writing here or write your answer on a tablet or computer.

☞Turn to page 146 and use the Marking checklist to check the student's writing. Also go to pages 165–166 where the sample pieces of writing (Intermediate and Advanced levels) can be used to see at what level the student is writing. These writing samples have been analysed based on the marking criteria used by markers to assess the NAPLAN Writing Test.

Year 7 Writing — Sample Online-style Test 2

Before you start, read the Tips for Writing on page 79.

Today you are going to write a narrative.

Your narrative will be about **water**.

Look at the picture to give you some ideas.

Your narrative could be about some water that you swim in or just look at. What sort of water is it? Don't just think of the beach. Perhaps you are doing something in the water, like fishing or on a boat.

Add some brief description of the water.

Your narrative may be serious or humorous.

Your writing will be judged on quality of expression and the structure of your narrative.

Before you start writing, give some thought to:

- where your narrative takes place (the setting)
- the characters and what they do in the narrative
- the events that take place in the narrative and the problems that have to be resolved
- how your narrative begins, what happens in your narrative, and how your narrative ends.

Don't forget to:

- plan your narrative before you start
- write in correctly formed sentences and take care with paragraphing
- choose your words carefully and pay attention to your spelling and punctuation
- write neatly but don't waste time
- quickly check your narrative once you have finished.

Start writing here or write your answer on a tablet or computer.

Turn to page 146 and use the Marking checklist to check the student's writing. Also go to pages 167–168 where the sample pieces of writing (Intermediate and Advanced levels) can be used to see at what level the student is writing. These writing samples have been analysed based on the marking criteria used by markers to assess the NAPLAN Writing Test.

Standard level questions

SPELLING Mini Test 1

1 bodies **2** ladies **3** leaves **4** knives **5** ankles **6** canvases **7** feet **8** princesses **9** dishes **10** mice **11** reef **12** hobbies **13** replies **14** individuals **15** exercises **16** activities **17** sports **18** downstairs **19** everybody **20** make-up (or makeup) **21** lifelike **22** excellent **23** Alongside **24** Moreover **25** commonplace

1 The adjective *many* indicates that more than one body of water is being referred to. Make plurals of words ending in ***y***, if there is a consonant before the ***y***, by changing the ***y*** to ***i*** before adding ***es*** (e.g. *body, bodies*).

2 The noun *ladies* indicates that more than one lady is being referred to. Make plurals of words ending in ***y***, if there is a consonant before the ***y***, by changing the ***y*** to ***i*** before adding ***es*** (e.g. *lady, ladies*). The word *ladies* does not have an apostrophe after it as it is being used in a descriptive rather than possessive sense.

3 The adjective *all* indicates that more than one leaf is being referred to. Make plurals of words ending in ***f*** or ***fe*** by changing the ***f*** or ***fe*** to ***v*** before adding ***es*** (e.g. *leaf, leaves*).

4 The ***s*** at the end of the word indicates that more than one knife is being referred to. Make plurals of words ending in ***f*** or ***fe*** by changing the ***f*** or ***fe*** to ***v*** before adding ***es*** (e.g. *knife, knives*).

5 The word *ankle* requires an ***e*** at the end. Other words that have a similar ***le*** final syllable include *bubble* and *cable*. The adjective *both* indicates that more than one ankle is being referred to. This is the most common way to make a plural and you should just add an ***s*** (e.g. *ankle, ankles*).

6 The adverb *a lot* indicates that more than one artist canvas is being referred to. Make plurals of words ending in ***x***, ***sh***, ***ch*** or ***s*** by adding ***es*** (e.g. *canvas, canvases*).

7 *Feet* is the plural of the singular *foot*. This is an example of an irregular plural that doesn't follow any particular rule.

8 The adjective *three* indicates that more than one princess is being referred to. Make plurals of words ending in ***x***, ***sh***, ***ch*** or ***s*** by adding ***es*** (e.g. *princess, princesses*).

9 The adjective *multiple* indicates that more than one dish is being referred to. Make plurals of words ending in ***x***, ***sh***, ***ch*** or ***s*** by adding ***es*** (e.g. *dish, dishes*).

10 *Mice* is the plural of the singular *mouse*. This is an example of an irregular plural that doesn't follow any particular rule.

11 The letters ***ee*** and ***ea*** often make the long ***e*** sound. There are no clear rules for when the different vowel combinations should be used and the words with these spellings just have to be learned. Some words spelt with an ***ee*** letter combination include *sleep* and *keep*. Words that have a similar sound but which are spelt with ***ea*** include *heat* and *meat*.

12 The verb *are* indicates that more than one hobby is being referred to. Make plurals of words ending in ***y***, if there is a consonant before the ***y***, by changing the ***y*** to ***i*** before adding ***es*** (e.g. *hobby, hobbies*).

13 The adjective *few* indicates that more than one reply is being referred to. Make plurals of words ending in ***y***, if there is a consonant before the ***y***, by changing the ***y*** to ***i*** before adding ***es*** (e.g. *reply, replies*).

14 The noun *number* indicates that more than one individual is being referred to. The most common way to make a plural is to simply add an ***s*** (e.g. *individual, individuals*).

15 The word *many* indicates that more than one exercise is being referred to. Simply adding an ***s*** is the most common way to make a plural (e.g. *exercise, exercises*).

16 The adjective *all* indicates that more than one activity is being referred to. Make plurals of words ending in ***y***, if there is a consonant before the ***y***, by changing the ***y*** to ***i*** before adding ***es*** (e.g. *activity, activities*).

17 The most common way to make a plural is to simply add an ***s*** (e.g. *sport, sports*).

18 This is an example of a 'closed form' compound noun, in which the words are joined together (e.g. *firefly, secondhand, softball* and *childlike*).

19 This is an example of a 'closed form' compound noun, in which the words are joined together (e.g. *firefly, secondhand, softball* and *childlike*). Pronounce *everybody* carefully to make it easier to spell. It is *ev* + *er* + *y* + *bo* + *dy*.

20 It is acceptable to write this compound word as either hyphenated or unhyphenated. It is necessary to spell *make* with an ***e*** at the end, however, as this ensures the word is pronounced correctly with a hard ***a*** sound. Examples of words with a similar spelling include *fake, take* and *lake*.

21 This is an example of a 'closed form' compound noun in which the words are joined together, such as *softball* and *childlike*. Adding an extra ***f*** into the word *life* would interfere with its pronunciation, making it 'liff' and not the hard ***i*** sounding *life*. Similar sounding words are *wife* and *knife*.

22 Although you only hear the sound ***x*** at the beginning of the word, the sound is actually formed by combining the letters ***ex***, as in *extract, exile, exam*. From the same word family is the verb *excel*, meaning 'to be very good at something', however you need to double the ***l*** before adding the suffix ***ent***.

23 This is an example of a 'closed form' compound noun, in which the words are joined together (e.g. *firefly, secondhand, softball* and *childlike*). *Alongside* needs to be spelt with the ***i–e*** vowel combination to give the long ***i*** sound.

24 This is an example of a 'closed form' compound noun, in which the words are joined together (e.g. *firefly, secondhand, softball* and *childlike*).

25 This is an example of a 'closed form' compound noun, in which the words are joined together (e.g. *firefly, secondhand, softball* and *childlike*). Pronounce *commonplace* carefully to make it easier to spell: *com + mon + place*.

Standard level questions

SPELLING Mini Test 2

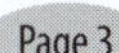

Page 3

1 chief **2** cough **3** bought **4** receipt **5** fruit **6** obtain **7** should **8** usually **9** beige **10** foreign **11** their **12** there **13** view **14** shrieked **15** table **16** feeling **17** ceiling **18** white **19** steal **20** purpose **21** loose **22** green **23** scream **24** lose **25** quiet

1 Sometimes it is difficult to remember whether a word is spelt with ***ie*** or ***ei***. There is a very simple rule to help you: 'I before E except after C'.

2 *Cough* and *trough* are the only two ***ough*** words pronounced *off*.

3 This word ends with the sound of ***ort*** but its spelling is similar to *thought, fought* and *brought*.

4 Sometimes it is difficult to remember whether a word is spelt with ***ie*** or ***ei***. There is a very simple rule to help you: 'I before E except after C'.

5 Other examples of words with the ***ui*** vowel combination include *bruise, recruit* and *juice*.

6 Words that have the long ***a + n*** sound can be difficult to spell. This sound is represented by the following spellings: ***ane*** as in *cane*, ***ain*** as in *obtain*, ***eign*** as in *reign*, ***ein*** as in *vein*.

7 *Could, would, should* are all examples of words ending in ***ould***.

8 A helpful way to remember how to spell this word is to break it down into its smallest form. This word is made up of the smaller word *usual* and the suffix ***ly***.

9 There are a number of exceptions to the I before E rule. Sometimes it is difficult to remember whether a word is spelt with ***ie*** or ***ei***. There is a very simple rule to help you: 'I before E except after C or when sounding like ***ay*** as in *neighbour* and *weigh*'.

10 There are a number of exceptions to the 'I before E except after C' rule that you will just have to remember. *Foreign* is one exception. Other examples are *neither, caffeine, codeine, counterfeit, forfeit, height, leisure, protein, their, weird, seize* and *seizure*.

11 Use *their* to indicate possession. It is a possessive adjective and indicates that a particular noun belongs to some people (e.g. *My friends have lost their tickets*). Remember that *they're* is a contraction of the words *they* and *are*. It can never be used as a modifier, only as a subject (who or what does the action) and verb (the action itself) (e.g. *Hurry up! They're closing the mall at 6 tonight!*) Use *there* when referring to a place, whether concrete (e.g. *over there by the building*) or more abstract (e.g. *it must be difficult to live there*).

12 Use *there* when referring to a place, whether concrete (e.g. *over there by the building*) or more abstract (e.g. *it must be difficult to live there*). Remember that *they're* is a contraction of the words *they* and *are*. It can never be used as a modifier, only as a subject (who or what does the action) and verb (the action itself) (e.g. *Hurry up! They're closing the mall at 6 tonight!*) Use *their* to indicate possession. It is a possessive adjective and indicates that a particular noun belongs to some people (e.g. *My friends have lost their tickets*).

13 Sometimes it is difficult to remember whether a word is spelt with ***ie*** or ***ei***. There is a very simple rule to help you: 'I before E except after C'.

14 Sometimes it is difficult to remember whether a word is spelt with ***ie*** or ***ei***. There is a very simple rule to help you: 'I before E except after C'.

15 The long ***a*** sound is most often written in an ***a–e*** combination (e.g. *state*). Usually there is only one letter between the ***a*** and the ***e***. However, sometimes there is more than one (e.g. *table*). It's the concluding ***e*** which makes the ***a*** have a long sound.

16 When you hear a long ***e*** sound, particularly in the middle of a word, it's often spelt ***ea*** or ***ee*** (e.g. *cheap, greet*). There are no rules to decide which one to choose so write both words down to help you decide which one 'looks' right.

17 Sometimes it is difficult to remember whether a word is spelt with ***ie*** or ***ei***. There is a very simple rule to help you: 'I before E except after C'.

18 As is usual with long vowel sounds, most long ***i*** sounds are written using an ***e*** at the end of the word. Take care as ***igh*** and ***y*** also make the long ***i*** sound.

19 When you hear a long ***e*** sound, particularly in the middle of a word, it's often spelt ***ea*** or ***ee*** (e.g. *cheap, greet*). There are no rules to decide which one to choose so write both spellings down to help you decide which one 'looks' right.

20 Although sounding like ***per***, the ***pur*** letter combination in *purpose* is common (e.g. *purchase, pursue* and *purple*). The ***pur*** letter combination can also make a long ***u*** sound (e.g. *pure*).

21 This is a common spelling error. *Lose* is a verb that is used to describe something mislaid. *Loose*, on the other hand, is an adjective that means 'not fastened or not contained', as seen in *the window catch is loose and so the window may fall down.*

22 When you hear a long ***e*** sound, particularly in the middle of a word, it's often spelt ***ea*** or ***ee*** (e.g. *cheap, greet*). There are no rules to decide which one to choose so write both spellings down to help you decide which one 'looks' right.

23 When you hear a long ***e*** sound, particularly in the middle of a word, it's often spelt ***ea*** or ***ee*** (e.g. *cheap, greet*). There are no rules to decide which one to choose so write both spellings down to help you decide which one 'looks' right.

24 *Loose* is an adjective used to describe when something is not tight (e.g. *This knot is too loose*). *Lose* is a verb used to describe when you have lost something (e.g. *Please do not lose my book*). One way to remember the difference between the two words is to think that *lose* has lost an ***o***.

25 This is a common spelling error. Sounding out the word's syllables *qui* + *et* will assist you in not mixing up the ***ie*** letter combination and spelling *quite* instead.

Intermediate level questions

SPELLING Mini Test 3

Page 5

1 stationary **2** currants **3** mourning **4** forth **5** aide **6** air **7** arc **8** banned **9** bear **10** beech **11** bough **12** brake **13** sense **14** two **15** our **16** their **17** time **18** through **19** naval **20** Pole **21** idle **22** blew **23** scene **24** humorous **25** vain

Note: a homophone is one of two or more words that have the same sound and often the same spelling but which differ in meaning, such as *bank* (embankment) and *bank* (place where money is kept). All the spelling words in this test are homophones.

1 *Stationary* is an adjective used to describe something that isn't moving. *Stationery* is a noun that relates to office and school supplies.

2 *Currants* are dried fruit, similar to sultanas, while a *current* is strong moving water.

3 *Mourning* means 'grieving the loss of someone or something', while *morning* is the earlier time of day.

4 *Forth*, when used in the expression *Stand forth*, means 'onward and forward in time'. *Fourth* shows the position of something coming after third.

5 *Aide* is a noun used to describe someone who helps someone else. *Aid* is a verb that means 'assist'.

6 *Air* is the mixture of gases which surround the earth and form its atmosphere. We commonly think of the air as the sky, the breeze, or wind. *Heir* is someone who is in line to succeed to a rank or to inherit.

7 An *arc* is something shaped like a curve or arch, while an *ark* is a large sea vessel.

8 To be *banned* means 'to be restricted or excluded from doing something', while a *band* describes a group of musicians or is a thin flat strip of some material, used especially to encircle and hold objects together (e.g. *a rubber band*).

9 *Bear*, in this context and as a verb, means 'sustain or tolerate something'. The verb *bare* means 'uncovered or exposed to view'. *Bear*, when used as a noun, is a shaggy coated animal.

10 *Beech* is a type of tree whose wood is used for flooring and furniture. *Beach* is a sandy place usually adjacent to water such as the ocean.

11 A *bough* is the long arm of a tree. Similarly sounding, but spelt *bow*, is the noun that means the front section of a ship or boat. The verb *bow* means 'bend politely from the waist, like a curtsy'.

12 A *brake* (noun) is a mechanism that stops or slows something that is moving, while *break* is a verb meaning 'destroy'.

13 *Sense* means 'the ability to make logical decisions', while *cents* relates to coins and money.

14 *Two* is the number after one, while *too* is an adverb meaning 'in addition, further, also'.

15 *Our* is a plural possessive pronoun to show ownership (e.g. *our car*), while *hour* relates to time of day.

16 *Their* shows belonging to 'them' (e.g. *This is their car*). *There* is an adverb used when referring to a place, whether concrete (e.g. *over there by the building*) or more abstract (e.g. *it must be difficult* to live there).

17 *Time* indicates a period or duration of something, while *thyme* is a herb that can be used in cooking.

18 *Through* is a preposition that means 'going in or starting at one side and coming out or stopping at the other side' (e.g. *a path through the wood*). *Threw* is the past tense of the word *throw*.

19 *Naval* is an adjective that describes something that belongs to the navy. *Navel* is a more formal noun for belly button.

20 A *pole* in this context relates to one of the two extremities of the earth's axis, while a *poll* is the casting and registering of votes in an election.

21 *Idle* is an adjective that describes someone who is not employed or busy, while *idol* is a noun that can describe something adored or worshipped.

22 *Blew* is the past tense of *blow*, meaning 'move along or be carried as if by the wind'. *Blue* is a noun used to describe the colour blue.

23 *Scene* is a noun used to describe the place where an action or event occurs, while *seen* is the past participle of *see*, meaning 'detect with the eye'.

24 *Humorous* is an adjective used to describe something witty or funny, while *humerus* is a noun that describes a long bone of the arm.

25 *Vain* means 'conceited or overly proud of your appearance', while *vein* is a noun used to describe the tubes that form a branching system which carry blood to the heart.

Intermediate level questions

SPELLING Mini Test 4

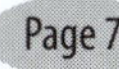

1 peaceful **2** wonderful **3** abandoning **4** achieving **5** accessing **6** exaggerating **7** revelled **8** anticipated **9** increased **10** levelled **11** crawled **12** renowned **13** travelling **14** common **15** heating **16** burning **17** famous **18** spiteful **19** vain **20** beautiful **21** preferring **22** friend **23** nothing **24** grey **25** similar

1 A letter or a syllable added to a word to form a new word is called a suffix (e.g. *hope* + ***ful*** = *hopeful*). There is no need to drop the final ***e*** before adding the suffix ***ful***.

2 A letter or a syllable added to a word to form a new word is called a suffix (e.g. *hope* + ***ful*** = *hopeful*). In this case, the suffix is simply ***ful*** and never *full*, which means 'containing as much or as many as possible'.

3 Adding ***ing*** to a verb gives you the present participle of the verb. In this case, the suffix ***ing*** is added to the verb *abandon*.

4 Adding ***ing*** to a verb gives you the present participle of the verb. In this case, the suffix ***ing*** is added to the verb *achieve*. The final ***e*** in *achieve* is dropped when adding the suffix ***ing***.

5 Adding ***ing*** to a verb gives you the present participle of the verb. In this case, the suffix ***ing*** is added to the verb *access*.

6 Adding ***ing*** to a verb gives you the present participle of the verb. In this case, the suffix ***ing*** is added to the verb *exaggerate*. The final ***e*** in *exaggerate* is dropped when adding the suffix ***ing***.

7 Regardless of the stress, words ending in a single ***l***, preceded by a single vowel, always have the ***l*** doubled before a suffix is added.

8 The word *anticipated* is created by adding the suffix ***ed*** to the base verb *anticipate* in order to form the past tense of the verb. First the ***e*** at the end of *anticipate* needs to be dropped. This word is similar to *participate* in that the ***c*** makes an ***s*** sound.

9 The word *increased* is created by adding the suffix ***ed*** to the base verb *increase* in order to form the past tense of the verb. Other words like *increase* whose ***ea*** letter combination makes an ***ee*** sound include *release* and *grease*.

10 Regardless of the stress, words ending in a single ***l***, preceded by a single vowel, always have the ***l*** doubled before a suffix is added.

Year 7 Literacy Mini Test Answers

11 The ***l*** is not doubled in *crawl* before the suffix ***ed*** is added as there is a ***w*** before the final ***l*** and not a vowel.

12 An ***ed*** is added to the noun *renown* to form an adjective.

13 Regardless of the stress, words ending in a single ***l***, preceded by a single vowel, always have the ***l*** doubled before a suffix is added.

14 *Common* in this example is not being used in a comparative sense so does not need the ***er*** suffix.

15 Adding ***ing*** to a verb gives you the present participle of the verb. In this case, the suffix ***ing*** is added to the verb *heat*.

16 Adding ***ing*** to a verb gives you the present participle of the verb. In this case, the suffix ***ing*** is added to the verb *burn*.

17 The suffix ***ous*** means 'full of' or 'possessing'. In this case, *famous* means 'possessing fame'. Other words with the same suffix include *contemptuous* and *preposterous*.

18 A letter or a syllable added to a word to form a new word is called a suffix (e.g. *spite* + ***ful*** = *spiteful*). There is no need to drop the final ***e*** before adding the suffix ***ful***.

19 The ***ai*** vowel combination is common. Other words spelt using this vowel combination include *gain* and *pain*.

20 When a suffix is added to a word ending in ***y***, the ***y*** usually changes to ***i*** (e.g. *beauty* + ***ful*** = *beautiful*).

21 This word is created by adding the suffix ***ing*** to the base verb *prefer*. Double a final single consonant before a suffix beginning with a vowel when a single vowel precedes the consonant: *prefer* + ***ing*** = *preferring*.

22 Sometimes it is difficult to remember whether a word is spelt ***ie*** or ***ei***. The simple rule 'I before E except after C' will help you to remember.

23 In this sentence *nothing* operates as a noun, meaning 'something that has no existence'. It has two syllables: *noth* + *ing*.

24 *Grey* is more commonly used in the UK, Australia, and other places that use British English. 'Gray' is the more popular spelling in America and countries which use American spelling.

25 'Similarer' is not a word.

Intermediate level questions

SPELLING Mini Test 5

Page 9

1 happiness **2** forgetfulness **3** valuable **4** adaptable **5** visible **6** illegible **7** flammable **8** avoidable **9** profitable **10** feasible **11** responsible **12** sensible **13** noisiness **14** religions **15** sadness **16** assess **17** faster **18** sleepiest **19** softer **20** lazier **21** sadder **22** tidiness **23** incomparable **24** goodness **25** shortest

1 When a word ends in ***y***, the ***y*** usually changes to ***i*** before the suffix is added (e.g. *baby, babies, copy, copies*).

2 This is best remembered as the joining of the word *forget* to the suffixes ***ful*** and then ***ness***.

3 As a general rule, most base words are not altered in any way when ***able*** is added (e.g. *suitable, peaceable, changeable*). *Valuable* is an exception to this rule as the final ***e*** is dropped. You will just need to remember this.

4 As a general rule, if you remove the suffix ***able*** from a word you should be left with a complete word, as seen here with *adapt*. If you remove ***ible*** from a word, you are not left with a complete word; however, *accessible, contemptible, digestible, flexible* and *suggestible* are exceptions to this rule.

5 The ***ible*** ending is used in words of Latin origin. As a general rule, if you remove ***ible*** from a word, you are not left with a complete word, unlike words that end in ***able*** (note that *accessible, contemptible, digestible, flexible* and *suggestible* are among the exceptions to this rule).

6 The ***ible*** ending is used in words of Latin origin. As a general rule, if you remove ***ible*** from a word, you are not left with a complete word, unlike words that end in ***able*** (note that *accessible, contemptible, digestible, flexible* and *suggestible* are among the exceptions to this rule). Note the prefix ***il*** has been added to the base word *legible* so the word is spelt with a double ***l***.

7 This word is an exception to the rule for ***ible/ able*** words, which is that if you remove the suffix ***able*** from a word you should be left with a complete word. That is not the case here, as 'flamm' is not a word. The base word is *flame*.

8 As a general rule, if you remove the suffix ***able*** from a word you should be left with a complete word, as seen here with *avoid*. If you remove ***ible*** from a word, you are not left with a complete word; however, *accessible, contemptible, digestible, flexible* and *suggestible* are exceptions to this rule.

9 As a general rule, if you remove the suffix ***able*** from a word you should be left with a complete word, as seen here with *profit*. If you remove ***ible*** from a word, you are not left with a complete word; however, *accessible, contemptible, digestible, flexible* and *suggestible* are exceptions to this rule.

10 The ***ible*** ending is used in words of Latin origin. As a general rule, if you remove ***ible*** from a word, you are not left with a complete word, unlike words that end in ***able*** (note that *accessible, contemptible, digestible, flexible* and *suggestible* are among the exceptions to this rule). Although *feasible* is pronounced with a ***z*** sound, it is spelt with an ***s***.

11 The ***ible*** ending is used in words of Latin origin. As a general rule, if you remove ***ible*** from a word, you are not left with a complete word, unlike words that end in ***able*** (note that *accessible, contemptible, digestible, flexible* and *suggestible* are among the exceptions to this rule).

12 The ***ible*** ending is used in words of Latin origin. As a general rule, if you remove ***ible*** from a word, you are not left with a complete word, unlike words that end in ***able*** (note that *accessible, contemptible, digestible, flexible* and *suggestible* are among the exceptions to this rule).

13 ***Ness*** is one of a number of noun suffixes. It is used to make nouns from adjectives, although not every adjective can be modified in this way. The ***y*** usually changes to ***i*** before the suffix is added (e.g. *ready, readiness, happy, happiness*).

14 If a word ends in ***x*** or ***s***, ***sh*** or ***ch***, then add ***es*** to form a plural noun (e.g. *church, churches, fax, faxes, gloss, glosses*). Otherwise, you usually just add ***s*** (e.g. *religion, religions*).

15 ***Ness*** is one of a number of noun suffixes. It is used to make nouns from adjectives, although not every adjective can be modified in this way. Simply add the suffix ***ness*** to the base form of the word *sad*.

16 You need to remember the double ***s*** letter combination at the beginning and end of this verb. Other words belonging to this family include *assessable, assessed, assessing* and *assessment*.

17 The comparative form of short adjectives is created by adding ***er*** and the superlative form is made by adding ***est***. This sentence's example is comparative, as seen by the use of *than*.

18 The comparative or superlative forms of short adjectives are created by adding ***er*** or ***est***. If the adjective ends in ***y***, the ***y*** should be dropped and changed to an ***i*** (e.g. *happy, happiest*).

19 The comparative form of short adjectives is created by adding ***er*** and the superlative form is made by adding ***est***. This sentence's example is comparative, as seen by the use of *than*.

20 The comparative form of short adjectives is created by adding ***er*** and the superlative form is made by adding ***est***. If the adjective ends in ***y***, the ***y*** should be dropped and changed to an ***i*** (e.g. *happy, happier*).

21 The comparative form of short adjectives is created by adding ***er*** and the superlative form is made by adding ***est***. This sentence's example is comparative, as seen by the use of *than*. If the adjective ends in a consonant + vowel + consonant then the last letter should be doubled (e.g. *mad, madder*).

22 ***Ness*** is one of a number of noun suffixes. It is used to make nouns from adjectives, although not every adjective can be modified in this way. If the adjective ends in ***y***, the ***y*** should be dropped and changed to an ***i*** (e.g. *ready, readiness, happy, happiness*).

23 The base word is *compare*, to which the prefix ***in*** and the suffix ***able*** have been added. When a word ends with ***e***, drop the ***e*** before adding a suffix if the suffix begins with a vowel. There are some exceptions to this rule.

24 ***Ness*** is one of a number of noun suffixes. It is used to make nouns from adjectives, although not every adjective can be modified in this way. The final consonant is only doubled when a suffix is added if there is one vowel before the single final consonant. In this case *good* has two vowels so ***d*** is not doubled.

25 The comparative form of short adjectives is created by adding ***er*** and the superlative form is made by adding ***est***.

Intermediate level questions

SPELLING Mini Test 6

Page 11

1 authors **2** stomach **3** behaviour **4** echoed **5** fibre **6** lunar **7** heir **8** pursuing **9** pursuit **10** technique **11** ravine **12** rogue **13** yacht **14** schnitzel **15** slaughter **16** wearisome **17** parallel **18** nutrition **19** hygiene **20** hoarse **21** gnawed **22** drought **23** thorough **24** height **25** shrieked

1 The word *author* is a noun that describes the writer of a book, article or other text. Similar words include *authoring* or *authored* and may help you to remember the spelling.

2 Although 'stumick' sounds as if it is spelt this way it is actually spelt *stomach*. This is a spelling you simply need to learn and remember.

Year 7 Literacy Mini Test Answers

3 The spelling of *behavior* is accepted in the USA. However, in Australia we follow the English spelling which uses an ***our*** ending: *behaviour*. Other examples of this variation include *colour/color, flavour/flavor* and *labour/labor*.

4 This word is created by adding the suffix ***ed*** to the base word *echo* in order to form the past tense of the word.

5 The spelling of *fiber* is accepted in the USA. However, in Australia we follow the English spelling which uses an ***re*** ending: *fibre*. Other examples of this variation include *centre/center* and *kilometre/kilometer*.

6 The adjective *lunar* means 'caused by or affecting the moon'. Other words that share a similar spelling and meaning are *lunacy* and *lunatic*, interestingly originally describing the effect of the moon on people.

7 Spelt with a silent ***h*** this word (*heir*) is pronounced *air*. It has the same ending and pronunciation as *their*.

8 Adding ***ing*** to a verb gives you the present participle of the verb. In this case, the suffix ***ing*** is added to the verb *pursue*, after dropping the final ***e*** in *pursue*.

9 You need to remember that although the word makes a *per* sound, the word is actually spelt *pur*.

10 The ***ch*** letter combination makes a ***k*** sound in this word.

11 This is an example of a word that ends in ***ine*** but makes a long ***ee*** sound. Other examples include *tangerine* and *gasoline*.

12 This is similar in sound and spelling to *vogue*.

13 A *yacht* is a light and fast-sailing ship, pronounced 'yot'. It is the only word in English that ends with an ***acht*** letter combination.

14 *Schnitzel* is specially prepared and crumbed meat. It is a unique word which must be learnt and remembered. Pronouncing the word correctly can help you to spell it: *sch + nit + zel*.

15 This is similar in spelling and sound to *daughter*. However, it is only similar in spelling to *laughter*.

16 When adding suffixes to words ending in ***y***, you should change the ***y*** to ***i*** before adding the suffix (e.g. *weary + some = wearisome*, *happy + ness = happiness*).

17 Remember to double the first ***l*** and not the ***r*** when you spell this word. ***Para*** is a common word beginning that is never spelt with a double ***r***. Other words with a similar spelling are *paralyse* and *parachute*.

18 Breaking this word into syllables can help you to spell it: *nu + tri + tion*. *Absorption* and *emotion* are examples of other words that end in ***tion***.

19 The ***iene*** letter combination is uncommon and must be remembered. The ***hy*** letter combination is most often pronounced ***hi***, but can also be a short ***i*** sound, as in *hypocrite* and *hypnotise*.

20 *Hoarse* and *horse* are homonyms, meaning they sound the same, but are spelt differently and have different meanings. *Hoarse* is similar in sound and spelling to *coarse*.

21 The ***g*** at the start of the word is silent as in *gnarled*, *gnash* and *gnome*. Sometimes the ***g*** in the middle of a word is silent (e.g. *design, reign* and *consign*).

22 Words that end in ***ought*** can be confusing as they can be pronounced differently. While the ***ought*** in *drought* is pronounced ***out***, most other words ending this way are pronounced ***ort***, including *thought, bought, sought* and *wrought*.

23 Words that end in ***ough*** can be confusing as they can be pronounced differently. ***Ough*** can be pronounced with a short ***u*** sound as in *thorough*, *tough* or with the long ***o*** sound, as in *although* and *dough*. It can also be pronounced ***off***, as in *cough*.

24 Most words that end in ***eight*** are pronounced ***ate***, as in *weight, eight* and *freight*. *Height* is an exception as it is pronounced ***ite***.

25 Sometimes it is difficult to remember whether a word is spelt ***ie*** or ***ei***. There is a very simple rule to help you: 'I before E except after C'.

Advanced level questions

SPELLING Mini Test 7

Page 13

1 vehicle **2** acquainted **3** sufficient **4** buoy **5** conscience **6** debris **7** cylinders **8** environment **9** explanatory **10** gauge **11** guaranteed **12** guillotine **13** psychic **14** descend **15** tempestuous **16** possessive **17** additional **18** decorating **19** incorporate **20** earliest **21** fundamental **22** commentary **23** diaries **24** typical **25** acknowledge

1 The ***h*** in *vehicle* is silent, which is common in English. Other words that contain a silent letter ***h*** are *mechanic, school* and *spaghetti*.

2 The ***acqu*** letter combination is fairly common, although pronounced ***ackw***. Other examples includes *acquit, acquire* and *acquisition*. A silent ***c*** may also occur before ***k*** (e.g. *acknowledge*).

3 The ***cient*** letter combination is fairly common, although pronounced ***shent***. Other examples include *proficient, ancient* and *deficient*.

4 *Boy* and *buoy* are homonyms, meaning they sound the same, but are spelt differently and have different meanings. A *buoy* is a float moored in water to mark a location or warn of danger.

5 This word can best be remembered as *con + science*. Other words that end in ***ience*** include *obedience* and *experience*.

6 The ***s*** in *debris* is silent, which is common in French where this word originates. Other words that contain a silent letter ***s*** are *aisle* and *island*.

7 The ***cy*** letter combination makes a short ***i*** sound in this word. Other examples include *cynical* and *cyst*. Other ***cy*** words include *cyclone* and *cycle*. However, these make a long ***i*** sound.

8 This word can best be remembered as *environ + ment*. Other words that contain a silent ***n*** include *autumn* and *solemn*.

9 This word can be confusing as it loses an ***i*** when being changed from the verb *explain* to the adjective *explanatory*. It can help to remember the same rule when forming the noun *explanation* from the verb *explain*.

10 Although pronounced as ***gage***, this word has a silent ***u*** and is spelt *gauge*.

11 The letter ***g*** is also sometimes followed by a silent ***u***, as in *guarantee, guard, beleaguered*.

12 The letter ***g*** is also sometimes followed by a silent ***u***, as in *guarantee, guard, beleaguered*.

13 Many words have silent letters, but the strangest of those is the silent ***p*** in words like *psycho, psalms, pneumonia, pseudonym* and *pterodactyl*.

14 Many words are spelt with a silent ***c*** following an ***s*** (e.g. *abscess, descend, omniscient, acquiesce, effervescent, convalescent*).

15 This can more easily be remembered as the noun and suffix: *tempest + uous*. Other words ending in the ***uous*** letter combination include *voluptuous, ambiguous* and *tortuous*.

16 This adjective is created by adding the suffix ***ive*** to the verb *possess*.

17 To spell this word, add the suffix ***al*** to the noun *addition* to form the adjective *additional*. Other words with the same suffix include *constitutional, hypothetical* and *ironical*.

18 When a word ends in a silent ***e***, drop the ***e*** before adding the suffix when the suffix begins with a vowel (e.g. *hope, hoping, crease, creasing*).

19 This is best remembered by adding the prefix ***in*** to the noun *corporate*. Words with the same prefix include *inability, inanimate* and *inflexible*.

20 When a word ends in ***y***, it usually changes to ***i*** before a suffix is added (e.g. *early + est = earliest*).

21 Breaking this word into its syllables can help you to spell it correctly: *fun + da + ment + al*. Other words from the same family include *fundamentalist* and *fundamentally*.

22 To form this word add the suffix ***ary*** to the noun *comment*. The ***ary*** ending begins with a vowel that is indistinct. The ***a*** is difficult to tell from an ***e*** when it is followed by the letter ***r***. The ending ***ary*** can sound almost like ***ery*** in *very*. Remember that the ending ***ary*** is more common than ***ery***.

23 *Diary* is often confused with *dairy*. Pronouncing the word correctly will help you spell *diaries* properly.

24 The ***ty*** letter combination makes a short ***i*** sound in this word. Other words with this letter combination include *tyrannical* and *typify*.

25 A silent ***c*** can occur before ***k*** or ***q*** (e.g. *acknowledge* and *acquire*). The prefix ***ac***, meaning 'towards', is here added to the noun *knowledge* to form the verb *acknowledge*.

Advanced level questions

SPELLING Mini Test 8

Page 15

1 absorption **2** bacteria **3** carbohydrate **4** ecosystem **5** element **6** genes **7** hormones **8** microscopic **9** nucleus **10** virus **11** evolution **12** haemoglobin **13** hypothesis **14** energy **15** chemical **16** bloodstream **17** condition **18** unique **19** mammals **20** habitat **21** extinct **22** calories **23** Health **24** unit **25** cells

1 This word is formed by adding the suffix ***tion*** to the base word *absorb*, although note the ***b*** changes to a ***p***.

2 Breaking this word into its syllables can help you to spell it correctly: *bac + ter + i + a*. There are few words in English that begin with ***bac*** as this sound is more often made by ***bach*** or ***back*** letter combinations.

3 This word is formed from two words *carbo + hydrate* (meaning water) and is a scientific term.

4 *Ecosystem* is a compound word that joins *eco* (ecology) + *system*.

5 Breaking this word into its syllables can help you to spell it correctly: *el + e + ment*. Other words that begin with the ***ele*** letter combination include *electric* and *elephant*. ***Ele*** words should not be confused with the similarly sounding ***ela*** words including *elaborate* and *elastic*.

6 This scientific noun should not be confused with the noun *jeans*, which is an article of clothing.

7 The ***one*** ending in *hormones* should not be confused with words that end in ***oan*** but sound the same (e.g. *loan*).

8 *Microscopic* is the adjective of the noun *microscope*.

9 Breaking *nucleus* into its syllables can help you to spell it correctly: *nu* + *cle* + *us*. This is a noun that describes a central or essential part or core.

10 *Virus* is a unique word that must be remembered. Most words beginning with ***vir*** are pronounced ***ver*** (e.g. *virtuous* and *virtual*). *Virus*, however, is pronounced ***vy***.

11 Breaking *evolution* into its syllables can help you to spell it correctly: *e* + *vo* + *lu* + *tion*. The suffix ***tion*** is added to a noun in order to show an action or process, as seen also by *education* and *frustration*. These words all have base verbs such as *educate, evolve* and *frustrate*.

12 *Haemoglobin* is a compound word with the ***ae*** letter combination which is seen in other words such as *archaeology* and *encyclopaedia*.

13 Other words which begin with ***hypo*** include *hypothermia, hypoallergenic* and *hypodermic*.

14 Breaking *energy* into its syllables can help you to spell it correctly: *en* + *er* + *gy*. Other forms of this word include the verb *energise* and the adjective *energetic*.

15 *Chemical* is the adjective of the noun *chemistry*. In *chemistry* the ***ch*** letter combination sounds like ***k***, not ***ch*** as in *chart*.

16 *Bloodstream* is a simple compound word that joins the two nouns *blood* + *stream*.

17 The suffix ***tion***, as seen in *alteration* and *demonstration*, should not be confused with words that end in ***sion***, such as *expansion* and *inclusion*.

18 Other words in English that are of French origin and end in ***ique*** include *antique, boutique* and *technique*.

19 *Mammals* are any of various warm-blooded vertebrate animals of the class *Mammalia*, including humans, characterised by the female milk-producing mammary glands for nourishing the young. Thinking of the word *mamma* will help you remember the double ***m***.

20 Other words that end in ***tat*** include *thermostat* and *photostat*.

21 Other words that end in ***tinct*** include *distinct, extinct* and *instinct*.

22 The ***ies*** ending is usually added when forming plurals (e.g. *babies*). In this case, the base noun is *calorie* and only ***s*** is added to form the plural.

23 Other words that end in ***ealth*** include *wealth* and *stealth*.

24 The noun *unit* describes a group regarded as a distinct entity within a larger group. This is similar in meaning to the verb *unite* and the noun *unity*.

25 The word *cells* is a homonym with the word *sells*. A *cell* is a noun in biology used for the smallest unit of an organism that is capable of independent functioning. The verb *sells* means 'exchange or deliver for money or an equivalent'.

Advanced level questions

SPELLING Mini Test 9

1 business **2** columns **3** lacerated **4** circuit **5** crevice **6** definitely **7** efficient **8** fascinating **9** fuchsia **10** grandeur **11** leisure **12** irrelevant **13** humanitarian **14** mesmerised **15** oxygen **16** purist **17** scissors **18** temporary **19** thoroughly **20** upholsterer **21** vulnerable **22** sewerage **23** smoulder **24** subsided **25** scavenger

1 *You take the bus to your business* is a trick that may help you remember the tricky beginning to this word. Similar words include *busied, busily* and *busier*.

2 When the ***mn*** combination occurs at the end of a word, the ***n*** is usually silent. Other words that contain a silent ***n*** include *autumn* and *solemn*.

3 Sometimes the ***c*** letter in words makes an ***s*** sound, as in *lace* and *lacerated*. At other times the ***c*** letter will create a ***k*** sound, as in *lacklustre* and *laconic*.

4 Other examples of words with the ***ui*** vowel combination include *bruise, pursuit, recruit* and *juice*.

5 Other words that end in ***ice*** but which are pronounced ***iss*** include *justice, accomplice* and *armistice*.

6 This word is often misspelt, but can be more easily remembered by adding the suffix ***ly*** to the adjective *definite*.

7 The ***cient*** letter combination is fairly common, although it is pronounced ***shent***. Other examples include *proficient, ancient* and *deficient*.

Year 7 Literacy Mini Test Answers

8 The ***sc*** letter combination in English is common. However, different sounds can be created. A ***sh*** sound is created in *fascism* but a distinct ***s*** then ***c*** sound in *conscript*. Most ***sc*** letter combinations make an ***ss*** sound as in *fascinating* (e.g. *convalesce* and *descend*).

9 This is a difficult word that simply must be remembered. This plant is named after a German botanist named Fuchs.

10 Words ending in ***eur*** come from the French. Other examples include *chauffeur, voyeur* and *liqueur*.

11 Words ending in ***ure*** come from the French. Other examples include *acupuncture, adventure* and *brochure*.

12 This word can best be remembered by adding the prefix ***ir***, meaning 'not' or 'opposite to', to the noun *relevant*.

13 The suffix ***arian*** is common and has a particular meaning. It relates to a person who is a part of something or describes a person's state or condition. Other examples include *barbarian, librarian* and *vegetarian*.

14 From the French *mesmérisme*, relating to magnetism. You must remember the ***mer*** in the second syllable.

15 ***Oxy*** is a prefix that describes scientific words that have a compound containing oxygen, including *oxyacids* and *oxygenic*.

16 The suffix ***ist*** is used in a noun to describe a person (e.g. *dentist*). In this case, when the suffix ***ist*** is added to the noun *pure*, the ***e*** is dropped.

17 This is a difficult word from the French *cisoires* and must be learnt and remembered.

18 Although this word sounds like it has an ***a*** in the middle it is spelt with an ***o***. Splitting *temporary* into syllables will help you spell it: *tem + po + ra + ry*.

19 Words that end in ***ough*** can be confusing as they can be pronounced differently. ***Ough*** can be pronounced with a short ***u*** sound as in *thorough*, *tough* or with the long ***o*** sound, as in *although* and *dough*. It can also be pronounced ***off***, as in *cough*.

20 An *upholsterer* is a person who upholsters furniture as a profession. This word, when sounded out correctly, should be more easily spelt.

21 As a general rule, if you remove ***able*** from a word, you are left with a complete word. *Vulnerable* is an exception to this rule that you will just need to remember.

22 To form the word *sewerage*, add the suffix ***age*** to the base word *sewer*. The suffix ***age*** is also present in *breakage, wastage* and *package*.

23 The word *smoulder* means 'burn with little smoke and no flame'. The American spelling of this word is slightly different: *smolder*.

24 The suffix ***ed*** is added to the base word *subside* to form the past tense of the word. First drop the ***e*** from *subside*.

25 The suffix ***er*** is often added to nouns to describe a person who undertakes that action (e.g. *advertiser* and *driver*). *Scavenger* is *scavenge + er*. First drop the ***e*** from *scavenge*.

Advanced level questions

SPELLING Mini Test 10

Page 19

1 archaeology **2** awkwardly **3** belligerent **4** unconscious **5** benefited **6** effervescent **7** euphoric **8** fluorescent **9** gouged **10** hallucinations **11** incandescent **12** kaleidoscope **13** lieutenant **14** litigious **15** manoeuvre **16** oscillated **17** plateau **18** psychiatrist **19** resuscitate **20** therapeutic **21** vicious **22** reminiscent **23** sovereign **24** facilities **25** medieval/mediaeval

1 The suffix ***logy*** relates to study, science or theory and is seen also in *biology, geology* and *neurology*. The ***ae*** letter combination is seen in other words such as *haemoglobin* and *encyclopaedia*.

2 The word *awkwardly* is formed by adding the suffix ***ly*** to the base noun *awkward*. Breaking this adverb into its syllables can help you to spell it correctly: *awk + ward + ly*.

3 Related words are *belligerence* or *belligerency*. Other words that end in ***erent*** include *coherent*, and *different*.

4 The word *unconscious* is formed by adding the prefix ***un*** meaning 'not' to the base word *conscious*. Other words that end in the ***scious*** combination include *luscious, precious* and *spacious*.

5 This word is formed by adding the suffix ***ed*** to the base noun *benefit*. It is an exception to the usual rule and there is no need to double the ***t*** as you would if changing, for example, the verb *fit* into the past tense *fitted*.

6 The word *effervescent* is from Latin meaning 'the action of boiling up'. There are many other words that end in ***scent***, including *fluorescent, descent* and *convalescent*.

7 The ***ph*** letter combination in *euphoric* makes an ***f*** sound. Other words which contain this combination include *telephone* and *photo*.

Year 7 Literacy Mini Test Answers

8 The word *fluorescent* can best be remembered by combining ***fluore*** with the suffix ***scent***. There are many other words that end in ***scent***, including *effervescent, descent* and *convalescent*.

9 *Gouged* is the past tense of the verb *gouge* meaning 'scoop or force something'. It is pronounced 'gowged' and is irregular from other ***ouge*** words, such as *rouge* which is pronounced 'rooge'.

10 The word *hallucinations* is formed by adding the suffix ***ations*** to the base word *hallucinate*. You drop the ***e*** at the end of the base word when adding the suffix.

11 The word *incandescent* can best be remembered by combining *incande* with the suffix ***scent***. There are many other words that end in ***scent***, including *effervescent, descent* and *convalescent*.

12 Breaking the noun *kaleidoscope* into its syllables can help you to spell it correctly: *kal + ei + do + scope*. It is a unique word that follows no particular rules.

13 *Lieutenant* is a French compound word joining *lieu*, meaning 'place', to *tenant*. We use the word *lieu* in English, in the expression 'in lieu of', meaning 'instead of or in place of'.

14 The suffix ***ous*** means to be 'full of' something, in this case lawsuits. This is also seen in *nervous, pompous* and *gracious*.

15 The difficult ***oe*** letter combination is also seen in *amoeba* and *diarrhoea*.

16 Related words include *oscillated* and *oscillating*.

17 *Plateau* is from the French, meaning 'an elevated, comparatively level expanse of land or tableland'. Other English words that end in ***eau*** and come from French include *tableau* and *bureau*.

18 There are many other words in English beginning with a silent ***p***, including *psalm* and *pseudo*.

19 The verb *resuscitate* is from the Latin *resuscit* meaning 'rouse again; revive'. The adjectival form is *resuscitative* and the noun *resuscitation*.

20 The suffix ***tic*** means 'pertaining to' and is seen also in *alphabetic* and *fanatic*.

21 The suffix ***ous*** means 'full of' or 'having'. In this case *vicious* is 'full of' wickedness. Other words with the suffix ***ous*** include *luxurious, mysterious* and *prestigious*.

22 This word can be best remembered by combining ***remini*** with the suffix ***scent***. There are many other words that end in ***scent***, including *effervescent, descent* and *convalescent*.

23 This is a French word that relates to authority. Other words in English that come from the French and end in ***eign*** include *feign* and *foreign*.

24 *Facilities* is the plural form of the noun *facility*. The ***y*** is changed to ***i*** when the suffix ***es*** is added.

25 This word can be spelt in two ways. The ***ae*** letter combination is seen in other words such as *haemoglobin* and *encyclopaedia*. This word means 'middle' and relates to the Middle Ages.

Standard level questions

GRAMMAR Mini Test 1

Page 21

1 C **2** B **3** pronoun, article, adjective, noun **4** cool, windy **5** hat, table, bed **6** B **7** C **8** B **9** D **10** D **11** cat **12** article, adjective, pronoun, noun **13** A **14** its **15** the students ran for cover **16** land-based, cool, enjoyable **17** frequently, never **18** B **19** B **20** B **21** B **22** C **23** might enjoy **24** C **25** A

1 *Cotton* is the most suitable adjective choice here to describe the noun *cushion*.

2 The modal auxiliary verb combination *would like to travel* is used to show the possibility of travelling to the Nile.

3 *She* is a pronoun, *an* is an article, *excellent* is an adjective and *teacher* is a noun.

4 Adjectives modify and describe nouns. In this case the noun being modified is *day*. Be careful as adjectives may not always be placed before their corresponding nouns.

5 *Hat, table* and *bed* are all concrete nouns. Concrete nouns refer to physical things.

6 The pronoun *who* is used here to link the first section of the sentence—*You had a phone call* (from someone)—to the sentence's second section—*but I can't remember who rang you.*

7 The definite article *the* is used as snow is never referred to generally. *From* is a preposition that indicates the starting or central point of an activity.

8 With *I* being the subject of this sentence, the only available object pronoun available is *her*.

9 We show continuous action with auxiliary verbs and the *ing* form of the verb: *had trouble walking*.

10 A preposition is a word that shows the relationship between a noun or pronoun and other words in a sentence. In this case *on* is the best preposition to show the position of the book. The definite article *the* is used when referring to a particular noun.

11 The pronoun *him* refers back to the noun *cat*.

12 *The* is an article, *tired* is an adjective, *their* is a pronoun and *teacher* is a noun.

13 The definite article *the* is used here when referring to a particular person: *the Australian Prime Minister.*

14 The pronoun *its* refers back to the noun *the swimming team.* The pronoun does not need an apostrophe.

15 The main clause is *the students ran for cover.* The other clauses are dependent, not independent.

16 Adjectives modify nouns. *Land-based* modifies *exercise* and *cool* and *enjoyable* modify *activity*.

17 Adverbs add meaning to verbs, adjectives and other adverbs. They often end in ***ly*** but not always. The adverbs *frequently* and *never* describe how often the action of swimming occurs.

18 The complete sentence is *That film was interesting.* It contains a subject, verb and object.

19 The present-tense verb *gives* is consistent with the verb *involves.*

20 The sentence requires the adjective *recreational* to be placed before the noun *activity.*

21 The adverb is *occasionally.* Adverbs often end in ***ly*** and add meaning to verbs, adjectives and other adverbs.

22 The modal auxiliary verb *might increase* indicates the possibility of the event.

23 The two verbs are: *might* and *enjoy*.

24 The past-tense verb *refreshed* is required to indicate that the action (*swimming*) has occurred in the past. The adverb *really* modifies *refreshed*.

25 Most nouns require an article in front of them. The articles are *a*, *an* and *the*. In this case, the noun *activity* is modified by the adjectives *low-impact* and *weightless.*

Intermediate level questions

GRAMMAR Mini Test 2

Page 25

1 A **2** B **3** pronoun, verb, noun, adjective **4** B **5** into, from, across **6** C **7** C **8** D **9** A **10** D **11** C **12** verb, adjective, preposition, noun **13** C **14** A **15** It is also possible to jump from a movable object **16** A, C **17** C **18** B **19** A **20** often **21** there **22** C **23** prowled, flapping **24** B **25** C

1 Prepositions of time rule that the word *on* is used for the days of the week, but *in* should be used for months, seasons, years and times of day.

2 The preposition *at* is used for night time, weekends and specific points in time.

3 *I* is a pronoun, *found* is a verb, *London* is a noun and *vibrant* is an adjective.

4 The preposition *by* is used to indicate where the crowd stood in relation to the road.

5 The prepositions *into*, *from* and *across* show relationships between people, places and things.

6 In sentences, subjects must agree with verbs. The subject *actions* is plural (meaning more than one) and so the verb that follows must agree with it, as *were* does.

7 *I'd have* is a contraction of *I would have.* The third conditional tense is used to show a hypothetical situation that might have occurred in the pas

8 In sentences, subjects must agree with verbs. The subject *book* is singular (meaning one) and so the verb that follows must agree with it, as *was* does.

9 *I'd* is a contraction of *I would.* The word *like* needs a helper verb and *would* is the correct helper verb to use in this sentence.

10 In this sentence, *will* indicates intention—something that is going to happen. As the action to take place is in the future, *will depart* is the correct future tense verb to use.

11 *Their is* a plural pronoun that refers back to *the brother and sister.*

12 *Were* is a verb, *red* is an adjective, *for* is a preposition and *family* is a noun.

13 The present perfect tense is used to indicate a link between the present and the past. The present perfect of any verb is composed of two elements: the appropriate form of the auxiliary verb *have* plus the past participle of the main verb *completed.*

14 The initial verb *is* sets the present tense for this sentence and for the present-tense verb *involves.* The preposition *from* shows the positional relationship between the person jumping and the building.

15 The main clause is *It is also possible to jump from a movable object.* The other two clauses are dependent on the main independent clause.

16 The only two phrases that make sense are: *in the morning* and *to get out of the house.*

17 *Sharon and I* is correct as they are the subjects, not the objects, of the sentence. It is polite to place the other person's name first before referring to yourself with *I.*

18 *The plant needs water* is the only complete independent sentence. It contains a subject, verb and object.

19 The modal auxiliary *would have liked* shows something the speaker wanted to do (see the show) but this was influenced by something that occurred in the past (tickets sold out).

20 The adverb *often* shows how frequently an action occurs.

21 The adverb *there* shows where the action occurs.

22 The adverb *well* is required. It is a common error to use an adjective (good) instead of an adverb.

23 The two verbs, *prowled* and *flapping*, are the action words in the sentence.

24 The comparative adjective is *cloudier*. It is unnecessary to add 'more'.

25 The conjunction *because* explains the relationship between the two events.

Intermediate level questions

GRAMMAR Mini Test 3

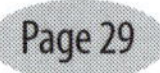

1 C **2** A, C **3** preposition, verb, adjective, noun **4** the **5** have, ring, complain **6** D **7** B **8** C **9** B **10** D **11** its, it's **12** adverb, verb, adjective, noun **13** A **14** B **15** I decided to become more active and outspoken about these issues **16** He, my, I, it **17** C **18** B **19** B **20** C **21** and **22** D **23** have been **24** C **25** wholeheartedly

1 The preposition *over* is used in this situation to mean 'overcoming an obstacle'.

2 An **idiom** is a phrase where the words together have a meaning that is different from the dictionary definitions of the individual words. If something is excessive or annoying, it is *a bit far*. It is also possible to go physically *far away*.

3 *By* is a preposition, *will* is a verb, *my* is an adjective and *assignment* is a noun.

4 The definite article *the* is used to refer to a specific person.

5 The three verbs *have*, *ring* and *complain* are the action words in this sentence.

6 Your verb choice here is based on points in time. You need to choose the verb that allows you to show an interrupted action: I had been … when …

7 Verb choices in this question are based on points in time. You need to choose the verbs that allow you to show a continuing action from the present into the future.

8 *Hand in hand* means 'work together closely'. When people in a group (e.g. in an office or in a project) work together with mutual understanding to achieve a target, it is said they work hand in hand.

9 Someone who's living from *hand to mouth* is very poor and needs the little money they have coming in to cover their expenses.

10 If someone is let off the hook, they have avoided punishment or criticism for something they have done.

11 *Its* is a possessive pronoun that stands for the main noun (the dog), while *it's* is a contraction of *it is*.

12 *Regularly* is an adverb, *visit* is a verb, *elderly* is an adjective and *lunch* is a noun.

13 The text is written in the present tense, as indicated by the initial verb *has*. Looking for a signal verb can help you decide what tense to use or identify, as consistency is important. The present-tense verb choice here is *extends*.

14 The text in this sentence is written in the past tense, as indicated by the initial verb *started*. Look for a signal verb to help you decide what tense to use, as consistency is important. The past-tense verb choice here is *saw*.

15 *I decided to become more active and outspoken about these issues* is the main independent clause. The other clauses are dependent.

16 The four pronouns are: *he, my, I* and *it*.

17 The preposition *on* is used here to describe a point in time.

18 *The actor had been practising his lines* is a complete sentence that contains a subject, verb and object.

19 *Who* and *that* are relative pronouns, which are used to refer back to a person or thing that was previously mentioned. As a general rule, *who* refers to people, while *that* may refer to people, animals, groups or things.

20 The present-tense verb choice here is *plans* and is the best choice to show that is what he wants to do, but hasn't done yet.

21 *And* is a conjunction used to join two adjectives.

22 *Green* is a colour that symbolises environmentally friendly behaviour, goods and services. A *green build* is a noun phrase that describes an environmentally sound building.

23 The two verbs are *have* and *been*.

24 The pronoun *them* stands for the main noun *hybrid cars*.

25 The adverb *wholeheartedly* describes how the students enjoy their time.

Year 7 Literacy Mini Test Answers

Advanced level questions

GRAMMAR Mini Test 4

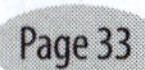

1 A **2** B **3** article, noun, adverb, verb **4** sadder **5** is, refuses, wash **6** B **7** B **8** A **9** A **10** B **12** noun, adjective, conjunction, adverb **11** D **12** A **13** C **14** D **15** males seldom live longer than 10 years **16** prepare, excite, terrify **17** lions, years, captivity **18** C **19** C **20** A **21** in, for **22** C **23** hopped, watched **24** car and licence **25** you, you

1 The verb *laid* in the sentence requires some further description. Choosing the option with the adverb *carefully* allows for a correctly worded description of how the table was laid.

2 *Urgently* is an adverb that is used to describe the verb *rang*.

3 *The* is an article, *sun* is a noun, *brightly* is an adverb and *has* is a verb.

4 *Sadder* is a comparative adjective.

5 The three verbs *is, refuses* and *do* are the action words in the sentence.

6 We make the superlative forms of short adjectives by adding ***est***. If the adjective ends in ***y*** it should be dropped and changed to an ***I***, e.g. *happy—happiest*. In this case, the speaker uses the superlative *hungriest* as she believes there is no one hungrier.

7 *However* is the best choice here as the speaker, in the context of the sentence, means 'in spite of that' or 'on the other hand'. The other choices do not suit this purpose.

8 *Despite* is used to connect two contrasting ideas. *Elder* and *eldest* can be used instead of *older* and *oldest* to talk about the order of birth of the members of a family. 'She is the elder' can be used to compare the ages of two sisters, while 'she is the eldest' implies that she is the oldest sister in the family.

9 *Smoothly* is an adverb that describes how the plane is landing. Not all adverbs appear next to the verb in a sentence or end in ***ly***.

10 *If the movie starts late, we will miss our dinner reservation* is the only sentence that shows verb consistency and subject-verb agreement.

11 This question asks you to consider redundancy in language. Redundancy occurs when words are repeated or duplicated unnecessarily in sentences. In the sentence, the second time the word *curtains* is used is unnecessary. The sentence would still make sense if this word was not repeated: *They put the yellow curtains up in the shop before hanging the red.*

12 *Assistant* is a noun, *honest* is an adjective, *and* is a conjunction and *accidentally* is an adverb.

13 *When the bus came, the students were required to stand for elderly passengers.* This question asks you to focus on tense consistency, with the verb *were* a clue for what tense to choose.

14 *Very* is an adverb that describes how quietly the students were working.

15 The main clause is *males seldom live longer than 10 years.* The other clauses are dependent on this main independent clause.

16 The three verbs *prepare, excite* and *terrify* are the action words in this sentence.

17 Nouns can refer to states of being such as *captivity,* as well as physical things like *lions*.

18 The complete sentence has both subject and verb.

19 You need to choose the correct tense to describe the lion. The present tense verb *is* is suitable as the lion is distinctive now, and not only in the past. *Is* is a verb and so any word that describes it must be an adverb. Most adverbs end in ***ly***, making *highly* the correct answer.

20 A superlative is used to show the highest degree of comparison: *The face of the male lion is one of the most widely recognised*. For words with only one syllable such as *fast,* the suffix ***est*** should be added to form the superlative (*the fastest*). For words with more than one syllable, e.g. *careful,* the words *most* or *least* should be added (*the most careful*).

21 The prepositions *in* and *for* describe what places (menageries and exhibitions) the lion occupies.

22 The plural verb *are* must be used with the plural word *zoos*. The definite article *the* is used when describing particular nouns and noun phrases, in this case *endangered Asiatic subspecies.*

23 The two verbs *hopped* and *watched* are the action words in this sentence.

24 The plural pronoun *them* stands for the main nouns *car and licence.*

25 The personal pronoun *you* is used twice here and can be used to refer directly to a specific person, object or group of things.

Year 7 Literacy Mini Test Answers

Advanced level questions

GRAMMAR Mini Test 5

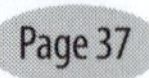

1 C **2** C **3** noun, conjunction, verb, noun **4** a, the **5** revved, shot, annoyed **6** B **7** C **8** B **9** B **10** We, it **11** B **12** D, A, C, B **13** A **14** but **15** The heat was stifling **16** yet, because **17** B **18** C **19** C **20** A **21** yet **22** C **23** cow, slope **24** Saturday **25** A

1 You must identify the correct preposition (a word used in front of a noun or pronoun) in this question. Alan is leaning on the wall, so the correct preposition is *against.*

2 In sentences, subjects must agree with verbs. The verb *has* refers to the noun *value,* not *goods.* In the second part of the sentence the plural verb *are* agrees with the plural noun *criteria.*

3 *Tori* is a proper noun, *but* is a conjunction, *had* is a verb and *money* is a common noun.

4 An article is a word preceding a noun and can be either definite (the) or indefinite (a, an, some).

5 The three verbs *revved, shot* and *annoyed* are the action words in the sentence.

6 The missing word is an adjective. The plural noun *flowers* indicates that the adjective must also be in plural form. *They* and *them* are personal pronouns and cannot be used as adjectives in this context.

7 *I would have completed my homework last night but I fell asleep. Of* is often confused as an auxiliary verb, however, it is always *have.*

8 It is common usage that we decide *on a course of action*, not *with* or *for.*

9 This is a tense question. *Shone* is the past tense of the verb *shine. Brightly* is an adverb that describes how the sun shone.

10 Pronouns stand for or refer to a noun, an individual or individuals, or a thing whose identity is made clearer in the text. In this case, who *we* are is not clear, only that *we* are in an unidentified group. The pronoun *it* replaces the soccer game.

11 *I will need to get a haircut before school starts next term.* The future tense verb *will* indicates something that needs to happen.

12 This question asks you to consider the logical order of ideas. *When summer comes, we usually visit the beach. However, if it I too hot, we go home to keep cool.*

13 You need to change the direct speech to reported speech as well as use the correct pronouns to make it clear who is saying what to whom and when. First remove the quotation marks to show reported speech and then change the pronouns *you* to *he* and *I* to *she.*

14 The coordinating conjunction *but* creates a relationship between the two ideas of the sentence.

15 The main clause is: *The heat was stifling.* It has a subject and verb.

16 Conjunctions such as *yet* can be used to connect two independent clauses. Conjunctions such as *because* are slightly different because they join dependent and independent clauses.

17 The standard rule for the past tense of *hang* is, in almost all situations, to use the word *hung.* However, in this instance we use *hanged* when referring to a person being suspended by a rope around the neck.

18 The complete sentence is: *He held office from 1994 to 1999.* It has a subject and verb.

19 Reflexive pronouns are used when the subject and object of a sentence are the same person or non-person, e.g. "*I talk to* myself *when I am nervous or excited*".

20 As a general rule, the use of *by which* is used to describe the effect of a process, whereas *in which* is used to describe what happens in a process. The use of *in which* in this example shows the speaker Nelson Mandela describing a society living *in* harmony.

21 *Yet* is a conjunction that connects two independent clauses. It allows the writer or speaker to express a contrast in their ideas.

22 *However* is the best choice here as the speaker, in the context of the sentence, means 'in spite of that' or 'on the other hand'. The other choices do not suit this purpose.

23 A *common noun* is the name for a person, place, or thing in a class or group. Unlike proper nouns, a *common noun* is not capitalised. In this example, a *cow* and a *slope* are both things.

24 Proper nouns need to be capitalised. Proper nouns name specific people, places or things, e.g. each part of a person's name, the names of places, buildings, months and days of the week.

25 The plural pronoun *them* refers to the sentence's main noun *the presents.*

Standard level questions

PUNCTUATION Mini Test 1

1 D **2** A **3** A **4** A **5** A **6** A **7** B **8** B **9** C **10** D **11** A **12** D **13** B **14** C **15** B **16** A **17** B **18** C **19** B **20** B **21** B **22** A **23** C **24** C **25** A

1 The date, written in this form, no longer requires a comma after any part of the date.

Year 7 Literacy Mini Test Answers

2 A colon is often used to introduce a list of items.

3 A colon can be used to introduce an explanation or a definition of something.

4 A colon is generally used to introduce a list, or lead from one point logically into another.

5 Expressions such as *Yes*, *No* and *Indeed* (usually at the start of a sentence) are known as interjections. Interjections can be followed by a comma.

6 Use commas to set off expressions that interrupt sentence flow.

7 Use a comma between dependent and independent clauses.

8 Use commas to separate the elements in a series of three or more things. The word *and* takes the place of the comma between the last two items. When referring to more than one item that the boy likes, use the plural form of the verb (*were*) and not the singular (*is*).

9 A colon can be used to introduce an explanation or a definition of something. In this sentence, the colon precedes the explanation of the *one thing* (*get out while you have the chance*).

10 Speech marks should be used around direct speech. A comma separates the two sections of the sentence.

11 Use a comma to divide non-restrictive parts of a sentence. A non-restrictive clause gives additional information that is not vital to the meaning of a sentence. In this sentence the words *who were fearless* give additional information about the sailors so should be inserted after the word *sailors*.

12 Titles of novels (*Pride and Prejudice*) require punctuation, either in the form of italics or underlining. Other titles that require this include the names of long poems, ships, plays, films and paintings. Short works and parts of long works are usually in quotation marks.

13 Use commas to separate the elements in a series (three or more things). The word *and* takes the place of a comma between the last two items.

14 Words that are spoken in direct speech should be punctuated using speech marks.

15 Only the words that are spoken are placed within speech marks. Commas separate the three sections of the sentence.

16 Use commas to separate the elements in a series (three or more things). The word *and* takes the place of a comma between the last two items.

17 Only the words that are spoken are placed within speech marks. A comma separates the two sections of the sentence.

18 Titles of long poems require punctuation, either in the form of italics or underlining. Other titles that require this include the names of novels, ships, plays, films and paintings. Short works and parts of long works are usually in quotation marks. As *The Man from Snowy River* identifies *which* poem is exciting, commas are not required.

19 Song titles should be in quotation marks. Use single quotation marks within speech marks. Speech marks should be used to punctuate direct speech.

20 Only the words that are spoken are placed within speech marks. A comma separates the two sections of the sentence.

21 Only the words that are spoken are placed within speech marks. A comma separates the two sections of the sentence.

22 Use commas to set off and enclose nonessential phrases or clauses.

23 A full stop is used at the end of a sentence unless it is a question or exclamation.

24 A full stop is used at the end of a sentence unless it is a question or exclamation.

25 A question mark is used at the end of a question.

Intermediate level questions

PUNCTUATION Mini Test 2

Page 45

1 A,D **2** B **3** A **4** B **5** B **6** D **7** A **8** A **9** A **10** D **11** A **12** C **13** B **14** C **15** A **16** A **17** A **18** C **19** C **20** C **21** A **22** A **23** B **24** C **25** C

1 One of the uses of apostrophes is to show missing letters in verb contractions. In most formal writing such contractions should be avoided. In this case, the contractions are who's (who is) and they're (they are).

2 An ellipsis can be used to indicate a pause in the flow of a sentence and is especially useful in quoted speech.

3 One of the uses of apostrophes is to show missing letters in verb contractions. In most formal writing such contractions should be avoided. In this case, the contraction is *let's* (*let us*).

4 An ellipsis can be used to indicate a pause in the flow of a sentence and is especially useful in quoted speech. In mid-sentence, a space should appear between the first and last ellipsis marks and the surrounding letters.

5 An ellipsis can be used to indicate a pause in the flow of a sentence and is especially useful in quoted speech. If words are omitted from the end of a sentence, indicate the omission with an ellipsis (preceded and followed by a space).

Year 7 Literacy Mini Test Answers

6 Ellipses can be used to indicate a reflective pause or hesitation. When spoken, the ellipsis becomes a pause or break in the flow of the sentence. This occurs in this sentence before *umm* to indicate the speaker's uncertainty.

7 Use commas to set off and enclose nonessential phrases or clauses. In this sentence commas should appear before and after *Nick and Dom.*

8 To make a plural noun possessive, simply add an apostrophe to the word. If the plural does not end in an ***s***, then add an apostrophe plus ***s***.

9 One of the uses of apostrophes is to show missing letters in verb contractions. In most formal writing such contractions should be avoided. In this case, the contraction is *you're* (*you are*).

10 One of the uses of apostrophes is to show missing letters in verb contractions. In most formal writing such contractions should be avoided. In this case, the contraction is *there'd* (*there had*).

11 One of the uses of apostrophes is to show missing letters in verb contractions. In most formal writing such contractions should be avoided. In this case, the contraction is *it's* (*it is*). The other *its* is a pronoun.

12 One of the uses of apostrophes is to show missing letters in verb contractions. In most formal writing such contractions should be avoided. In this case, the contraction is *they'd* (*they had*).

13 To make a plural noun possessive, simply add an apostrophe to the word. If the plural does not end in an ***s***, then add an apostrophe plus ***s***. In this case *room* belongs to the *men*. As *men* is already a plural noun, the apostrophe comes before ***s***.

14 An apostrophe is used to form the plurals of alphabetical letters to avoid confusion with the words that would appear if the apostrophe was omitted. In this case the apostrophe prevents *A's* being read as the word *As*.

15 An apostrophe is normally used with the letter ***s*** to show ownership or possession. With most singular nouns, simply add an apostrophe plus the letter ***s*** to do this.

16 To make a plural noun possessive, simply add an apostrophe to the word. If the plural does not end in an ***s***, then add an apostrophe plus ***s***. In this case *shoes* belongs to the *children*. As *children* is already a plural noun, the apostrophe comes before the ***s***.

17 One of the uses of apostrophes is to show missing letters in verb contractions. In most formal writing such contractions should be avoided. In this case, the contraction is *they'll* (*they will*).

18 One of the uses of apostrophes is to show missing letters in verb contractions. In most formal writing such contractions should be avoided. In this case, the contraction is *would've* (*would have*).

19 One of the uses of apostrophes is to show missing letters in verb contractions. In most formal writing such contractions should be avoided. In this case, the contraction is *wouldn't* (*would not*). In the other examples the apostrophes are not in the place of the missing letters.

20 Expanding the contractions can help you decide which response to choose. *There'll* (*there will*) is the best option.

21 Expanding the contractions can help you decide which response to choose. *Didn't* (*did not*) is the best option. The words *did you* can also help you decide.

22 Use commas to set off and enclose nonessential phrases or clauses.

23 An opening speech mark needs to begin the spoken words. The word *said* indicates that the following words are the spoken words.

24 A full stop is used at the end of a sentence unless it is a question or exclamation.

25 A comma goes after the beginning adverbial phrase.

Intermediate level questions

PUNCTUATION Mini Test 3

Page 48

1 D **2** C **3** A **4** A, B **5** D **6** C **7** D **8** A, B **9** B **10** B **11** C **12** A **13** B **14** C **15** A **16** C **17** D **18** D **19** B **20** D **21** C **22** B **23** C **24** A **25** C

1 A question mark should be used at the end of a direct question. A tag question is a device used to turn a statement into a question. It nearly always consists of a pronoun, a helping verb and sometimes the word *not*.

2 A question mark should be used at the end of a direct question.

3 Speech marks are used to enclose direct speech.

4 Add an apostrophe and the letter ***s*** to most singular nouns to show ownership or possession.

5 A question mark should be used at the end of a direct question. A tag question is a device used to turn a statement into a question. It nearly always consists of a pronoun, a helping verb and sometimes the word *not*.

6 A question mark should be used at the end of a direct question. Any punctuation should be contained within speech marks, including exclamation marks, question marks and full stops.

Year 7 Literacy Mini Test Answers

7 Speech marks are used to enclose direct speech.

8 Speech marks are used to enclose direct speech.

9 A question mark should be used at the end of a direct question. A tag question is a device used to turn a statement into a question. It nearly always consists of a pronoun, a helping verb and sometimes the word *not*.

10 A question mark should be used at the end of a direct question.

11 Speech marks are used to enclose direct speech.

12 Speech marks are used to enclose direct speech. A comma separates the two sections of the sentence.

13 A question mark should be used at the end of a direct question. A tag question is a device used to turn a statement into a question. It nearly always consists of a pronoun, a helping verb and sometimes the word *not*.

14 The sentence *Oh no* is an exclamation and should end with an exclamation mark. The sentence *I think I may have dropped my keys* is not a question and should not end with a question mark.

15 This is an example of reported (or indirect) speech—the actual words spoken by the waiter have not been repeated. Therefore no speech marks are required.

16 This is an example of reported (or indirect) speech—the actual words spoken by the walker have not been repeated. Therefore no speech marks are required.

17 You need to enclose all words spoken by Peter in speech marks.

18 Sometimes speech mark punctuation is broken up by other information—in this case by the writer telling us who is speaking. Look for the words being spoken to help guide you.

19 This is an example of reported (or indirect) speech—the actual words spoken by the toddler have not been repeated. Therefore no speech marks are required. The pronoun *I* has been converted to the third person *he*.

20 The adverb *immediately* is included in the words spoken by the male and needs to be included within the speech marks.

21 A closing speech mark needs to end the spoken words. The word *told* indicates that the preceding words were the spoken words.

22 A full stop is used at the end of a sentence unless it is a question or exclamation. The capital letter in the following word indicates that the first sentence has ended.

23 A closing speech mark needs to end the spoken words. The word *said* indicates that the preceding words were the spoken words.

24 Commas need to surround the nonessential clause.

25 An exclamation is used at the end of an exclamation.

Advanced level questions

PUNCTUATION Mini Test 4

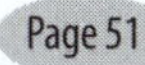
Page 51

1 A, B **2** C **3** C **4** A **5** C **6** B **7** A **8** C **9** B **10** D **11** A **12** D **13** D **14** B **15** A **16** C **17** A **18** A **19** C **20** D **21** A **22** B **23** B **24** B **25** B

1 An apostrophe is normally used with the letter ***s*** to show ownership or possession. In this example, there are two nouns, *Steven* and *team*, that need an apostrophe. It is *Steven's team* and the *team's win*. *Steven* is a singular noun and so an apostrophe and then ***s*** is added to show possession. *Team* is a collective noun and as it does not end in ***s***, an apostrophe and then ***s*** is added.

2 A colon is generally used to introduce a list or lead from one point logically into another.

3 Words that are spoken in direct speech should be punctuated using speech marks. The teacher's words finish after the exclamation mark.

4 Placing commas in different locations affects the meaning of the sentence. A comma should be placed after the verb *fall*, otherwise the sentence's meaning becomes unclear.

5 Only words actually spoken by an individual should be enclosed in speech marks. Ideas enclosed in speech marks should begin with a capital letter, making option B incorrect.

6 Apostrophes can be used to show possession as well as to contract (shorten) words. *Could've* is a contraction of *could have* and *I'd* is a contraction of *I had*. Option A requires no punctuation as *rocks* in this example is plural and not possessive. Option C requires the plural form of *baby* which is *babies*. Option D omits the apostrophe in *we've*.

7 Brackets are used to enclose (or set off) supplementary information, or afterthoughts. In these examples, option A is the only sentence that could have the bracketed information removed and the sentence still make grammatical sense.

8 The single quotation marks are used here to imply a meaning other than what is written. The single quotation marks surrounding 'unsinkable' are to show the statement's irony, as the *Titanic* actually did sink.

9 A dash can be used to separate parts of a sentence. The information that surrounds the words within the dashes (*soccer and league*) can act as a complete sentence on its own: *There are two main sports that are popular in this country*.

10 The semicolon is used to connect independent clauses and indicates a closer relationship between the clauses than a full stop does.

11 One of the uses of apostrophes is to show missing letters in verb contractions. In most formal writing such contractions should be avoided. In this question, the contraction is *they'll* (*they will*).

12 A colon is generally used to introduce a list, or lead from one point logically into another. In this case the colon introduces the *two choices* (*dinner or bed*).

13 The semicolon is used to connect independent clauses and indicates a closer relationship between the clauses than a full stop does.

14 The Winter Olympics refers to a specific event and is considered a proper noun, although winter can also operate as a common noun depending on the context.

15 Brands are considered proper nouns and should be capitalised. *Sandra* is a proper name, but *sales assistant* is a common noun and should not be capitalised.

16 The definite article *the* preceding the title *School Principal* indicates that a specific principal is being referred to and so the words should be capitalised.

17 An apostrophe is normally used with the letter ***s*** to show ownership or possession. With most singular nouns, simply add an apostrophe followed by the letter ***s*** to do this. For plural nouns it is necessary to place the apostrophe *after* the final ***s*** (e.g. *The teachers' room*). However, words like *children* and *men* are nouns that refer to 'more than one' which cannot be made singular. For these examples, the apostrophe follows the rule for singular nouns and precedes the final ***s*** (*children's*/*men's*).

18 One of the uses of apostrophes is to show missing letters in verb contractions. In most formal writing such contractions should be avoided. In this case, the contraction is *would've* (*would have*).

19 Direct speech should be punctuated using speech marks. An exclamation mark is a suitable punctuation choice when someone is shouting.

20 A full stop is used at the end of a sentence unless it is a question or exclamation.

21 A comma precedes the phrase at the end of the sentence.

22 A comma is used to end the direct speech that is followed by the word *said*.

23 A comma precedes the phrase at the end of the sentence.

24 An exclamation mark is a suitable punctuation choice when someone is shouting or saying something emotional.

25 Use commas to set off expressions that interrupt sentence flow.

Advanced level questions

PUNCTUATION Mini Test 5

1 D **2** B **3** A **4** A **5** A, D **6** A, C **7** A, B **8** B **9** D **10** C **11** A **12** A **13** A **14** B **15** B **16** C **17** A **18** A **19** B **20** A **21** C **22** A **23** B **24** B **25** A

1 Also known as parentheses, these brackets contain material that could be omitted without destroying or altering the meaning of the sentence. Identifying the United Kingdom as (UK) in this sentence will allow for subsequent references to the United Kingdom to be just UK.

2 To show plural possession, make the noun plural first, then immediately use the apostrophe. The noun in this case is *car*, which should have an ***s*** added to it followed by an apostrophe. This has been determined by the following plural noun *drivers* which shows that there is more than one car and more than one driver.

3 Use commas to divide non-restrictive parts of a sentence. A non-restrictive clause gives additional information that is not vital to the meaning of a sentence. As the words *which was the family's treasured pet* describes the cat they should be placed after the word *cat*.

4 The punctuation mark must always come inside the closing speech mark; in this case it is a question mark. Only the words that are actually spoken by someone should be contained within speech marks.

5 The punctuation mark must always come inside the closing speech mark; in this case it is an exclamation mark. Only the words that are actually spoken by someone should be contained within speech marks. The titles of films or books should be written in italics or underlined.

6 To show plural possession, make the noun plural first, then immediately use the apostrophe. The noun in this case (*women*) is already plural so the apostrophe should be added and then the ***s***.

Other examples of similar plural nouns are *men* and *children*. For single possession, place the apostrophe before the ***s*** (*Melinda's*).

7 Use commas to divide non-restrictive parts of a sentence. A non-restrictive clause gives additional information that is not vital to the meaning of a sentence. In this question, the information between the commas could be removed, and the main points of the sentence would not change.

8 To show plural possession, make the noun plural first, then immediately use the apostrophe. The noun in this case (*children*) is already plural so the apostrophe should be added and then the ***s***. Other examples of similar plural nouns are *men* and *women*.

9 A colon has the main purpose of introducing ideas and information. It can introduce a small amount of information or a large amount: a word, a phrase, a sentence, a quotation or a list. In this sentence the colon introduces the *one thing* (*profit*).

10 The semicolon cuts and divides parts of a sentence into easily recognised pieces. Use a semicolon between independent clauses if the clauses are closely related.

11 This sentence is missing an exclamation mark after *edge*. An exclamation mark usually shows strong feeling, such as surprise, anger or joy. Using an exclamation mark when writing is rather like shouting or raising your voice when speaking. Exclamation marks are most commonly used in written quoted speech. You should avoid using exclamation marks in formal writing, unless absolutely necessary.

12 This sentence is missing a question mark after *sugar*. Use the question mark when posing a direct query in an interrogative sentence. This shows that the speaker is seeking information. The sentence may begin with an interrogative pronoun such as *do*, *who*, *when* or *where*.

13 Ellipses are three full stops that are used to indicate omitted parts of quotations. This is convenient when you wish to leave out unnecessary parts of a longer quotation. Ellipses are also used to show indecision on the part of a speaker, as in this sentence. The ellipsis in this sentence is best placed after the first *Umm*. This type of usage is common in informal texts, such as in dialogue, but rare in academic writing.

14 This sentence is missing a full stop after *pens*. Use full stops between independent sentences which both contain a noun and verb, and are not directly related to each other in meaning.

15 The dialogue in this sentence is *"The crowd went wild when the band came on stage."* but it is divided into two sections, separated by the information about the speaker, so it is really only one sentence. A comma must come before the end of the first set of speech marks to indicate the continuation of the sentence, and similarly before the second piece of dialogue to indicate that the dialogue continues. Only words actually spoken should be contained by speech marks.

16 The dialogue in this answer is two sentences *"Can you get the door? I'm in the shower!"* which are separated by information about who is speaking. The question mark must come before the end of the first set of speech marks, but *he* does not require a capital letter as this is considered to be a continuation of the first sentence. Speech marks are needed again around the second piece of dialogue, *"I'm in the shower!"* Only words actually spoken should be contained by speech marks.

17 The sentence is an example of indirect speech, as the actual words spoken were not repeated. Speech marks are therefore unnecessary.

18 Use commas to separate three or more consecutive listed items. Do not use a comma where only two things are listed (*flour or cocoa*). The word *and* takes the place of the comma before the last item in the first list.

19 There are two sentences. When there are speech marks the closing punctuation should come before the closing speech mark as seen by the comma after *umbrella* and the full stop after *rain*. Only the words that are actually spoken by someone should be contained within speech marks, which is why *said Mum* is not within the speech marks.

20 The punctuation mark must always come inside the closing speech mark; in this case it is a full stop to indicate the end of the spoken sentence. Only the words that are actually spoken by someone should be contained within speech marks. Titles of long poems should be italicised or underlined.

21 Two commas are required in this sentence as there is additional information added to the middle of the sentence. The sentence would have made sense as *Our school is performing at the Sydney Opera House,* but the additional information *along with five other schools* has been added to the middle of the sentence, and requires a comma on either side.

Year 7 Literacy Mini Test Answers

22 The colon is used to introduce information. It can introduce many things including a word, a phrase, a sentence, a quotation or a list.

23 The semicolon cuts and divides parts of a sentence into easily recognised pieces. Use a semicolon between independent clauses if the clauses are closely related. In academic writing, the semicolon is used most commonly to divide long elements of a list.

24 The semicolon cuts and divides parts of a sentence into easily recognised pieces. Use a semicolon between independent clauses if the clauses are closely related. In academic writing, the semicolon is used most commonly to divide long elements of a list.

25 The colon is used to introduce information. It can introduce many things including a word, a phrase, a sentence, a quotation or a list.

Standard level questions

READING Mini Test 1: Information report

1 C **2** D **3** A, C **4** B **5** D **6** B **7** Many dogs are easily and quickly trained. **8** D

1 This is an **inferring type of question**. To find the answer you have to 'read between the lines'. You need to make a judgement about the meaning of the text as a whole and not consider its sections individually.

2 This is a **fact-finding type of question**. The answer is a fact in the text. You read that *Law requires that owners register their dogs with their local council (see line 4)*. This sentence contains the key word *registered* that will help you answer this question correctly.

3 This is a **fact-finding type of question**. The answers are facts in the text. You read that *Yearly veterinarian trips for a medical exam and annual vaccinations keep dogs happy and healthy (see lines 7–8)*. You also read that *A dog…needs to see a vet for diagnosis and treatment (lines 8–9)*.

4 This is a **judgement type of question**. You read *Dogs need fresh water daily, as well as one or two meals per day (see line 16)*. Combining the possible answers with your own knowledge you can work out that the best answer to describe *nourishment* is *survival*, meaning 'to live, carry on or endure'.

5 This is an **inferring type of question**. To find the answer you have to 'read between the lines'. You read *A fenced-in backyard allows dogs to run freely without the risk of escape (see lines 12–14)*. You also read that this sentence comes under the heading Safety *(see line 10)*. The answers provided are all possibilities. However, the best response to this question is that the fenced-in backyard stops dogs from getting hit by cars.

6 This is a **judgement type of question**. You read *The type of food depends on the dog's tastes (see lines 16–17)*. *Depends* is a verb that states what type of food dogs like. It implies that dogs' choices may change depending on their individual likes and dislikes.

7 This is a **judgement type of question**. You read *Many dogs take to training quickly (see line 20)*. *Take to* is a phrasal verb that means 'become fond of or attached to'. This means that many dogs are easily and quickly trained.

8 This is a **judgement type of question**. You read the title *Caring for dogs responsibly*. You also read *a responsible dog owner knows that caring for pets is a top priority (see lines 1–2)*. You have to use your experience to help answer this question. The opening paragraph contains an overview of how to care for dogs responsibly. Its purpose is to teach people the best ways to care for their dogs.

Standard level questions

READING Mini Test 2: Explanation

1 A, C **2** A **3** C **4** A **5** D **6** C **7** D **8** What are clouds for: to inform and to explain; Caring for dogs: to inform and to persuade

1 This is a **fact-finding type of question**. The answer is a fact in the text. You read *the air around us is moist. That means that it contains water in the form of vapour (see line 1)*.

2 This is a **judgement type of question**. You read *Water can exist in three states: liquid (water), solid (ice) and gas (water vapour) (see line 3)*. Combining the possible answers with your own knowledge you can work out that the best answer to describe *state* is *condition*, meaning 'circumstances or situation'.

3 This is a **fact-finding type of question**. The answer is a fact in the text. You read *water vapour has no smell, you can't pick it up, and it's invisible (see line 4)*.

4 This is an **inferring type of question**. To find the answer you have to 'read between the lines'. You read *This doesn't mean that you can't feel it though (see lines 4–5)*. The idea is presented as a negative. In order to get the right answer you need to interpret the idea in a positive way: that you can feel the vapour.

5 This is an **inferring type of question**. To find the answer you have to 'read between the lines'. You read clouds *[are] tiny water droplets condensing out of the air to form liquid water* (see line 10). In order to answer this question correctly, you need to change the verb *condensing* to the noun *condensation*.

6 This is a **judgement type of question**. You read *Perhaps you can remember a hot and sticky day in summer* (see line 6). You have to use your own knowledge to help answer this question. A rhetorical question is a question that is asked to make a point or highlight an idea, but does not necessarily require an answer.

7 This is a **fact-finding type of question**. The answer is a fact in the text. You read *We've all seen fog and steam, but why does water condense out of air and become visible?* (see line 11). You then read the answer to this question: *Well, warm air can hold more water vapour than cool air, so if warm air starts to cool, it can no longer hold as much water vapour. The extra water vapour has to go somewhere, so it condenses out as water* (see lines 11–13).

8 This is a **judgement type of question**. You have to use your experience to help answer this question. Both texts contain factual information that is informative. In *What are clouds for* its purpose is to explain a scientific process. The purposes of *Caring for dogs* are to inform and persuade. It uses persuasive language such as *happy, healthy and friendly* (line 2) to persuade the reader to care for their dog correctly.

Intermediate level questions

READING Mini Test 3: Book blurb

Page 61

1 B **2** A **3** C **4** C **5** D **6** B **7** D **8** 2, 5, 3, 1, 4

1 This is an **inferring type of question**. To find the answer you have to 'read between the lines'. You read *Asian-Australians have often been written about by outsiders* (see lines 1–2). *Outsiders* means 'people not belonging to a particular group', the group in this question being Asian-Australians. The most likely answer to the question is Australians whose cultural background is not Asian. The answer wouldn't be Alice Pung or Benjamin Law, as they are authors in this book and would not be considered outsiders.

2 This is a **judgement type of question**. You read *they tell their own stories with verve, courage and a large dose of humour* (see lines 4–5). Other words besides *verve* used in the sentence include *courage* and *humour*. These are positive words that make *energy* the best response given the possible answers. Or you might already know that *verve* means 'enthusiasm or energy'.

3 This is a **judgement type of question**. You read *They tell tales of leaving home, falling in love and finding one's feet* (see lines 6–7). The other life experiences listed in this sentence (*leaving home* and *falling in love*) give you a clue that 'discovering who you are' is the best response out of the possible answers. *Finding one's feet* is an idiom that means 'adjusting or settling down' or, in this context, 'discovering who you are'.

4 This is a **fact-finding type of question**. The answer is a fact in the text. You read *Benjamin Law has a close encounter with some angry Australian fauna* (see lines 12–13). *Fauna* means 'animals of a particular region or era'.

5 This is a **judgement type of question**. You read *Kylie Kwong makes a moving pilgrimage to her great-grandfather's Chinese village* (see lines 13–14). *Moving* in this sentence is an adjective that describes the noun *pilgrimage*. A *pilgrimage* is a 'journey to a sacred place as an act of devotion'. The word *moving* here would therefore mean 'moving the emotions', rather than physically moving. Of the options the best answer would be *had an emotional experience*.

6 This is a **judgement type of question**. You read *Here are … exciting new voices, spanning several generations and drawn from all over Australia. In sharing their stories, they show us what it is really like to grow up Asian* (see lines 15–19). From these words you can work out that the exciting new voices are writing about many different experiences and stories so the best option is *have new and interesting perspectives*.

7 This is an **inferring type of question**. To find the answer you have to 'read between the lines'. You read *In sharing their stories, they show us what it is really like to grow up Asian* (see lines 18–19). You also read *In this collection … they tell their own stories* (see lines 3–4). Summarising the overall meaning of the text will help you answer the question rather than focus on individual sentences. The book shares the experiences of a range of Asian-Australians.

8 This is a **fact-finding type of question**. The answer is a fact in the text. You read the text and work out the order in which each sentence appears.

Year 7 Literacy Mini Test Answers

Intermediate level questions

READING Mini Test 4: News report

1 D **2** B **3** D **4** A **5** 3, 2, 4, 1 **6** Aboriginal students: headline, quotation, statistics; Book blurb: headline, anecdote, emotional language **7** Aboriginal students: to inform, to report; Book blurb: to inform, to persuade **8** novel, newspaper

1 This is a **judgement type of question**. You read *Aboriginal students make short work of success.* Alliteration is the repetition of consonant sounds at the beginning of a word. There are three words beginning with ***s*** in this title. Alliteration is a common device used in headlines.

2 This is a **fact-finding type of question**. The answer is a fact in the text. You read *a special school called Gawura for Aborigines (see lines 6–7).*

3 This is an **inferring type of question**. To find the answer you have to 'read between the lines'. You read *A Sydney private school's investment in Aboriginal children is starting to pay off, with dramatically improved literacy and numeracy results (see lines 1–4).* Summarising the overall meaning of the text, rather than focusing on individual sentences, will help you answer the question. The school makes a number of investments in the students it is trying to help.

4 This is an **inferring type of question**. To find the answer you have to 'read between the lines'. You read *A snapshot of results for this year's first national literacy and numeracy tests shows the year 5 Gawura pupils achieved results in writing (see lines 13–15).* You also read *Reading results were below the state average but well above the state average for indigenous students (see lines 18–20)* and *numeracy results were 411.6 compared to the state average of 489.1 (see lines 26–27).* These are general results, rather than a detailed description, making a *snapshot* an overview or summary.

5 This is a **fact-finding type of question**. The answer is a fact in the text. You read the text and work out the order in which each sentence appears.

6 This is a **judgement type of question**. You have to use your own knowledge of text features to answer this question. *Aboriginal students* contains a headline, a quotation and statistics. The book blurb uses a headline, contains anecdotes and uses emotional language (*courage, angry, exciting*).

7 This is a **judgement type of question**. You have to use your own experience to answer this question. The purposes for *Aboriginal students* are to inform and to report. This text contains factual information that is informative. Its purpose is to report on a factual event. The purposes for the book blurb are to inform and persuade. The book blurb contains information about the book that is informative. It also uses persuasive language such as *well-known authors and exciting new voices (line 15)* to create interest in the book and to persuade the audience to read it.

8 This is a **judgement type of question**. You have to use your own experience to answer this question. It is most likely that the book blurb would appear in a novel or on its back cover, while *Aboriginal students make short work of success* would appear in a newspaper, as it is a news article.

Intermediate level questions

READING Mini Test 5: Interview

1 C **2** A **3** B **4** D **5** B **6** C **7** question and answer, interview **8** C

1 This is a **fact-finding type of question**. The answer is a fact in the text. You read *Hating Alison Ashley deals with issues like friendship and acceptance (see lines 1–2).*

2 This is a **fact-finding type of question**. The answer is a fact in the text. You read *Saskia Burmeister, who plays Erica (see line 4).* This means she is an actor in the film.

3 This is a **fact-finding type of question**. The answer is a fact in the text. Go to paragraph 3. You read *You're twenty at the moment and the character you're playing is fourteen (line 7).*

4 This is a **fact-finding type of question**. The answer is a fact in the text. You read *She has this obsession with Romeo and Juliet and I read the script and went 'That's me' (see line 12).*

5 This is an **inferring type of question**. To find the answer you have to 'read between the lines'. You read *it was that moment that it clicked and I had a name for something that I knew I was going to be doing for the rest of my life (see lines 16–17).* Saskia had seen Meryl Streep acting and suddenly she realised this career made sense to her, that it was what she wanted to do.

6 This is a **judgement type of question**. You have to use your experience to help answer this question. This text uses bold to highlight the differences between the questions and answers.

7 This is a **judgement type of question**. You have to use your experience to help answer this question. This text uses paragraphing and bold text to indicate the question and answer format, rather than explicitly stating 'question' and 'answer'. The questions indicate that this is an interview.

8 This is a **judgement type of question**. You read *Hating Alison Ashley deals with … Things that young people understand (see lines 1–2)* which is typical of the factual yet persuasive information in this text. Its purpose is to provide information on the film and actors, while recommending it as a film that you should see.

Intermediate level questions

READING Mini Test 6: Narrative

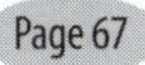
Page 67

1 B **2** C **3** B **4** A, C **5** D **6** Behind the news: first-person perspective, conversational language, idiom; How the leopard got his spots: descriptive adjectives, made-up words, third-person perspective **7** Behind the news: to inform, to create interest; How the leopard gots his spots: to recount, to tell a story **8** magazine, novel

1 This is a **fact-finding type of question**. The answer is a fact in the text. You read *the Leopard lived in a place called the High Veldt (see line 1)*.

2 This is a **judgement type of question**. You read *the 'sclusively bare, hot shiny High Veldt (see lines 2–3)*. You also read *they were 'sclusively sandy-yellow-brownish all over (see lines 5–6)* and *the Leopard 'sclusively with his teeth and claws (see line 24)*. The word *exclusively* is an adverb that is used here to mean that the High Veldt is only bare, hot and shiny, the colour of the animals was only sandy-yellow-brownish and the Leopard only used his teeth and claws. *Exclusively* in this sense means 'not including any other quality'.

3 This is a **fact-finding type of question**. The answer is a fact in the text. You read *hot shiny High Veldt, where there was sand and sandy-coloured rock (see line 3)*.

4 This is a **fact-finding type of question**. The answer is a fact in the text. You read *the Leopard, he was the 'sclusivest sandiest-yellowest-brownest of them all—a greyish-yellowish catty-shaped kind of beast (lines 7–9)*.

5 This is an **inferring type of question**. To find the answer you have to 'read between the lines'. You read *he would lie down by a 'sclusively yellowish-greyish-brownish stone or clump of grass, and when the Giraffe or the Zebra … came by he would surprise them (see lines 13–17)*. The Leopard was camoflauged by his environment, which meant that the Giraffe and Zebra didn't see him and it was easier for him to hunt them.

6 This is a **judgement type of question**. You have to use your knowledge of text features to help answer this question. *Behind the news* contains first-person perspective (*I*), conversational language (*And yeah it was that moment (line 16)*) and idiom (*that it clicked (line 16)*). *How the leopard got his spots* uses descriptive adjectives (*bare, hot, shiny*), made-up words (*jumpsome (line 18)*) and third-person perspective (*the leopard*).

7 This is a **judgement type of question**. You have to use your knowledge of text types to help answer this question. *Behind the news* is an informative interview about a film. Its purpose is to provide information and to create interest in the film. The purposes for *How the leopard got his spots* are to recount and to tell a story. The text is a narrative or story. It also uses past tense to recount a particular incident.

8 This is a **judgement type of question**. You have to use your knowledge of text types to help answer this question. It is most likely that *Behind the news* would appear in a magazine as it is a media text, while *How the leopard got his spots* would appear in a novel as it is a narrative.

Advanced level questions

READING Mini Test 7: Diary entry

Page 69

1 A **2** 4, 1, 3, 2 **3** simile **4** C **5** C **6** D **7** D **8** C

1 This is an **inferring type of question**. To find the answer you have to 'read between the lines'. You read that the students *go aimlessly in different directions (see lines 3–4)*. If you read on, the text states that *Then … all the paths coalesce (see lines 5–6)*. This implies that the aimlessness has stopped and that the students are now coming together.

2 This is a **fact-finding type of question**. The answer is a fact in the text. You read the text and work out the order in which each event appears.

3 This is an **inferring type of question**. To find the answer you have to 'read between the lines'. The writer says the school seems *familiar*, however if you read on she uses this simile *like a game of Dungeons and Dragons (line 14)* to describe her initial experience.

4 This is a **fact-finding type of question**. The answer is a fact in the text. You read *Sophie, who's so bubbly and lively but who finds me so irritating (see line 17)*.

Year 7 Literacy Mini Test Answers

5 This is an **inferring type of question**. To find the answer you have to 'read between the lines'. You read Lisa is *so private inside her cold Scandinavian marble mountain* (see lines 18–19). A clue is given in the word *private* that shows Lisa is not friendly, disappointed or overseas. *Aloof* means 'distant, cold and remote'.

6 This is an **inferring type of question**. To find the answer you have to 'read between the lines'. A 'voice' is not necessarily always 'heard' but may represent more general forms of communication.

7 This is a **judgement type of question**. You have to use your experience to help answer this question. A rhetorical question here allows the writer to consider the result of someone else reading her diary.

8 This is a **judgement type of question**. You have to use your experience to help answer this question. This text contains personal information that is emotional in nature. For example, you read *I write too much in this Journal. But it seems that I cannot help myself* (see line 21). The purpose of this text is to reveal the thoughts and feelings of the writer.

Advanced level questions

READING Mini Test 8: Fable

Page 71

1 C **2** A **3** D **4** B **5** D **6** diary entry: first-person perspective, simile, metaphor; The fox and the goat: direct speech, coda, third-person perspective **7** Diary entry: to reveal emotions and feelings, to entertain; The fox and the goat: to entertain, to instruct **8** novel, collection of short stories

1 This is a **fact-finding type of question**. The answer is a fact in the text. You read *A Fox one day fell into a deep well and could find no means of escape* (see line 1).

2 This is a **judgement type of question**. You read *Concealing his sad plight under a merry guise* (see line 3). This suggests the fox is hiding (*concealing*) his bad situation (*plight*) under a cheerful or happy (*merry*) face or appearance (*guise*).

3 This is a **fact-finding type of question**. The answer is a fact in the text. You read *'I will run up your back and escape'* (see line 7). You also read *the Fox leaped upon his back* (see line 10).

4 This is an **inferring type of question**. To find the answer you have to 'read between the lines'. The question is asking you to consider what moral or coda the story holds for the reader.

5 This is an **inferring type of question**. To find the answer you have to 'read between the lines'. You read that the fox says to the goat *'If you had as many brains in your head as you have hairs in your beard, you would never have gone down'* (see lines 18–22). He is implying that the goat is hairy, but that he doesn't have the same amount of brains or intelligence, as he behaved quite stupidly.

6 This is a **judgement type of question**. You have to use your experience to help answer this question. The diary entry contains first-person perspective (*I*), a simile (*like a game of Dungeons and Dragons*) and a metaphor (*inside her cold Scandinavian marble mountain*). *The fox and the goat* uses direct speech, contains a coda (a moral to the story) and uses third-person perspective (*the goat*).

7 This is a **judgement type of question**. You have to use your experience to help answer this question. The diary entry reveals the author's emotions and feelings and is entertaining. The fox and the goat teaches about life in an interesting way.

8 This is a **judgement type of question**. You have to use your experience to help answer this question. The diary entry is most likely to appear in a novel, as it is a narrative text, while *The fox and the goat* would appear in a collection of short stories, as it tells a complete story in a compacted form.

Advanced level questions

READING Mini Test 9: Narrative

1 B **2** D **3** B **4** C **5** D **6** A **7** B **8** C

1 This is a **fact-finding type of question**. The answer is a fact in the text. You read *Marley was dead … There is no doubt whatever about that. The register of his burial was signed by the clergyman, the clerk, the undertaker, and the chief mourner* (see lines 1–2).

2 This is a **fact-finding type of question**. The answer is a fact in the text. You read *a coffin-nail as the deadest piece of ironmongery in the trade* (see lines 6–7).

3 This is a **judgement type of question**. You read *Old Marley was as dead as a doornail. Mind! I don't mean to say that I know of my own knowledge, what there is particularly dead about a doornail* (see lines 3–6). *Mind* is used here as an interruption, or interjection, that allows the narrator to contradict himself, i.e. disagree with his previous argument about the meaning of *dead as a doornail*.

4 This is a **judgement type of question**. You read *Old Marley was as dead as a doornail* (see lines 3–4). Similes are examples of imagery, along with metaphors and personification, which create an 'image' in our minds. A simile can be recognised by the words *like* or *as*, which create a comparison between two things; in this case, comparing *dead* to *a doornail*.

5 This is an **inferring type of question**. To find the answer you have to 'read between the lines'. You read *permit me to repeat, emphatically, that Marley was as dead as a doornail* (see lines 8–9). Summarising the overall meaning of the sentence rather than focusing on individual words will help you answer the question. The narrator is trying to impress upon the reader just how dead Marley is. He does this by repeating himself, as well as using the word *emphatically*, meaning 'definitely'.

6 This is an **inferring type of question**. To find the answer you have to 'read between the lines'. You read *Scrooge was not so dreadfully cut up by the sad event but that he was an excellent man of business on the very day of the funeral, and solemnised it with an undoubted bargain* (see lines 12–14). The fact that Scrooge did business on the funeral day shows he was not very upset, which is the meaning of the words *not so dreadfully cut up*.

7 This is a **fact-finding type of question**. The answer is a fact in the text. You read *Scrooge and he were partners* (see line 10).

8 This is a **judgement type of question**. You have to use your experience to help answer this question. This paragraph contains examples of features of Scrooge's personality and how he reacts to different events.

Advanced level questions

READING Mini Test 10: Poem

Page 75

1 D **2** C **3** D **4** A **5** B **6** Marley's ghost: old-fashioned language, exclamation, rhetorical question; In the playground: rhetorical question, third-person plural pronoun, instructional verbs
7 Marley's ghost: to entertain, to recount; In the playground: to question, to entertain
8 novel, collection of poems

1 This is a **fact-finding type of question**. The answer is a fact in the text. You read *In the playground / At the back of our house* (see lines 1–2).

2 This is an **inferring type of question**. To find the answer you have to 'read between the lines'. You read *They said the climbing frame was / NOT SAFE* (see lines 4–5). There is no specific name given to describe who *they* are. In this case you must generalise and say all adults fit this category.

3 This is an **inferring type of question**. To find the answer you have to 'read between the lines'. You read *They said the climbing frame was / NOT SAFE* (see lines 4–5). The use of capitals allows the persona to show the adult opinion that he or she disagrees with. It creates the feeling that the children are always being told what to do and aren't allowed to make any decisions for themselves.

4 This is a **fact-finding type of question**. The answer is a fact in the text. You read *They said the see-saw was / NOT SAFE / So they took it away* (see lines 10–12).

5 This is a **judgement type of question**. You read *Sawed down / Drained dry / Taken away / Fenced in / Locked up* (see lines 19–23). The ideas in this section of the poem have already been used in the poem, making this an example of repetition.

6 This is a **judgement type of question**. You have to use your knowledge of text features to help answer this question. *Marley's ghost* contains old-fashioned language (*unhallowed hands*), an exclamation (*Mind!*) and a rhetorical question (*How could it be otherwise*?). *In the playground* uses a rhetorical question (*How do you feel?*), third-person plural pronouns (*They*) and instructional verbs (*sawed*, *drained*, *taken*, *fenced*).

7 This is a **judgement type of question**. You have to use your experience to help answer this question. *Marley's ghost* is a story. Its purpose is to recount the experiences of the characters and to entertain. The purposes for *In the playground* are to question and to entertain. The text is a poem that highlights an issue within society.

8 This is a **judgement type of question**. You have to use your knowledge of text types to help answer this question. It is most likely that *Marley's ghost* would appear in a novel, as it is a narrative text, while *In the playground* would appear in a collection of poems, as it is a poem. Poems that are published are often printed in a group as a collection.

Year 7 Literacy Mini Test Answers

WRITING Mini Test 1: Persuasive text

Page 78

Marking checklist for a persuasive text

Tick each correct point. Read the student's work through once to get an overall view of their response.

Focus on general points

- ☐ Did it make sense?
- ☐ Did it flow? Were the points logical and relevant?
- ☐ Did the points arouse any reactions?
- ☐ Was the body of the writing mainly in third person?
- ☐ Did you want to read on?
- ☐ Were the arguments convincing?
- ☐ Has the writer been assertive (e.g. the use of *is* rather than a less definite term)?
- ☐ Was the handwriting readable?
- ☐ Was the writing style suitable (i.e. objective, and not casual or dismissive) for a persuasive text?

Now focus on the detail. Read each of the following points and find out whether the student's work has these features.

Focus on content

- ☐ Did the opening sentence(s) focus on the topic?
- ☐ Was the writer's point of view established early in the writing?
- ☐ Did the writer include any evidence to support his or her opinion?
- ☐ Did the writer include information relevant to his or her experiences?
- ☐ Were the points/arguments raised by the writer easy to follow?
- ☐ Did the writing follow the format with an introduction, the body of the text and a conclusion?
- ☐ Were personal opinions included?
- ☐ Was the concluding paragraph relevant to the topic?

Focus on structure, vocabulary, grammar, spelling, punctuation

- ☐ Was there a variety of sentence lengths, types and beginnings?
- ☐ Was a new paragraph started for each additional argument or point?
- ☐ Has the writer used any similes (e.g. *as clear as crystal*) to stress a point raised?
- ☐ Did the writer avoid approximations such as *probably, perhaps* and *maybe*?
- ☐ Did the writer use such phrases as *I know* and *It is important to*?
- ☐ Did the writer refer to the question in the points raised? (A good way to do this is to use the keywords from the question or the introduction.)
- ☐ Has the writer used any less common words correctly?
- ☐ Was indirect speech used correctly?
- ☐ Were adjectives used to improve descriptions (e.g. *<u>expensive</u> buildings*)?
- ☐ Were adverbs used effectively (e.g. *firstly*)?
- ☐ Were capital letters used where they should have been?
- ☐ Was punctuation correct?
- ☐ Was the spelling of words correct?

Writing samples

Go to **pages 159–160** for Intermediate and Advanced Writing samples for Mini Test 1.

WRITING Mini Test 2: Narrative text

Page 80

Marking checklist for a narrative text

Tick each correct point. Read the student's work through once to get an overall view of their response.

Focus on general points

- ☐ Did it make sense?
- ☐ Did it flow?
- ☐ Did the story arouse any feeling?
- ☐ Did you want to read on?
- ☐ Did the story create suspense?
- ☐ Was the handwriting readable?

Now focus on the detail. Read each of the following points and find out whether the student's work has these features.

Focus on content

- ☐ Did the opening sentence(s) 'grab' the reader's interest?
- ☐ Was the setting established (i.e. where the action takes place)?
- ☐ Was the reader told when the action takes place?
- ☐ Was it clear who the main character(s) is/are? (The story can be in first person using *I*.)
- ☐ Was there a 'problem' to be solved early on in the writing?

- ☐ Was a complication or unusual event introduced?
- ☐ Did descriptions refer to any of the senses (e.g. *cold air, strange smell*)?
- ☐ Was there a climax (a more exciting part near the end)?
- ☐ Was the conclusion (resolution of the problem) believable?

Focus on structure, vocabulary, grammar, spelling, punctuation

- ☐ Was there a variety of sentence types, lengths and beginnings?
- ☐ Was a new paragraph begun for each change in time, place or action?
- ☐ Were conversations or direct speech in separate paragraphs for each change of speaker?
- ☐ Was a range of *said* words used for speech?
- ☐ Were any similes used (e.g. *as clear as glass*)?
- ☐ Were less common words used correctly?
- ☐ Were adjectives used to improve descriptions (e.g. *careful steps*)?
- ☐ Were adverbs used to make actions more interesting (e.g. *shook his head sadly*)?
- ☐ Were capital letters used where they should have been?
- ☐ Was punctuation correct?
- ☐ Was the spelling correct?

Writing samples

Go to **pages 161–162** for Intermediate and Advanced Writing samples for Mini Test 2.

WRITING Mini Test 3: Recount text

Page 82

Marking checklist for a recount

Tick each correct point. Read the student's work through once to get an overall view of their response.

Focus on general points

- ☐ Did it make sense?
- ☐ Did it flow?
- ☐ Did the writing arouse any feeling?
- ☐ Did you want to read on? (Were the events interesting?)
- ☐ Was the handwriting readable?

Now focus on the detail. Read each of the following points and find out whether the student's work has these features.

Focus on content

- ☐ Did the opening sentence(s) introduce the subject of the recount?
- ☐ Was the setting established (i.e. when and where the action takes place)?
- ☐ Was it clear who the main character(s) was/were?
- ☐ Were personal pronouns used (e.g. *I, we, our*)?
- ☐ Were the events recorded in chronological (time) order?
- ☐ Was the recount in the past tense?
- ☐ Did the writing include some personal comments on the events (e.g. *feeling cold, disappointed*)?
- ☐ Did descriptions make any reference to any of the senses (e.g. *loud commentary, salty air*)?
- ☐ Were interesting details included?
- ☐ Was the conclusion satisfactory?

Focus on structure, vocabulary, grammar, spelling, punctuation

- ☐ Was there a variety of sentence lengths and beginnings?
- ☐ Did a new paragraph begin with every change in time, place or action?
- ☐ Were subheadings used (optional)?
- ☐ Were adjectives used to improve descriptions (e.g. *frozen ground*)?
- ☐ Were adverbs used to make actions more interesting (e.g. *swam strongly*)?
- ☐ Were adverbs used for time changes (e.g. *later, soon, then*)?
- ☐ Were similes used (e.g. *as clear as glass*)?
- ☐ Were less common words used correctly?
- ☐ Was direct and indirect speech used appropriately?
- ☐ Were capital letters used where they should have been?
- ☐ Was the punctuation correct?
- ☐ Was the spelling correct?

Writing samples

Go to **pages 163–164** for Intermediate and Advanced Writing samples for Mini Test 3.

Year 7 Literacy Sample Test Answers

CONVENTIONS OF LANGUAGE

Sample Test 1

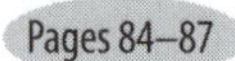
Pages 84–87

1 A **2** B **3** A **4** B **5** article, noun, verb, adverb **6** C **7** D **8** B **9** A **10** C **11** D **12** up, into **13** B **14** D **15** A **16** B **17** A **18** D **19** A **20** gymnastics is considered to be a hazardous sport **21** C **22** B **23** A **24** B **25** A **26** familiar **27** combination **28** exhibit **29** apologised **30** accessory **31** occasions **32** separate **33** writing **34** skilful **35** success **36** hoping **37** weird **38** vicious **39** nowhere **40** waste **41** planting **42** sufficient **43** growth **44** Too **45** require **46** opportunities **47** maximum **48** standards **49** suppose **50** accident

1 In English it is usual to use certain prepositions with particular verbs. It is usual to say *stood by*. You needed to also match the past tense verb *stood* with the sentence's second verb *watching* in order to show an activity that has occurred in the past.

2 This question relies on subject-verb agreement. The subject *much to be gained* is considered singular and not plural, and requires the corresponding singular verb *was*.

3 This question requires correct verb choice. The verb *might* is modal and indicates low possibility or certainty.

4 Combining these examples into one sentence is logical as all information relates to the one place, *the house*. Option C is an unclear option. Without the *and* between the two last locations it appears as if the house is behind the school on Smith Street. This is incorrect.

5 *The* is an article, *robber* is a noun, *ran* is a verb and *eventually* is an adverb.

6 Adverbs provide more information about verbs. They often end in ***ly***, although not always. The verb *waited* contains the further information *patiently*. The other options do not contain examples of verbs where further information is provided. Words like *local* and *excited* are adjectives.

7 The words *its* and *it's* are easily confused. The word *its* is a pronoun and *it's* is a contraction of the words *it is*. In this sentence, *its* should be used twice to indicate that both the tank and water bowl are owned by the turtle.

8 This question asks you to consider redundancy in language. Redundancy occurs when words are repeated or duplicated unnecessarily in sentences. In the sentence, the word *free* is considered redundant, as gifts by definition should already be free and not something we are charged for.

9 Punctuation for direct speech should only be placed around the actual words spoken by an individual. *Asked the librarian of her class* is supplementary unspoken information about the event.

10 This question asks you to consider pronouns. A pronoun is used to replace a noun (person, place or thing) that has preceded it. In this case, the pronoun *they* replaces the noun *crowd* in the previous sentence. The crowd are showing their appreciation by throwing flowers on the stage.

11 A reflexive pronoun refers back to the subject of a sentence. The reflexive pronouns are *herself, himself, itself, myself, ourselves, themselves* and *yourselves*. *I learned a lot about myself at summer camp* (*myself* refers back to *I*).

12 A preposition is a word such as *after*, *in*, *to*, *on*, and *with*. Prepositions are usually used in front of nouns or pronouns and they show the relationship between the noun or pronoun and other words in a sentence.

13 A pronoun is used in place of a noun or nouns. Common pronouns include *he, her, him, I, it, me, she, them, they, us* and *we*. Here is a sentence using the pronoun *they*: *Is your family coming to dinner? No, they are not.* To find a pronoun's antecedent, ask yourself what that pronoun refers to. In this example, *they* refers to the noun *family*.

14 *During* is a preposition that means 'throughout a period or event'. To correctly replace *during* you need to choose the option that best describes the relationship between other ideas in the sentence. *In the course of* best describes the event of the page being torn occurring *throughout* or *during* a period of time—the annual stocktake.

15 Apostrophes can be used to show possession as well as to contract (shorten) words. In this case, the plural noun *walks* indicates there is more than one walk and consequently more than one dog. Apostrophes for plural possession are placed after the final ***s*** in *dogs* (*dogs'*).

Year 7 Literacy Sample Online-style Test Answers

16 The expression *to a certain extent* expresses the range or magnitude of something, in this case the level to which the man disagreed.

17 Apostrophes can be used to show possession, that is, something belonging to something else. In this case, the leash is something owned or possessed by the dog. The other examples use apostrophes to show contractions (shortened words) and are not examples of possession.

18 The correct answer is *helped the younger students get on the bus. It* is a pronoun that replaces a main idea within the sentence. In this case *it* is what the students are doing: helping the younger ones get on the bus.

19 You will often have to make tense choices when writing. Continuity of tense is important. The past-tense choice of *included* is based on the tense of a previous verb, *developed,* which is also in the past tense.

20 The other two clauses are dependent and do not form complete sentences on their own.

21 This sentence requires an adverb that will introduce a counterbalancing consideration. *However* means *nevertheless* or *but* and is required to show that even though the students have lost permission notes, they will still be able to attend the event.

22 This question requires correct use of the apostrophe for both possession and contraction. The prescriptions belong to the doctor, explaining the apostrophe in *doctor's*. *Prescriptions* is just plural and requires no punctuation. *Won't* is a contraction of *will not* and requires an apostrophe as well.

23 *Since* is an adverb that means 'from the time when'. The speaker has not ridden a bike for some time.

24 *By* in this sentence is a preposition that indicates cause. The father in this case is causing a situation and a reaction in his daughter.

25 Use a comma to divide non-restrictive parts of a sentence. A non-restrictive clause gives additional information that is not vital to the meaning of a sentence. In this sentence, the information between the commas could be removed, and the main points of the sentences would not change. In this case, the information *who had been given free tickets* is an addition to the already complete sentence *Simon asked if Peter knew when …* The pronoun *who* refers to *Simon*, so this extra information should come directly after the sentence subject *Simon*.

26 Breaking *familiar* into syllables can help you spell it: *fa* + *mil* + *i* + *ar*. Other words ending in ***iar*** include *peculiar* and *caviar*.

27 The suffix ***ation*** is common and is used to create a sense of process or action. This is also seen in *accumulation, celebration* and *decoration*.

28 *Exhibit* has a silent ***h***. The ***h*** is often silent in English, according to the derivation of the word concerned.

29 Spell *apologised* and the related word *apology* with ***olo*** in the middle.

30 Spell *accessory* with a double ***c*** and a double ***s***; the ending is spelt ***ory***.

31 The word *occasions* is spelt with a double ***c***, not a double ***s***.

32 The word *separate* is spelt with ***par*** in the middle. Remember: The apple cut into two se***par***ate ***par***ts.

33 Adding a suffix to words ending with a consonant + ***e*** requires you to drop the ***e*** before you add the suffix (e.g. *write/writing*).

34 Remember that *skilful* is spelt with one ***l*** in the middle (the US spelling has a double ***l***). The rule for adding suffixes which begin with a consonant to words which end with a double ***l*** is to drop the last ***l*** before you add the suffix.

35 Spell *success* and the related word *successful* with a double ***c*** and a double ***s***.

36 Adding a suffix to words ending with a consonant + ***e*** requires you to drop the ***e*** before you add the suffix (e.g. *hope/hoping*).

37 Remember that *weird* is spelt with the ***e*** before the ***i***. It does not follow the usual rule of ***i*** before ***e*** except after ***c***.

38 Although *vicious* sounds like it contains the ***sh*** sound, it is spelt with a ***c*** instead. Remember: ***vici****ous* begins with ***vici***.

39 *Nowhere* is a compound noun made up of two nouns: *no* + *where*. Some compound nouns have a space in between, some have a hyphen and some, like this example, are joined. Unfortunately, compound nouns follow no regular pattern.

40 The word *waste* is an example of a homonym, where there are two words that sound the same but which have different spellings and meanings. The word *waste* means 'something not put to good use', while a *waist* is the circumference around a person's stomach.

41 For many short words that end with two consonants or two vowels followed by a consonant, simply add the suffixes ***er***, ***ing***, ***ed*** or ***est***. In this question the word is *plant + ing*.

42 Spell *sufficient* with a double *f*. Although the word sounds like it contains the letters ***sh***, it is actually spelt with a ***cient*** ending.

43 Sounding out *growth* properly will help you identify the ***th*** sound.

44 *Too, two* and *to* are homonyms, meaning they sound like one another but have different spellings. *To* is a preposition that always comes before a noun, *two* means the number two and *too* is a synonym for also, or in this case it means 'more than enough'.

45 Other words containing ***quire*** include *acquire, reacquire* and *inquire.*

46 Break *opportunities* into syllables to make it easier to spell: *opp + or + tu + ni + ties*. The singular of this word is *opportunity*. Other words beginning with ***opp*** include *opponent, opposite* and *oppressor*.

47 Break *maximum* into syllables to make it easier to spell: *max + i + mum*.

48 If you remember to repeat the initial ***a*** you will spell this word correctly: *standards*.

49 There are two syllables in *suppose*. The first syllable has a short vowel and the second stressed syllable has a long vowel sound and begins with a double ***pp***. Other words beginning with ***supp*** include *support, supplement* and *supplier*.

50 There is a soft ***c*** in the middle of *accident* so the word sounds like it begins with ***axe*** but it is spelt ***acc***, like *accelerate, accent, accessory*.

CONVENTIONS OF LANGUAGE

Sample Test 2

Pages 88–91

1 B **2** C **3** A **4** C **5** B **6** C **7** A **8** B **9** A **10** agitated **11** C **12** A **13** B **14** C **15** C, D **16** B **17** computer, acronym, 'puter **18** C **19** B **20** truthfully **21** adjective, noun, verb, preposition **22** Computers **23** computers also contained smaller and cheaper parts **24** Bill **25** A **26** conserving **27** recycled **28** environment **29** buying **30** increasing **31** properly **32** competitive **33** enjoyable **34** balance **35** sensitive **36** excellent **37** beginning **38** measured **39** projects **40** received **41** confirm **42** performance **43** boating **44** aggressive **45** absence **46** amateur **47** embarrassed **48** exaggerate **49** irresistible **50** maintenance

1 The word *from* is a preposition that is used as a function word to indicate a difference between two things—in this case *walking* and *other possible ways of getting home*.

2 The correct answer is *Jane spoke to Natalie excitedly*. It is the only example of an independent clause that contains a subject, verb and object.

3 A colon is punctuation that is used in a sentence to indicate that a list is following.

4 You need to add the adverb *quickly* to describe the verb, in this case how the liquid *spread*.

5 *Better* is an adjective in this sentence that describes the noun *pianist*. It refers to something or someone greater in excellence or higher in quality.

6 The first-person singular pronoun is *I* when it is a subject of a sentence and *me* when it is an object in a sentence. It is easy to work out which to use by breaking the sentence into two: *Sally will take the lunch basket* and *I will take the lunch basket*. Common practice is to put oneself last in a pair, so it should be *Sally and I*, not *I and Sally*.

7 The exclamation mark is punctuation that is commonly used to show heightened emotion and expression. The words *fantastic* and *loved it* are good examples of words that deserve an exclamation mark.

8 *Who's* is a contraction of *Who is*, whereas *whose* is an adjective that can be used in questioning (e.g. *Whose hat is that?*).

9 Remember that only the actual words spoken by an individual should be contained by speech marks.

10 An adjective is a word that describes a noun, in this case *woman*.

11 The question asks you to combine the sentences into one sentence so it is not possible to choose options A or D. The word *which* in the correct answer is used to connect an independent clause *There's a letter and a parcel…* to a dependent clause *which arrived for you today*, forming one meaningful sentence.

12 It is appropriate to use the present tense *comes* in a text like this. Although you could argue that the word *film* was named in the past and should be referred to in the past tense, the fact that it is still in current use makes the present tense more suitable.

13 The word that is missing is an adverb as it describes the verb *has* that comes before it. *Historically* is an adverb that can be recognised here by its ***ly*** ending.

Year 7 Literacy Sample Online-style Test Answers

14 *Neither* in the usage *neither ... nor* can take either a singular or plural verb but if both things being compared are singular usually a singular verb is used. In this sentence *team* is a collective noun and can take either a singular or plural verb depending on whether you see the team as individuals or as a whole. So you could use either *was* or *were* in this sentence. The only option is *was*.

15 Remember that only the actual words spoken by an individual should be contained by speech marks.

16 *Who* is used to describe people, while *that* is used when describing things and animals.

17 The three common nouns are *computer*, *acronym* (an acronym is an abbreviation formed from the initial letters of other words but pronounced as a word on its own e.g. NASA) and *'puter*. This is a bit tricky to identify as *'puter* is a contracted and informal way of expressing the noun *computer*.

18 *That* introduces essential information, while *which* is used to introduce information that is considered non-essential, in other words the beginning sentence could stand on its own. In this case, the sentence requires a *which*, as its beginning sentence could stand alone *It is an electronic device*.

19 Comparative adjectives are used to compare differences between the two objects they modify (*larger, smaller, faster, higher*). It is not necessary to use the word *more* before a comparative adjective ending in ***er***.

20 Adverbs modify adjectives, verbs, or other adverbs. They tell us how, when, and where things happen. They express quantity, intensity, frequency, and opinions. The verb being modified is *know*.

21 *First* is an adjective that describes the noun *computer*, *called* is a verb and *during* is an adverb that tells us 'when' the action occurred.

22 *They* is a pronoun that replaces a main idea within the sentence. In this case *they* is a plural pronoun referring to something already mentioned in the sentence: in this case *computers*.

23 The main clause is *computers also contained smaller and cheaper parts.* This is the only independent sentence. The other clauses are dependent and cannot stand on their own as independent sentences.

24 The answer is *Bill*. This is provided as an extra piece of information within the sentence and shows us an alternative, more well-known name that William is known as.

25 The correct answer is *Peter, leaving the shop, looked around to make sure he hadn't left anything behind.* A comma is used to break up the parts of the sentence. If you took the section out 'leaving the shop', the remaining information would form a complete sentence.

26 For words ending with a consonant and ***e***, drop the ***e*** before you add the suffix ***ing*** (*conserve/ conserving*).

27 Even though *recycled* has an ***i*** sound, it is spelt with a ***y*** instead. It is not pronounced like the similarly spelt *bicycle*.

28 The word *environment* has a silent ***n*** in the middle of it. Break the word up to make it easier to spell: *en + vi + ron + ment*.

29 There is no need to add an ***e*** to the end of *buy* when adding ***ing***, as the word *buy* does not end with an ***e***. This is a word you need to learn and remember how to spell.

30 For words ending with a consonant and ***e***, drop the ***e*** before you add the suffix ***ing*** (*increase/ increasing*).

31 Remember to spell *properly* by adding the suffix ***ly*** to *proper*. Breaking the word into syllables will help you spell it: *pro + per + ly*.

32 The short ***a*** in the ending of words like *imaginative* sounds very much like the short ***i*** in *competitive*, so it is easy to end up with spelling mistakes. Common words ending in ***itive*** include *acquisitive*, *sensitive*, *fugitive*, *inquisitive*, *intuitive* and *repetitive*.

33 The prefix ***in*** means 'not' or 'the opposite of' (e.g. *inflexible*). However, the prefix ***en*** (or ***em***) means 'put into, provide with' (e.g. *empower* and *enlighten*). So it is easy to remember how to spell *enjoyable* because it refers to the experience of joy in an activity.

34 There is no clear rule regarding the use of the suffixes ***ence*** or ***ance***. You should use a dictionary if in doubt. Some words ending in ***ance*** include *abundance*, *defiance* and *entrance*. Some words ending in ***ence*** include *absence*, *experience* and *science*.

35 The short ***a*** in the ending of words like *imaginative* sounds very much like the short ***i*** in *sensitive*, so it is easy to end up with spelling mistakes. Common words ending in ***itive*** include *acquisitive*, *competitive*, *fugitive*, *inquisitive*, *intuitive* and *repetitive*.

36 The word *excellent* is formed by adding the suffix ***ent*** to the base verb *excel*. It is necessary to double the consonant ***l*** before adding the suffix.

37 The word *beginning* is formed by adding the suffix ***ing*** to the base word *begin*. If the base word ends in a consonant followed by a vowel and then another consonant, double the last letter (e.g. *mad/madder*).

38 The word *measured* is formed by adding the suffix ***ed*** to the base word *measure* in order to form the past tense. Other words that contain an ***ea*** letter combination include *pleasure* and *feather*.

39 Words spelt with a ***j*** like *projects* are easily confused with words that have the soft ***g*** sound like *giraffe* and *geometry*. You just have to learn and remember them.

40 The spelling of *received* follows a common rule: ***i*** before ***e*** except after ***c***. There are a few exceptions to this rule (e.g. *weird*).

41 Pronouncing *confirm* properly will help you with correct spelling. If you break the word down into its two syllables it becomes more manageable: *con + firm*.

42 The word *performance* is created by adding the suffix ***ance*** to the base verb *perform*.

43 The word *boating* is created by adding the suffix ***ing*** to the base noun *boat*. Other words containing the ***oa*** letter combination include *moat* and *throat*.

44 Remember that *aggressive* is spelt with a double ***g*** and double ***s***.

45 The word *absence* is difficult to spell as both the ***s*** and the ***c*** make a soft ***s*** sound. Remember that the ***c*** always comes last in similar nouns such as *licence*, *science* and *conscience*.

46 The word *amateur* is exactly the same in French. Other English words that come from French and end in ***eur*** include *chauffeur* and *voyeur*.

47 The word *embarrassed* is difficult to spell as the ***em*** is often pronounced as ***am***. Try to remember the double ***r*** and double ***s***.

48 The word *exaggerate* has a double ***g*** that has a soft ***g*** sound. Split the word into syllables to help you spell it: *ex + agg + er + ate*.

49 The word *irresistible* is a difficult word that can best be remembered by breaking up the main parts. The prefix is ***ir***, the base word is *resist* and the suffix is ***ible***. Remember the suffix is ***ible***, not ***able***.

50 The noun *maintenance* comes from the verb *maintain*. The ***ain*** is dropped to add the suffix ***enance***.

READING Sample Test 1

Pages 92–105

Go to the **inside back cover** for a guide to question types.

1 C **2** A **3** C **4** D **5** B **6** A **7** B, D **8** C **9** B **10** C **11** D **12** A **13** D **14** A **15** D **16** Peafowl: to inform, to explain; Movie review: to inform, to give an opinion **17** C **18** A **19** C **20** Using a diversity of mulches will vary the nutrients being provided to the garden by the mulches. **21** C **22** B **23** A **24** D **25** A **26** C **27** C **28** A, C **29** Magic of Mulch: instructional verbs, scientific terms; Dive Australia's depths: images, descriptive adjectives **30** Magic of Mulch: poster; Dive Australia's depths: website **31** B **32** D **33** B **34** D **35** C **36** D **37** B **38** C **39** B **40** D **41** B **42** D **43** B **44** A **45** C **46** A **47** C **48** Running infographic: poster; Tips to improve maths skills: website

Peafowl

1 This is an **inferring type of question**. To find the answer you have to 'read between the lines'. You read *The peafowl are forest birds that nest on the ground. The Pavo peafowl are terrestrial feeders but roost in trees* (see lines 2–3). Combining this with your own knowledge of the meaning of *terrestrial*, which is 'living or growing on land', you can work out the final answer that the Pavo Peafowl eat only on the ground.

2 This is a **judgement type of question**. You read *it has been suggested that 'females' entering a male Green Peafowl's territory are really his young* (see lines 4–5). Combine this with your own knowledge that an animal's young are their children to work out the final answer—that the '*females*' in the Green Peafowl's territory are really his children.

3 This is a **fact-finding type of question**. The answer is a fact in the text. You read *The male (peacock) Indian Peafowl* (see line 9). The answer is given indirectly within parentheses, *The male (peacock)*, which means 'also known as'.

4 This is a **fact-finding type of question**. The answer is a fact in the text. You read *The Green Peafowl is different in appearance to the Indian Peafowl. The male has green and gold plumage and has an erect crest* (see lines 17–18).

5 This is a **fact-finding type of question**. The answer is a fact in the text. You read *The so-called 'tail' of the peacock, also termed the 'train', is not the tail quill feathers but highly elongated upper tail coverts (see lines 9–11)*.

6 This is a **judgement type of question**. You read *The wings are black with a sheen of blue (see line18)*. Combining the possible answers with your own knowledge you can work out that the best answer to describe *sheen* is *lustre*.

7 This is a **fact-finding type of question**. The answer is a fact in the text. The image shows the bird and the section called **Plumage** describes the appearance. *Plumage* is a word that means the feathery covering of a bird.

8 This is a **judgement type of question**. You need to use your knowledge of word meanings to answer this question. *Iridescent* is closest in meaning to *lustrous* because they both indicate a sheen.

Harry Potter and the Half-Blood Prince

9 This is an **inferring type of question**. To find the answer you have to 'read between the lines'. You read *The Half-Blood Prince is, by all accounts, the sparsest in the series (see line 1)*. *Sparsest* means 'thinnest', or 'briefest'.

10 This is a **fact-finding type of question**. The answer is a fact in the text. You read *Harry's godfather, Sirius Black (Gary Oldman) (see line 6)*. The name in brackets is the name of the actor who plays the character of Sirius Black.

11 This is a **fact-finding type of question**. The answer is a fact in the text. You read *Harry is 'the chosen one'. Meaning that either he has to kill Voldemort, or Voldemort has to kill him (see lines 8–9)*.

12 This is an **inferring type of question**. To find the answer you have to 'read between the lines'. You read *Honestly, there are so many spinning and whirling romantic entanglements in this film (see lines 10–11)*. The words *spinning* and *whirling* are used to describe romantic entanglements that are changing and constantly fluctuating. It is hard to keep track of who is seeing whom.

13 This is a **judgement type of question**. You need to form an opinion about the text's overall meaning. The review writer has an overall positive attitude towards the film, largely as a result of the acting abilities of the main actors.

14 This is an **inferring type of question**. To find the answer you have to 'read between the lines'. You read *And the one ringing criticism of the Harry Potter films—that the kids can't act—can now be well and truly buried (see lines 25–27)*. The writer reveals his positive attitude towards the actors indirectly by saying that the criticism of the kids—that they can't act—can now be buried, which means it is no longer true.

15 This is an **inferring type of question**. To find the answer you have to 'read between the lines'. You read *So how does it compare to the book? Well, it's quite different in many ways, which is actually a good thing (see lines 21–23)*. This is a positive comment about the film. Other clues that the writer approves of this film are in words such as *brilliantly (see line 16)* and *wonderful (see line 18)*. The four-star rating at the end of the review also provides another clue.

16 This is a **judgement type of question**. You need to use your knowledge and experience to answer this question. The purposes of *Peafowl* are to inform and to explain. This text is an information text about an animal. Its purpose is to provide factual information and to explain why and how a peafowl behaves and looks. The purposes of the movie review are to inform and to give an opinion. Movie reviews contain information about the story and the reviewer's thoughts and feelings about the movie.

The Magic of Mulch

17 This is a **judgement type of question**. You read *The Magic of Mulch*. Two words begin with the consonant ***m***, making the technique used alliteration. Alliteration is the repetition of initial consonant sounds and is often used to create catchy and memorable headings.

18 This is a **fact-finding type of question**. The answer is a fact in the text. You read that *Mulch is a material that covers the soil to stop weed growth and promote healthy plants (see lines 1–3)*. *Used over* is another way of saying *covers*, and *inhibits* means 'stop the growth of weeds'.

19 This is a **fact-finding type of question**. The answer is a fact in the text. You read in the second text box under the subheading *Killer Mulch*: *Avoid making mulch with materials that have had weed killer or pesticides used on them (see lines 21–25)*. It is implied that these will kill your plants.

20 This is an **inferring type of question**. To find the answer you have to 'read between the lines'. You read *Mulch can be made from a wide variety of organic material (see lines 4–5)*. You also read *Mulch can be made from common organic items found around the garden and the kitchen. Some examples*

are: LEAVES—Leaves provide a fibrous organic benefit to the soil (see lines 26–28). Then you read the benefits of each of the different mulches listed. Use your own knowledge to work out that using a diversity of mulches will vary the nutrients being provided to the garden by the mulches. Words like *variety* and *assortment* or *range* would be suitable synonyms for the key word *diversity* in this statement.

21 This is an **inferring type of question**. To find the answer you have to 'read between the lines'. The poster has a persuasive purpose that encourages people to use mulch by focusing on its positive benefits. It does this through the use of words such as *promote*, *helps* and *healthier*.

22 This is an **inferring type of question**. To find the answer you have to 'read between the lines'. You read *This makes the clippings break down quickly* (see line 30). Another way of saying *break down* in this sentence would be to say *decompose*.

23 This is a **judgement type of question**. You read *Mulch can be made from a wide variety of organic material* (see lines 4–6). This text contains ideas that are informative. Its purpose is to provide factual ideas and information about the topic, *mulch*. While the text creator has used some examples of persuasive language, such as *magic*, in order to encourage mulching, the overriding purpose is to provide information.

Dive Australia's depths

24 This is a **fact-finding type of question**. The answer is a fact in the text. You read *Completely surrounded by water and rich in islands and reefs, Australia is a diver's dream* (see line 1).

25 This is an **inferring type of question**. To find the answer you have to 'read between the lines'. You read *Our temperate waters are calling* (see line 7). The temperate waters are presented as inviting and positive. This makes *moderate* and *pleasant* the best response.

26 This is a **fact-finding type of question**. The answer is a fact in the text. You read *It stretches almost 2000 kilometres* (see lines 11–12).

27 This is an **inferring type of question**. To find the answer you have to 'read between the lines'. You read *Kick through coral canyons filled with turtles, sea stars and crabs* (see lines 19–20). The text is informally describing an activity you can do there. Use your own knowledge to work out that to see turtles and the other sea creatures described you would have to be underwater. *Kick* in this context means 'snorkel'.

28 This is a **judgement type of question**. You have to use your experience to help answer this question. The images presented have the purpose of supporting the information presented in the text. They depict aspects of diving in Australia and show images of coral.

29 This is a **judgement type of question**. You need to use your knowledge and experience to answer this question. *The Magic of Mulch* contains instructional verbs, e.g. *take care* (line 16) and *avoid* (line 22), and scientific terms, e.g. *nutrients* (line 7) and *microbes* (line 11). *Dive Australia's depths* contains images and descriptive adjectives to create a picture in the readers' minds, e.g. *giant, gentle* (line 3) and *kelp-encrusted* (line 6).

30 This is a **judgement type of question**. You need to use your knowledge and experience to answer this question. It is most likely that *The Magic of Mulch* would appear in a poster as it is an information text that has a community purpose. *Dive Australia's depths* would appear in a website as it contains information about a place that people might search for.

Beowulf

31 This is an **inferring type of question**. To find the answer you have to 'read between the lines'. You read *praise of the prowess of people-kings* (see line 1). Many words in this text have been used to show the greatness of the people being described, resulting in feelings of awe. Examples include *prowess* (see line 1) and *honour* (see line 3).

32 This is a **judgement type of question**. You read *Prelude of the Founder of the Danish House*. The information in the prelude gives some background information about the main character, Beowulf, as it talks about his family and father. In this way, a prelude then acts as an introduction to the rest of the story.

33 This is a **fact-finding type of question**. The answer is a fact in the text. You read *spear-armed Danes* (see line 2).

34 This is an **inferring type of question**. To find the answer you have to 'read between the lines'. You read *Famed was this Beowulf: far flew the boast of him* (see line 19). The adjective *famed* is used here to describe Beowulf. The other examples given, while positive, are not used in the poem to describe Beowulf, which is who the question asks you to focus on.

35 This is a **fact-finding type of question**. The answer is a fact in the text. You read that Beowulf is *son of Scyld* (see line 20). You also read his full name *Scyld the Scefing* (see line 5).

Year 7 Literacy Sample Online-style Test Answers

36 This is a **judgement type of question**. You read *praise of the prowess of people-kings (see line 1)*. Three words begin with the consonant ***p***, making the technique used alliteration. Alliteration is the repetition of initial consonant sounds.

37 This is a **judgement type of question**. You have to use your experience to help answer this question. The text contains creative information that is entertaining. Its purpose is to entertain you and provide you with an enjoyable reading experience.

Running infographic

38 This is a **judgement type of question**. You need to make a judgement based on the best definition of the pictures available. A dumbbell is a piece of exercise equipment that is used to build strength.

39 This is a **fact-finding type of question**. The answer is a fact in the text. You need to read the information under 'Calories' to learn that calories are burned by the body during running.

40 This is an **inferring type of question**. To find the answer you have to 'read between the lines'. Thinking about the overall purpose of the text will help you decide that *simple graphics and words combine to create an overview of the benefits of running*.

41 This is an **inferring type of question**. To find the answer you have to 'read between the lines'. You read the heading *Running infographic* The text contains factual information that is unbiased and objective. Its 'tone' or 'attitude' is factual.

Tips to improve maths skills

42 This is a **fact-finding type of question**. The answer is a fact in the text. You read in *Step 6: Change your attitude to a positive one if you find that you do not like maths (see lines 21–23)*.

43 This is a **judgement type of question**. You read *Make, Learn, Buy, Make, Write, Change (see lines 2, 6, 9, 13, 17, 22)*. Each word is a verb. A feature of instructional texts is the use of verbs that tell you what you need to do.

44 This is a **judgement type of question**. You read *Tips to improve maths skills*. This heading indicates that the text is instructional. It provides a series of steps to help you improve your maths skills.

45 This is an **inferring type of question**. To find the answer you have to 'read between the lines'. You read *This will help you to continue increasing your aptitude in the subject (see lines 3–4)*. *Increasing your aptitude* means 'increasing your ability in the subject'.

46 This is a **judgement type of question**. You need to make a judgement based on the best definition of the pictures available. The pictures are mathematical symbols—characters used to indicate a mathematical problem or operation.

47 This is a **judgement type of question**. You need to decide on the best summary of the ideas in Step 6 to find the answer. The key words *attitude … positive … confidence … encouraged (see lines 22–27)* indicate that your personal attitude influences success in maths.

48 This is a **judgement type of question**. You need to use your knowledge and experience to answer this question. It is most likely that *Running Infographic* would appear on a poster as it communicates information in a visual way. *Tips to improve maths skills* would appear in a website as it is an example of an information text that might be searched for on the internet.

READING Sample Test 2

Pages 106–117

1 C **2** B **3** D **4** B **5** A **6** C **7** C **8** D **9** C **10** A **11** D **12** D **13** B **14** D **15** A **16** Origami: jargon, present tense; The cyclone: descriptive adjectives, past tense **17** B **18** C **19** C **20** B **21** A **22** D **23** A **24** C **25** C **26** B **27** A **28** A **29** C **30** A **31** A **32** B **33** A **34** B **35** C **36** D **37** A **38** A **39** The song: to recount, to entertain; Eve's diary: to reflect, to entertain **40** The song: collection of poems; Eve's diary: collection of short stories **41** B **42** C **43** C **44** B **45** C **46** A **47** B **48** C

Origami

1 This is a **fact-finding type of question**. The answer is a fact in the text. You read *Origami (from ori meaning 'folding', and kami meaning 'paper') (see lines 1–2)*.

2 This is a **fact-finding type of question**. The answer is a fact in the text. You read *It has since then evolved into a modern art form (lines 4–5)*. *Modern* indicates it is popular in the present day.

3 This is a **fact-finding type of question**. The answer is a fact in the text. You read *The most well-known origami model is probably the Japanese paper crane (see lines 11–13)*.

4 This is a **fact-finding type of question**. The answer is a fact in the text. You read *These [basic origami techniques] include simple diagrams of basic folds like valley and mountain folds, pleats, reverse folds, squash folds, and sinks (see lines 20–21)*. You need to search also for the subheading *Techniques (see line 18)* in order to locate the correct paragraph for this question.

5 This is a **fact-finding type of question.** The answer is a fact in the text. You read *Origami paper is sold in pre-packaged squares of various sizes* (lines 24–25) and *weighs slightly less than copy paper* (line 30). You are also told that *the use of cuts and glue are not considered to be part of origami* (lines 8–9) and is only sometimes dual-coloured and patterned.

6 This is a **fact-finding type of question**. The answer is a fact in the text. You read *Heavier weight papers can be wet-folded. This technique allows for a more rounded sculpting of the model* (see lines 33–35).

7 This is a **judgement type of question**. You read *Origami (from ori meaning 'folding', and kami meaning 'paper') is the traditional Japanese folk art of paper folding* (see lines 1–2). This opening sentence gives a clue that the text contains useful information about origami. It does not give you instructions on how to make origami models.

8 This is a **judgement type of question**. You need to decide what the purpose of the images is. The images show paper that is flat and unfolded; this is an example of the material used. There are also images of different animals and folded creations; these are the designs.

The cyclone

9 This is a **fact-finding type of question**. The answer is a fact in the text. You read *Uncle Henry, who was a farmer* (see line 1).

10 This is a **fact-finding type of question**. The answer is a fact in the text. You read *There were four walls, a floor and a roof, which made one room; and this room contained a rusty looking cook stove* (see lines 3–4).

11 This is an **inferring type of question**. To find the answer you have to 'read between the lines'. You read *a cyclone cellar, where the family could go in case one of those great whirlwinds arose, mighty enough to crush any building in its path* (see lines 7–8). If the family went into the cyclone cellar when the whirlwinds came, the whirlwinds must be cyclones. The only option that talks about the whirlwinds describes how they could crush any building—this shows the strength of the cyclones.

12 This is a **fact-finding type of question**. The answer is a fact in the text. You read *The sun had baked the ploughed land into a grey mass* (see lines 18–19).

13 This is a **fact-finding type of question**. The answer is a fact in the text. You read *When Aunt Em came there to live she was a young, pretty wife. The sun and wind had changed her, too. They had taken the sparkle from her eyes and left them a sober grey* (see lines 26–27). You also read *She was thin and gaunt, and never smiled now* (see line 28).

14 This is a **judgement type of question**. You read in the text about Dorothy and her family and also about the prairie life. However, the main purpose of the story is to entertain by narrating a fictional story.

15 This is a **judgement type of question**. You need to decide which word group communicates the feelings of the story. *Austere* means 'bare, harsh and grim' and is a good word to describe the room in the house. *Arid* means 'dry, parched and waterless' and is a good word to describe the extreme landscape.

16 This is a **judgement type of question**. You need to use your knowledge and experience to answer this question. *Origami* contains jargon, e.g. *sculpting techniques* (line 7) and *squash folds* (line 21) and is written in the present tense, e.g. *Origami … is* (lines 1–2). *The cyclone* contains descriptive adjectives to create a picture in the readers' minds, e.g. *great, grey prairie* (line 13) and is written in the past tense, e.g. *Dorothy lived* (line 1).

Seagrass

17 This is an **inferring type of question**. To find the answer you have to 'read between the lines'. You read *Seagrass … is a marine plant which grows like terrestrial grass* (see lines 1–2). This sentence is making a comparison between seagrass and terrestrial grass. *Terrestrial* means 'relating to earth', which makes 'grass that grows on land' the best possible response. This idea is supported by *the plants often grow in large 'meadows' which look like grassland* (see lines 18–20).

18 This is a **fact-finding type of question**. The answer is a fact in the text. You read *Detritus, formed by the breakdown of seagrass* (see line 11).

19 This is a **fact-finding type of question**. The answer is a fact in the text. You read *Seagrass … is a marine plant which grows like terrestrial grass* (see lines 1–2). You also read that *it is the main food source for Green Turtles* (see lines 5–6).

20 This is a **fact-finding type of question**. The answer is a fact in the text. Looking closely at the images will help you decide that there are a variety of images presented in the text, including plant life and animal life.

Year 7 Literacy Sample Online-style Test Answers

21 This is an **inferring type of question.** To find the answer you have to 'read between the lines'. Thinking about the overall purpose of the images will help you choose the best response, which is to generally support the information presented in the text.

22 This is a **judgement type of question.** You read *a myriad of captivating and striking aquatic creatures (see lines 12–13).* There are a variety of marine creatures being described in the text. The adjective *numerous* is the most logical possibility to replace the noun *myriad.*

23 This is a **judgement type of question.** You read *Seagrass ... is a marine plant which grows like terrestrial grass (see lines 1–2).* This is only one of the facts about seagrass presented in the text. This text contains factual information that is informative. Its purpose is not only to inform readers about seagrass but to provide further information on its place in the ecosystem. This is supported by information on detritus, animals that eat seagrass and reference to *a complex marine food chain (see line 12).*

24 This is a **fact-finding type of question.** The answer is a fact in the text. You read *the plants often grow in large 'meadows' which look like grasslands (see lines 18–20).* Another word for *meadow* and *grasslands* is *field.*

The song of wandering Aengus

25 This is an **inferring type of question.** To find the answer you have to 'read between the lines'. You read *I went out to the hazel wood, / Because a fire was in my head (see lines 1–2).* There is no mention in the poem of any real fire or urgency. After reading stanza one, the reader gains the impression of a persona who needs to escape something bothering him and who goes fishing.

26 This is an **inferring type of question.** To find the answer you have to 'read between the lines'. You read *And cut and peeled a hazel wand, / And hooked a berry to a thread (see lines 3–4).* You also read *I dropped the berry in a stream / And caught a little silver trout (see lines 7–8).* While the words *fishing pole* are never used, the description of the wand with the berry on the end that he uses to catch a fish sounds like a fishing pole.

27 This is a **fact-finding type of question.** The answer is a fact in the text. You read *someone called me by my name: / It had become a glimmering girl (see lines 12–13).*

28 This is a **judgement type of question.** You read *someone called me by my name: / It had become a glimmering girl (see lines 12–13).* The girl is *glimmering* which means she is *radiant.* The word *shiny* may seem like a possible choice, but it means more a glossy appearance, rather than the light-filled appearance that both *glimmering* and *radiant* imply.

29 This is a **fact-finding type of question.** The answer is a fact in the text. You read *Though I am old with wandering (see line 17).*

30 This is a **judgement type of question.** You read lines 18 and 20 and the words *lands* and *hands* and use your own knowledge of language to make a judgement that the author is using rhyme. Rhyme in poetry is when the word at the end of lines sound the same.

31 This is an **inferring type of question.** To find the answer you have to 'read between the lines'. You read *Though I am old with wandering (see line 17).* The persona uses the word *wandering*, however, he is not being literal. He is referring to being old and tired from living.

32 This is an **inferring type of question.** To find the answer you have to 'read between the lines'. You read *Though I am old with wandering / Through hollow lands and hilly lands (see lines 17–18).* You also read *And walk among long dappled grass, / And pluck till time and times are done (see lines 21–22).* The poem focuses on feelings of sadness about the past (nostalgia) when an old man looks back to his past and thinks about his life as a young man.

Eve's diary

33 This is a **judgement type of question.** You read the beginning of the text *SATURDAY.—I am almost a whole day old, now (see line 1).* The text continues writing in first person using the pronoun *I.* This is a usual feature of a diary because diaries contain mostly personal and emotional information. The text is not giving chronological or factual information about what happened on the Saturday, but is generally talking about Eve's reflections.

34 This is a **fact-finding type of question.** The answer is a fact in the text. You read *I am almost a whole day old, now (see line 1).* This means that Eve is less than a day old. The question is not asking when she arrived but how old she is.

Year 7 Literacy Sample Online-style Test Answers

35 This is a **fact-finding type of question**. The answer is a fact in the text. You read *I feel exactly like an experiment (see lines 6–7)*. You also read *that is what I am—an experiment; just an experiment (see line 8)*.

36 This is a **judgement type of question**. You read *Then if I am an experiment, am I the whole of it? (see line 10)*. Eve is writing in her diary so she would not expect a response to this question. A question is indicated by the use of a question mark, and a rhetorical question is one that does not usually demand a response but is used to highlight a point or issue.

37 This is an **inferring type of question**. To find the answer you have to 'read between the lines'. You read *eternal vigilance is the price of supremacy. (That is a good phrase, I think, for one so young.) (see lines 12–13)*. Brackets (parentheses) are used here to indicate Eve's thoughts: she thinks she sounds impressive, despite her age.

38 This is a **judgement type of question**. You read *this majestic new world is indeed a most noble and beautiful work (see lines 20–21)*. The adjective *majestic* is used here to describe the new world that Eve sees before her. It is used in this sense as *magnificent*, more than having any royal connotations.

39 This is a **judgement type of question**. You need to use your knowledge and experience to answer this question. The purposes for *The song of wandering Aengus* are to recount and to entertain. This text is a poem about an old man. He is recounting events of his youth in an entertaining way. The purposes for *Eve's diary* are to reflect and to entertain. The text is a narrative or story written in the style of a diary. The main character reflects on her experiences in an entertaining way for the reader.

40 This is a **judgement type of question**. You need to use your knowledge and experience to answer this question. It is most likely that *The song of wandering Aengus* would appear in a collection of poems as it is a poem. Poems are often published as a group in a collection. *Eve's diary* would most likely appear in a collection of short stories as it is a narrative text.

Butterflies

41 This is a **fact-finding type of question**. The answer is a fact in the text. You read *A butterfly is any of several groups of mainly day-flying insects (see lines 1–2)*.

42 This is a **fact-finding type of question**. The answer is a fact in the text. You read *butterflies in their adult stage can live from a week to nearly a year (see lines 6–8)*.

43 This is a **fact-finding type of question**. The answer is a fact in the text. You read *Each egg contains a number of tiny funnel-shaped openings at one end, called micropyles; the purpose of these holes is to allow sperm to enter and fertilise the egg (see lines 19–22)*.

44 This is an **inferring type of question**. To find the answer you have to 'read between the lines'. You read *Butterfly eggs are fixed to a leaf with special glue, which hardens rapidly (see line 24)*. You also read *This glue is so hard that the silk pad, to which the setae are glued, cannot be separated (see lines 27–28)*. The glue hardens in order to fix the egg to a leaf.

45 This is a **fact-finding type of question**. The answer is a fact in the text. You read *The nature of the glue is unknown and is a suitable subject for research (see line 26)*.

46 This is a **judgement type of question**. You read *Each species of butterfly has its own host plant range (see line 29)*. The answers given for this question are all possible definitions of *host* but only *the animal or plant on which or in which another organism lives* relates to the context of the text, butterflies and plants.

47 This is a **judgement type of question**. This text contains factual information on butterfly life spans and reproduction. The headings *Life spans (see line 4)* and *Eggs (see line 13)* give you a clue of the purpose of the text.

48 This is a **judgement type of question**. You need to use your knowledge and experience to answer this question. *Contracts* is a synonym for *shrinks*. In the text it states: *As* [the butterfly egg] *hardens, it contracts, deforming the shape of the egg (line 24)*.

WRITING Sample Tests 1 and 2

Pages 118–119

Go to **pages 165–168** for Intermediate and Advanced Writing samples for Sample Tests 1 and 2.

Go to **pages 146–147** for Marking Checklists for Samples Tests 1 and 2:

- Persuasive Text (page 146)
- Narrative Text (pages 146–147)

Writing Mini Test 1

Intermediate level — Sample of Persuasive Writing

Park or car park?

Dear Sir/Madam

I am writing to express my anger at my local council's recent decision to bulldoze a local nature reserve and create a concrete car park. It is my firm belief that this will have a negative effect on our local community.

The council's recent decision to bulldoze Affron Park will result in the loss of a much loved and used nature reserve. The park is visited by at least one hundred persons daily and is the only park within three surrounding suburbs that allows off-leash dog walking. This removal will result in fewer people exercising and socialising in a beautiful, quiet and free environment.

The council's investigations into the park have been a joke. They say, in their community newsletter dated last month, that the car park will generate business for the locally owned SouthFields centre and ensure the commercial success of the region. The idea of a car park designed to profit a few local business owners is horrible.

One thousand locals will rally at Affron Park on Saturday, 3 August, with thanks to the organisation of Friends of Affron Park. I wish all locals who value their right to a park to walk together to show the council that we will not be ignored on this issue!

Yours sincerely

Frank Jones

Structure

Audience
The writer's purpose is clearly stated. This acts to position, engage and convince the reader.

Text structure
The information is presented in a suitable and effective text structure. The text contains a clear introduction, main body with development of ideas, and conclusion.

Paragraphing
The organisation of information into clear paragraphs helps the reader follow the line of argument.

Cohesion
The writing's meaning is clear and it flows well in a consistent piece of writing.

Persuasive techniques
The use of persuasive techniques such as emotive language, statistics and facts add power to the writer's argument and influence the reader.

Language and ideas

Vocabulary
A variety of verbs and adjectives are used to persuade. Precise word choices and a range of effective words and phrases enhance the tone of the letter.

Sentence structure
Sentences are varied in length and structure, which creates pace and atmosphere. Sentence types are varied and include complex clauses.

Ideas
Clear ideas relating to a central event, the car park, are crafted to create the effect of a well-structured and persuasive text.

Punctuation
Correct and appropriate punctuation aids in the effectiveness of the text.

Spelling
The text contains no errors and includes the use of difficult vocabulary (*investigations*, *environment*).

Please note that this sample has not been written under test conditions. However, it gives you a standard to aim for.
The writing sample on this and the following page have been analysed based on the marking criteria used by markers to assess the NAPLAN Writing Test.

Writing Mini Test 1

Advanced level — Sample of Persuasive Writing

Park or car park?

Dear Sir/Madam

I am writing to express my dismay at my local council's recent decision to bulldoze a local nature reserve and erect a concrete car park. It is my firm belief that this will have a detrimental effect on our local community.

The council's recent decision to bulldoze Affron Park will result in the loss of a much loved and utilised nature reserve. The park is frequented by at least one hundred individuals daily and is the only park within three surrounding suburbs that allows off-leash dog walking. This removal will result in fewer people exercising and socialising in a beautiful, serene and free environment. A park is surely of more benefit to a community than a car park, isn't it?

The council's investigations into the park viability have been utterly ridiculous. They state, in their community newsletter dated last month, that '… the car park will generate business for the locally owned SouthFields centre and ensure the commercial success of the region …' The idea that a concrete jungle designed to line the pockets of a few questionably local business owners is disgusting and offensive.

One thousand locals will rally at Affron Park on Saturday, 3 August, with thanks to the organisation of Friends of Affron Park. I encourage all locals who cherish their right to a clean and green park to march together to show the council that we will not go unheeded on this issue!

Yours sincerely

Frank Jones

Structure

Audience
The writer's purpose is clearly stated. This acts to position, engage and convince the reader.

Text structure
The information is presented in a suitable and effective text structure. The text contains a clear introduction, main body with development of ideas, and conclusion.

Paragraphing
The organisation of information into clear paragraphs helps the reader follow the line of argument.

Cohesion
The writing's meaning is clear and it flows well in a consistent piece of writing.

Persuasive techniques
The use of persuasive techniques such as emotive language, statistics, facts and rhetorical questions add power to the writer's argument and influence the reader.

Language and ideas

Vocabulary
A variety of verbs and adjectives are used to persuade. Precise word choices and a range of effective words and phrases enhance the tone of the letter.

Sentence structure
Sentences are varied in length and structure, which creates pace and atmosphere. Sentence types are varied and include complex clauses.

Ideas
Clear ideas relating to a central event, the car park, are crafted to create the effect of a well-structured and persuasive text.

Punctuation
Correct and appropriate punctuation aids in the effectiveness of the text.

Spelling
The text contains no errors and uses both difficult (*questionably, viability*) and challenging vocabulary (*detrimental*).

Please note that this sample has not been written under test conditions. During a test you might not have the time to produce such a polished piece of writing. However, this sample gives you a standard to aim for.

Writing Mini Test 2

Intermediate level — Sample of Narrative Writing

Structure

Audience
The use of description and some tension engages the reader, and the setting and situation support the dramatic events.

Character and setting
Time and setting are established early in the text. The reader is encouraged to sympathise with the main character, through the use of the personal pronoun *I* and through description.

Text structure
Connecting words join and order ideas.

Paragraphing
The story is organised into paragraphs that focus on one idea or a group of related ideas.

Cohesion
The story is written with a beginning and a complication.

Journey

It was summer two years ago when Dad decided to drive to Melbourne, rather than fly. "We'll be there in no time," he stated. Long car journeys have never really been my thing. But it was decided and so there was no going back.

The day we departed, Dad, Mum, Henry and I piled into the car, books and other bits already scattered on the back seat. We were prepared for any real boredom. Dad adjusted his seat and we were off. We made it out of the city in no time and soon were cruising down the Princes Highway, ticking off the kilometres of our journey.

Nothing much happened until we were past the Victorian border. We'd had a couple of stops—one at a place with a submarine, which was weird. Another to taste the 'Best Pies in Australia'. It was at the pie place that Mum started talking to Sarah, a young girl not much older than me. I was shocked when Mum invited her into the car. Apparently she was coming with us over the border.

Sarah was quiet and no trouble—in fact she barely said a word. We dropped her off at her small town and she smiled shyly as she waved us off. Mum was silent for a moment then looked back at us, and with a tear in her eye squeezed both our legs.

"Sarah's been kicked out of her house by her stepfather. She's travelling south to her aunt's where she'll hopefully be looked after. She's been on the streets for four nights, sleeping at the local park," she said.

"Wow," I thought. It was pretty scary to see Mum upset like that. The journey was one I would never forget.

Language and ideas

Vocabulary
A variety of verbs, adverbs and adjectives are used to create interest in the story. Accurate words or groups of words are used to describe events and ideas.

Sentence structure
Sentences are varied in length and structure, which creates pace and atmosphere.

Ideas
Clear ideas relating to a central event, the journey, are crafted.

Punctuation
All sentences are punctuated correctly with capital letters and full stops. More complex punctuation marks are used some of the time.

Spelling
Common words are correctly spelt and some difficult words are included with less regular spelling patterns and silent letters.

Please note that this sample has not been written under test conditions. However, it gives you a standard to aim for.
The writing sample on this and the following page have been analysed based on the marking criteria used by markers to assess the NAPLAN Writing Test.

Advanced level — Sample of Narrative Writing

Structure

Audience
The use of description and some tension engages the reader and a well-controlled setting and situation supports the dramatic events.

Character and setting
Time and place are established early in the text. The reader is encouraged to sympathise with the main character through the use of the personal pronoun *I* and through access to the character's inner thoughts and feelings.

Text structure
The information is presented chronologically, allowing for a surprising resolution.

Paragraphing
Paragraph use is appropriate and each begins with a new event or location within the narrative. They are visible and assist the reader to negotiate the events of the story.

Cohesion
Word associations and connectives are used to tie events of the story together. The ending is swift but satisfying.

Journey

It was summer two years ago when Dad decided to drive to Melbourne, rather than fly. "We'll be there in no time," he stated, I felt, optimistically. Long car journeys have never really been my thing. But it was decided and so there was no going back.

The day we departed dawned crisp and brisk. Dad, Mum, Henry and I piled into the car, books and other paraphernalia already scattered on the back seat. We were prepared for any real boredom. Dad adjusted his seat and we were off. We made it out of the city in no time and soon were cruising down the Princes Highway, ticking off the kilometres of our journey.

Nothing much happened until we were past the Victorian border. We'd had a couple of stops—one at a place with a submarine, which was weird. Another to taste the 'Best Pies in Australia', which turned out to be somewhat of an exaggeration. It was at the pie place that Mum started talking to Sarah, a young girl not much older than me. I was shocked when Mum invited her into the car, after a serious and private discussion with Dad. Apparently she was coming with us over the border, and with a couple of meaningful 'don't say a word' looks shot in my direction, we all piled into the car.

Sarah was quiet and no trouble—in fact she barely said a word. Not the axe-wielding maniac of my nightmares. We dropped her off at her small town and she smiled shyly as she waved us off. Mum was silent for a moment then looked back at us, and with a tear in her eye squeezed both our legs.

"Sarah's been kicked out of her house by her stepfather. She's travelling south to her aunt's where she'll hopefully be looked after. She's been on the streets for four nights, sleeping at the local park." She paused. "I'm just thankful every day that you don't have to experience anything like that. I'm glad we could help her in some small way."

"Huh," I said to myself, "What do you know". It was pretty scary to see Mum upset like that. It was even scarier to think that there were young people, children like me, who were out there alone. The journey had turned out to be thought-provoking after all.

Language and ideas

Vocabulary
A variety of verbs, adverbs and adjectives are used to create interest in the story. A range of effective words and phrases enhance the tone and mood of the story.

Sentence structure
Sentences are varied in length and structure, which creates pace and atmosphere. Sentence types are varied and include complex clauses.

Ideas
Clear ideas relating to a central event, the journey, are crafted to create the effect of some tension and, ultimately, surprise.

Punctuation
There are no errors in punctuation.
All direct speech is correctly punctuated.
Apostrophes and question marks are used correctly.

Spelling
The text contains no errors and includes use of both difficult (*optimistically, exaggeration*) and challenging vocabulary (*paraphernalia*).

Please note that this sample has not been written under test conditions. During a test you might not have the time to produce such a polished piece of writing. However, this sample gives you a standard to aim for.

Writing Mini Test 3

Intermediate level — Sample of Recount Writing

Last holidays

Last holidays were terrible. They began with the conversations with those relatives you see once a year.

"My, haven't you grown!" someone shouts. As you can see, I'm not the strong family type.

The morning of their visit got worse, as it always does, when my mother entered the kitchen. She always tries to do too much and black clouds of smoke and a burning smell filled the house. This forced us to open all the windows as widely as possible and to hope for wind.

At lunch we all tried to calm the cook but I had fun blacking out my teeth with black pieces of meat. This didn't go down well. Relatives grinned at each other, which was fairly good really, given the thickness of the meat they were trying to chew. Even the dog wasn't under the table and he eats anything, even carrots.

"Yes … yes … lovely to see you … thanks for the socks/scarf." Can't wait to do it all again next year!!!!

Structure

Audience
The title informs the reader of the event to be recounted
The situation is quickly established in the first paragraph.
The past tense is used.
The use of the pronoun ***I*** indicates that this is a personal recount.

Character and setting
Time and place are quickly established.
The writer is aware of the feelings of others.

Text structure
Events happen in order using adverbs of time.
Precise words are used for details.

Paragraphing
New paragraphs start with changes in time.
New paragraphs are used for a personal opinion and speech.

Cohesion
A personal comment is used to round off the recount.

Language and ideas

Vocabulary
Better words than *said* are used (*shouts*).
Adjectives and verbs are well chosen.

Sentence structure
The writer uses a variety of sentence beginnings, types and lengths.
The writer has a controlled use of *I* as a sentence beginning.

Ideas
The writer is writing about a familiar subject.

Punctuation
Commas are used correctly.
Punctuation is well handled.
An exclamation sentence is used effectively.
Capital letters are correctly used at the beginning of sentences.

Spelling
The text contains no spelling mistakes in common or unusual words.

Please note that this sample has not been written under test conditions. However, it gives you a standard to aim for.
The writing sample on this and the following page have been analysed based on the marking criteria used by markers to assess the NAPLAN Writing Test.

Writing Mini Test 3

Last holidays

Last holidays were a bit of a nightmare, really. They began, as always, with the uncomfortable conversations with those who I like to call 'annual relatives', i.e. those relatives you see once a year.

"My, haven't you grown!" etc. etc. insert clichéd remark here. As you can see, I'm not the strong family type.

The morning of their visit descended steadily south, as it always does, when my mother entered the kitchen. She always tries to do too much, or too little, depending on your perspective, and black clouds of smoke and an excruciating burning acrid smell permeated the house. This forced us to open all the windows as widely as possible and to hope for wind.

At lunch we all tried to placate the cook but I had fun blacking out my teeth with charred pieces of meat. This didn't go down well. Relatives grinned and smirked at each other, which was fairly impressive really, given the density and toughness of the meat they were trying to masticate. Even the dog wasn't under the table and he eats anything, even carrots.

"Yes … yes … lovely to see you … thanks for the socks/scarf/multi-coloured knitted jumper that has one long arm and a too-wide collar." Can't wait to do it all again next year!!!!

Structure

Audience
The title informs the reader of the event to be recounted.
The situation is quickly established in the first paragraph.
The past tense is used.
The use of the pronoun I indicates that this is a personal recount.

Character and setting
Time and place are quickly established.
The writer is aware of the feelings of others.

Text structure
Events happen in order using adverbs of time.
Precise words are used for details.

Paragraphing
New paragraphs start with changes in time.
New paragraphs are used for a personal opinion and speech. Each paragraph has a specific point. Paragraphs are of varying lengths.

Cohesion
A personal comment is used to round off the recount.

Language and ideas

Vocabulary
Adverbs, adjectives and verbs are well chosen.

Sentence structure
Good use is made of direct speech.
The writer uses a variety of sentence beginnings, types and lengths.

Ideas
The writer correctly includes unusual words.
The writer is writing about a familiar subject.

Punctuation
Punctuation is well handled.
An exclamation sentence is used effectively.
Commas are used correctly.
Capital letters are correctly used at the beginning of sentences.

Spelling
The text contains no spelling mistakes in common or unusual words.

Please note that this sample has not been written under test conditions. During a test you might not have the time to produce such a polished piece of writing. However, this sample gives you a standard to aim for.

Writing Sample Test 1

School uniform or not?

Fellow students

Today is an awful day for all students as today marks the day our school will attempt to introduce the wearing of the School Uniform! I'm here today to encourage all of us to get together and make sure that the school uniform is not allowed to be introduced into our school!

The school has tried to tell us that wearing a school uniform will make daily dressing easier. I find this rude. The school often encourages us to 'grow up' and 'behave like adults' and yet here they are treating us like children all over again. Who do you want to be treated as? A child or an adult?

The school reduces our choices in so many ways—they tell us what to do, where to go and what to study. I think that making us wear a school uniform will make us act like children again and that the school will regret their decision!

So I ask you, fellow students, to do something! Don't sit around while important decisions such as this are being made around us! Sign the petition and write to the school so that we can show them what we think!

Thank you for listening.

Structure

Audience
The writer's purpose is stated. This acts to position, engage and convince the reader.

Text structure
The information is presented in a suitable text structure. The text contains a clear introduction, main body with development of ideas, and conclusion.

Paragraphing
The organisation of information into clear paragraphs helps the reader follow the line of argument.

Cohesion
The writing's meaning is clear and it flows well in a consistent piece of writing. This is achieved through words that link ideas.

Persuasive techniques
The use of persuasive techniques such as emotive language, repetition and rhetorical questions add power to the writer's argument and influence the audience.

Language and ideas

Vocabulary
A variety of verbs are used to persuade. Pronoun choices are inclusive and persuasive.

Sentence structure
Sentences are varied in length and structure, which creates pace and atmosphere. Sentence types are varied and include complex clauses.

Ideas
Clear ideas relating to a central event, the school uniform, are crafted to create the effect of a well-structured and persuasive speech.

Punctuation
Correct and appropriate punctuation aids in the effectiveness of the text.

Spelling
The text contains no errors and includes use of difficult vocabulary (*encourage, decision*).

Please note that this sample has not been written under test conditions. However, it gives you a standard to aim for.

The writing sample on this and the following page have been analysed based on the marking criteria used by markers to assess the NAPLAN Writing Test.

Writing Sample Test 1

School uniform or not?

Fellow students

Today dawns a wretched and tragic day for all students. For today marks the day our school will attempt to introduce that most vile and restrictive of garments onto our persons—the School Uniform! I'm here today to encourage all of us to band together, take action, and ensure that the school uniform never rears its foul head to impinge upon our freedom to dress with independence and choice.

The school has tried to persuade us that wearing a school uniform will make us more equal and make daily dressing easier. They have even suggested that wearing a uniform will reduce bullying within the school. I find these suggestions insulting to our intelligence. The school often encourages us to 'grow up' and 'behave like adults' and yet here they are treating us like children all over again. So I ask you—who do you want to be treated as? A child or an adult?

The school system limits our choices in so many ways—they tell us what to do, where to go, what to study, what to say—and now they want to tell us what to wear. I believe we are modern students in a modern age and that we should be given the choice. I believe that enforcing a school uniform upon us is a step backwards in our development and that the school will eventually regret their decision!

So I encourage you, fellow students, to take action! Don't sit idly by while important decisions such as this are being made around us! Sign the petition and write to the school so that we can show that we are a force to be reckoned with!

Thank you for listening.

Structure

Audience
The writer's purpose is clearly stated. This acts to position, engage and convince the reader.

Text structure
The information is presented in a suitable and effective text structure. The text contains a clear introduction, main body with development of ideas, and conclusion.

Paragraphing
The organisation of information into clear paragraphs helps the reader follow the line of argument.

Cohesion
The writing's meaning is clear and it flows well in a consistent piece of writing. This is achieved through words that link ideas.

Persuasive techniques
The use of persuasive techniques such as emotive language, repetition, hyperbole and rhetorical questions add power to the writer's argument and influence the audience.

Language and ideas

Vocabulary
A variety of verbs are used to persuade. Pronoun choices are inclusive and persuasive. A range of effective words and phrases enhances the tone of the speech.

Sentence structure
Sentences are varied in length and structure, which creates pace and atmosphere. Sentence types are varied and include complex clauses.

Ideas
Clear ideas relating to a central event, the school uniform, are crafted to create the effect of a well-structured and persuasive speech.

Punctuation
Correct and appropriate punctuation aids in the effectiveness of the text.

Spelling
The text contains no errors and includes use of both difficult (*restrictive, reckoned*) and challenging vocabulary (*wretched*).

Please note that this sample has not been written under test conditions. During a test you might not have the time to produce such a polished piece of writing. However, this sample gives you a standard to aim for.

Writing Sample Test 2

Intermediate level — Sample of Narrative Writing

Structure

Audience
The use of description and some tension engages the reader, and the setting and situation support the dramatic events.

Character and setting
Time and setting are established early in the text. The reader is encouraged to sympathise with the main character through the use of the personal pronoun *I* and through description.

Text structure
Ideas are joined and ordered using connecting words.

Paragraphing
The story is organised into paragraphs that focus on one idea or a group of related ideas.

Cohesion
The story has a beginning and a complication.

Ocean swim

During the sear of summer, I loved to dive off the rocks and cut through the deep, clear water, making as small a splash as I could. Below the sea line, the world above was silent, the local buildings bent. I particularly enjoyed the way my hair floated under water—fine, weightless, soft yet soon to be a burden I turned to grin at the mermaid statue that rested on the rocks' edge. Her gaze, as always, was hard to understand.

That day's swim was no different from any other—perhaps the water a little cleaner with the salt burning my eyes under water, however, I saw a flash out of the corner of my eye that I was too slow to catch and my head whipped around. My eyes searched, chest beginning to swell and hurt now; I held on for as long as I could before bursting to the surface.

The mermaid was gone. It was impossible, I knew, but my eyes confirmed the fact as I searched the shoreline. There were no men carrying her off for repairs. No children to push her in. In fact, there were few people, with only one lone dog walker in the distance. I was confused.

I trod water for a few minutes, thinking of the possibilities, trying to decide what to do when something soft brushed my leg. I jumped, scanning the water for seaweed, a plastic bag, anything … but was rewarded with a flash of a tail of something large swimming away.

I got out of the water then, a southerly breeze making me shiver. The laugh of a child woke me up and I crammed my feet into my thongs, the sun and the people making my fear go away, like the tide. I blinked and somehow, inexplicably, the mermaid was back, her gaze just as unreadable. "Spending too much time in the sun," I warned myself, moving off home.

Language and ideas

Vocabulary
A variety of verbs, adverbs and adjectives are used to create interest in the story. Accurate words or groups of words are used to describe events and ideas.

Sentence structure
Sentences are varied in length and structure, which creates pace and atmosphere.

Ideas
Clear ideas relating to a central event, the ocean swim, are crafted.

Punctuation
Nearly all sentences are correctly punctuated with capital letters and full stops. Only a couple of errors occur. More complex punctuation marks are used some of the time.

Spelling
Common words and some difficult words with less regular spelling patterns and silent letters are correctly spelt.

Please note that this sample has not been written under test conditions. However, it gives you a standard to aim for.
The writing sample on this and the following page have been analysed based on the marking criteria used by markers to assess the NAPLAN Writing Test.

Writing Sample Test 2

Advanced level — Sample of Narrative Writing

Ocean swim

During the sear of summer, I loved to dive off the rocks and cut through the deep, clear, iridescent water, making as small a splash as I could. Below the sea line, the world above was silent and distorted, the local buildings looming and bending like the wonky mirrors at Luna Park. I particularly enjoyed the way my hair floated under water—fine, weightless, soft yet soon to be a burden, plastered over my eyes as I emerged, with me no longer the sylph-like beauty of my underwater imaginings. I turned to grin at the mermaid statue that rested on the rocks' edge. Her gaze, as always, was indecipherable, impenetrable and unyielding.

That day's swim was unremarkable from any other—perhaps the water a little cleaner, the salt searing my eyes with its usual intensity. Under water, however, I saw a flash out of the corner of my eye that I was too slow to catch, my head whipping with exaggerated slowness in my eagerness. My eyes searched, chest beginning to swell and hurt now; I held on for as long as I could before bursting, projectile-like, to the surface.

The mermaid was gone. It was impossible, I knew; however, my eyes confirmed the fact as I searched the shoreline. There were no men carrying her off for repairs. No children to push her in. In fact, there were remarkably few people, with only one lone dog walker in the distance. I was stumped.

I trod water for a few minutes, thinking of the possibilities, trying to decide what to do when something soft brushed my leg. I jumped, eyes bulging, scanning the water for seaweed, a plastic bag, anything … but was rewarded with a playful flash of a tail of something large swimming away.

I got out of the water then, heart yammering, a southerly breeze making me shiver. The tinkle of a child laughing jolted me out of my reverie and I crammed my feet into my thongs, the sun and the people making my fear ebb away, like the tide. I blinked and somehow, inexplicably, the mermaid was back, her stony gaze just as unreadable. "Spending too much time in the sun," I warned myself, trudging home forgetfully.

Structure

Audience
The use of description and some tension engages the reader and a well-controlled setting and situation support the dramatic events.

Character and setting
Time and place are established early in the text. The reader is encouraged to sympathise with the main character, through the personal pronoun *I* and through access to the character's inner thoughts and feelings.

Text structure
The information is presented chronologically, allowing for a surprising resolution.

Paragraphing
Paragraph use is appropriate and each begins with a new event or location within the narrative. They are visible and help the reader negotiate the events of the story.

Cohesion
Word associations and connectives are used to tie events of the story together. The ending is swift but satisfying, as the complication is resolved.

Language and ideas

Vocabulary
A variety of verbs, adverbs and adjectives are used to create interest in the story. Precise word choices are made. A range of effective words and phrases, seen in similes, enhance the tone and mood of the story.

Sentence structure
Sentences are varied in length and structure, which creates pace and atmosphere. Sentence types are varied and include more complex clauses.

Ideas
Clear ideas relating to a central event, the ocean swim, are crafted to create the effect of some tension and, ultimately, surprise.

Punctuation
No errors in punctuation occur. All direct speech is correctly punctuated.
Apostrophes and question marks are used correctly.

Spelling
There are no spelling errors and both difficult (*intensity, remarkably*) and challenging vocabulary (*indecipherable, impenetrable* and *unyielding*) is included.

Please note that this sample has not been written under test conditions. During a test you might not have the time to produce such a polished piece of writing. However, this sample gives you a standard to aim for.

SPELLING WORDS FOR CONVENTIONS OF LANGUAGE TESTS

To the teacher or parent

First read and say the word slowly and clearly. Then read the sentence with the word in it. Then repeat the word again. Give the student time to write their answer. If the student is not sure, then ask them to guess. It is okay to skip a word if it is not known.

Spelling words for Mini Test 1

Word	Example
1. bodies	The earth has many large bodies of water.
2. ladies	The ladies luncheon was a huge success.
3. leaves	The gardener worked hard to rake up all the leaves.
4. knives	Take care when working with sharp knives.
5. ankles	I have twisted both ankles in my running career.
6. canvases	As an artist, I tend to use a lot of canvases.
7. feet	My feet are growing so much, soon I'll need new shoes
8. princesses	My daughter's favourite story is the one with the princesses.
9. dishes	The waiter found carrying multiple dishes difficult.
10. mice	The mice had chewed a large hole in the hessian sacking.
11. reef	The Great Barrier Reef is gorgeous!
12. hobbies	What are your favourite hobbies?
13. replies	I am still waiting on a few replies to my party invitation.
14. individuals	The number of individuals interested in sport is increasing.
15. exercises	People do many exercises to stay in good physical condition.

Spelling words for Mini Test 2

Word	Example
1. chief	Getting a good result in the exam was my chief concern.
2. cough	I tried not to cough during the politician's speech.
3. bought	Thanks to Mum, the cake we bought was a huge success.
4. receipt	You need to have your receipt to receive a refund.
5. fruit	Fruit and vegetables are required in a healthy diet.
6. obtain	I had to visit an official office in order to obtain my certificate.
7. should	"You really should make an effort," I reminded myself.
8. usually	Unless the traffic is bad, it doesn't usually take long to get home.
9. beige	The beige coloured walls were unremarkable.
10. foreign	I have always wanted to study at a foreign school.
11. their	I couldn't wait to see their new computer.
12. there	"What are you doing over there?" called the supervisor.
13. view	I sat down at the edge of the cliff to enjoy the view.
14. shrieked	The shop owner shrieked and chased after the thief.
15. table	I needed to quickly set the table for dinner.

SPELLING WORDS FOR CONVENTIONS OF LANGUAGE TESTS

Spelling words for Mini Test 3

Word	Example
1. stationary	The train was stationary for twenty minutes.
2. currants	Scones with currants are my favourite type of cake.
3. mourning	The widow had been in mourning for two years.
4. forth	"Go forth!" exclaimed the preacher.
5. aide	The teacher's aide was there to assist anyone who needed help.
6. air	The air was still smoky after the fires had cleared.
7. arc	The light on the table threw a strong arc of colour around the room
8. banned	The children were banned from the cinema for unruly behaviour.
9. bear	I couldn't bear waiting a moment longer for my present!
10. beech	The chair was a lovely golden beech colour.
11. bough	The tree's bough was weakened in the storm.
12. brake	It's important to know where the car's brake is.
13. sense	I think some people have a lack of common sense.
14. two	I love it when my two uncles come to visit us.
15. our	We had a group of people visit our house for lunch yesterday.

Spelling words for Mini Test 4

Word	Example
1. peaceful	The evenings are so peaceful during summer.
2. wonderful	I thought last night's play was simply wonderful.
3. abandoning	He felt terrible about abandoning the class but could no longer find time for it.
4. achieving	Achieving a high result was her primary concern.
5. accessing	I sometimes have difficulties accessing the Internet.
6. exaggerating	Without exaggerating too much, I feel I did the best.
7. revelled	The actor revelled in the glory of winning an Oscar.
8. anticipated	The soccer goalie anticipated the ball and caught it.
9. increased	My study workload has increased now I'm in high school.
10. levelled	The town was completely levelled by the disaster.
11. crawled	She crawled into the narrow opening, hoping she could squeeze through.
12. renowned	A renowned singer is visiting our town.
13. travelling	We are thinking of travelling north this winter.
14. common	A Bunsen burner is a common piece of laboratory equipment.
15. heating	It is commonly used for heating chemical substances, sterilisation and combustion.

SPELLING WORDS FOR CONVENTIONS OF LANGUAGE TESTS

Spelling words for Mini Test 5

Word	Example
1. happiness	Everybody deserves happiness in their lives.
2. forgetfulness	Such forgetfulness in a person is difficult to excuse.
3. valuable	Last year held some valuable experiences for me.
4. adaptable	You need to be adaptable in today's job market.
5. visible	By opening the door, the room was made visible.
6. illegible	The writing was so hard to read it was illegible.
7. flammable	Take care around flammable materials.
8. avoidable	Most accidents are avoidable.
9. profitable	The business was deemed a success when it became profitable.
10. feasible	It is not feasible to be in two places at once.
11. responsible	I hope you are responsible for making your own bed.
12. sensible	Crossing the road against the lights is not sensible.
13. noisiness	The neighbour's noisiness is disturbing my sleep.
14. religions	Buddhism is one of the major religions of the world.
15. sadness	There was a lot of sadness in the office when we learnt of his illness.

Spelling words for Mini Test 6

Word	Example
1. authors	The authors were more than happy to sign copies of their book.
2. stomach	I was unable to attend the event due to a stomach complaint.
3. behaviour	The children's behaviour was exceptionally good.
4. echoed	The sound of my voice echoed off the rocks and back towards me.
5. fibre	Fibre is essential in a balanced diet.
6. lunar	I am hoping to see the lunar eclipse later tonight.
7. heir	Prince Charles is the rightful heir to the throne.
8. pursuing	She insisted on pursuing a career on the stage.
9. pursuit	The police gave up their pursuit of the thief
10. technique	There is a special technique to life drawing.
11. ravine	The walkers came dangerously close to falling into the ravine.
12. rogue	A rogue is a deceitful and unreliable person.
13. yacht	It is my dream to one day sail around the world in a yacht.
14. schnitzel	Chicken schnitzel is my favourite meal for dinner.
15. slaughter	I cannot agree with the mindless slaughter of animals.

Spelling words for Mini Test 7

Word	Example
1. vehicle	The vehicle was towed after being parked illegally.
2. acquainted	I hope to get better acquainted with the new boy on my street.
3. sufficient	There was sufficient space in my room for a desk and bookcase.
4. buoy	The bobbing red buoy marked the swimmer's turning point.
5. conscience	Your conscience tells you when you have done something wrong.
6. debris	Rubble and debris littered the road after the crash.
7. cylinders	I am learning about cylinders in geometry.
8. environment	It is important that we take care of our environment.
9. explanatory	The teacher had an explanatory manner that was very helpful.
10. gauge	A fuel gauge is an instrument used to indicate the level of fuel contained in a tank.
11. guaranteed	My new TV was guaranteed not to break down for three years.
12. guillotine	The guillotine is a device used to chop off peoples' heads.
13. psychic	The psychic told me I would win the lotto this year!
14. descend	Courageous and daring, people born in the Year of the Tiger rarely descend into shyness.
15. tempestuous	Some people can be unpredictable and tempestuous.

Spelling words for Mini Test 8

Word	Example
1. absorption	Absorption allows substances to enter the body through the skin.
2. bacteria	Bacteria have a wide range of shapes including spheres.
3. carbohydrate	The word carbohydrate often means any food that is rich in starch.
4. ecosystem	An ecosystem is generally an area within the natural environment.
5. element	A heating element is a device that changes electricity to heat.
6. genes	All living things depend on genes.
7. hormones	Hormones in animals are often transported in the blood.
8. microscopic	Microscopic is a word used to describe objects that are very small.
9. nucleus	The ice nucleus is the centre of an ice crystal
10. virus	I hope I don't get the virus that's going around.
11. evolution	It is interesting to consider the evolution of humankind.
12. haemoglobin	The doctor checked my haemoglobin levels.
13. hypothesis	In science, a hypothesis needs to be tested to establish a new theory.
14. energy	Our body's primary source of energy takes the form of glucose.
15. chemical	This type of sugar comes from digesting carbohydrates into a chemical that we can easily convert to energy.

SPELLING WORDS FOR CONVENTIONS OF LANGUAGE TESTS

Spelling words for Mini Test 9

Word	Example
1. business	I would like to one day open my own business.
2. columns	There were four columns holding the roof up.
3. lacerated	Her leg was lacerated by the flying glass.
4. circuit	The jogger followed a familiar circuit.
5. crevice	The tourist dropped his sunglasses down a crevice.
6. definitely	I hope definitely to travel to Paris next summer.
7. efficient	My new vacuum cleaner is quite efficient.
8. fascinating	I find the natural world fascinating.
9. fuchsia	The fuchsia is my favourite flower.
10. grandeur	The queen was used to grandeur and fine things.
11. leisure	In my leisure time I like to read.
12. irrelevant	Whether I like school or not is irrelevant as I have to go.
13. humanitarian	The students were concerned about humanitarian issues.
14. mesmerised	The visitor was mesmerised by the beauty of the harbour.
15. oxygen	I love to breathe the uncontaminated oxygen of the mountains.

Spelling words for Mini Test 10

Word	Example
1. archaeology	I find Egyptian archaeology fascinating.
2. awkwardly	After breaking a leg, Henry moved awkwardly around.
3. belligerent	Belligerent means having an aggressive or fighting attitude.
4. unconscious	She was unconscious during the whole ordeal.
5. benefited	The student benefited from the extra reading.
6. effervescent	People described him as happy and effervescent.
7. euphoric	I was euphoric upon receiving excellent test results.
8. fluorescent	The fluorescent light flickered irritatingly.
9. gouged	The glass on the road gouged a hole in my tyre.
10. hallucinations	People who remain awake may experience hallucinations.
11. incandescent	The light was incandescent and glowed with a white heat.
12. kaleidoscope	I love the pattern of shapes and colours in a kaleidoscope.
13. lieutenant	The lieutenant discharged his soldiers at midday.
14. litigious	The litigious nature of the case made it controversial.
15. manoeuvre	I had to manoeuvre the car around the fallen bin.

SPELLING WORDS FOR CONVENTIONS OF LANGUAGE TESTS

Spelling words for Sample Test 1

Word	Example
26. familiar	I thought the man looked familiar.
27. combination	The thief didn't know the safe's combination.
28. exhibit	The art exhibit was well worth the trip.
29. apologised	My daughter apologised for breaking the vase.
30. accessory	I would like to buy a new hair accessory.
31. occasions	It is worthwhile to remember special occasions.
32. separate	My knee injury requires a separate specialist.
33. writing	I finished writing my essay last night.
34. skilful	The skilful footballer manoeuvred the ball.
35. success	Tina's birthday party was a complete success.
36. hoping	I was hoping for a new bike for my birthday.
37. weird	People think my brother and I are very weird.
39. vicious	There is a vicious looking dog down the road.
39. nowhere	Peter was nowhere to be seen.
40. waste	I felt the activity was a waste of time.

Spelling words for Sample Test 2

Word	Example
26. conserving	Salvaging is an excellent way of saving energy and conserving the environment.
27. recycled	There is still a great deal of waste which could be recycled.
28. environment	This is harmful to the environment.
29. buying	More money means that people are buying more products and creating more waste.
30. increasing	The number of people interested in sport is increasing.
31. properly	People need to exercise properly to stay in good physical condition.
32. competitive	The term *sport* refers to all competitive activities.
33. enjoyable	I find playing soccer very enjoyable.
34. balance	The gymnast lost her balance performing on the beam.
35. sensitive	Some people are sensitive about revealing private information.
36. excellent	I find reading the newspaper an excellent way to spend Saturday morning.
37. beginning	It was the beginning of the summer holidays.
38. measured	The carpenter measured the length of wood before sawing it.
39. projects	I enjoy working on group projects.
40. received	The women received a standing ovation for their performance.